The Planet Earth

A spectacular waterfall in Iceland

The World Book
Encyclopedia of Science

Volume
4

The
Planet Earth

World Book, Inc.

a Scott Fetzer company

Chicago

Acknowledgments

Consultant Editor   Dougal Dixon

Consultants and Contributors

Brian Beeley   Michael Kelly
Geoffrey Brown   Alexander Mather
John Davies   Alan Mussett
Dougal Dixon   Jim Somerville
John Downes   Sandra Smith
John Farrington   Francis Stephenson
Eric Hearn   Fred Vine
Fiona Hyden   Zuza Vrbova

Artists and Designers

Terry Allen   Mick Saunders
Stephen Bull   Marnie Searchwell
Chris Forsey   Graham Smith
Mick Gillah   Michelle Stamp
Alun Jones   Charlotte Styles
Aziz Khan   Lisa Tai
Colin Salmon

Bull Publishing Consultants Ltd

Harold Bull   Kate Duffy
Brian Carter   Nicola Okell
John Clark   Martyn Page
Michael and   Hal Robinson
  Anneli Darton   Sandy Shepherd

Printed in the United States of America
Library of Congress Catalog Card No. 51260
ISBN: 0-7166-3212-8
J/HI

Contents

Preface

The quest to map the known world and to describe its creation and subsequent story is nearly as old as mankind. In the Western world, the best known creation story comes from the book of Genesis. It tells how God created the earth and all living things. Modern religious thinkers interpret the Biblical story of creation in various ways. Some believe that creation occurred exactly as Genesis describes it. Others think that God's method at creation is revealed through scientific investigation. *The Planet Earth* describes what most scientists believe to be the story of the earth and its history.

The editorial approach

The object of this series is to explain for an average family readership, adults and children alike, the many aspects of science that are not only fascinating in themselves but are also vitally important for an understanding of the world today. To achieve this the books have been made straightforward and concise, accurate in content, and are clearly and attractively presented. They are also a readily accessible source of scientific information.

The often forbidding appearance of traditional science publications has been completely avoided. Approximately equal proportions of illustrations and text make even the most unfamiliar subjects interesting and attractive. Even more important, all of the drawings have been created especially to complement the text, each explaining a topic that can be difficult to understand through the printed word alone.

The application of these principles thoroughly and consistently has created a publication that encapsulates its subject in an interesting and stimulating way and that will prove to be an invaluable work of reference and education for many years to come.

The advance of science

One of the most exciting and challenging aspects of science is that its frontiers are constantly being revised and extended, and new developments are occurring all the time. Its advance depends largely on observation, experimentation, and debate, which generate theories that have to be tested and even then stand only until they are replaced by better concepts. For this reason it is difficult for any science publication to be completely comprehensive. It is possible, however, to provide a thorough foundation that ensures any such advances can be comprehended—and it is the purpose of each book in this series to create such a foundation, by providing all the basic knowledge in the particular area of science it describes.

How to use this book

This book can be used in two basic ways.

The first, and more conventional, way is to start at the beginning and to read through to the end, which gives a coherent and thorough picture of the subject and opens a resource of basic information that can be returned to for rereading and reference.

The second allows the book to be used as a library of information presented subject by subject, which the reader can consult piece by piece as required.

All articles are prepared and presented so that the subject is equally accessible by either route. Topics are arranged in a logical sequence, outlined in the contents list. The index allows access to more specific points.

Within an article scientific terms are explained in the main text where an understanding of them is central to the understanding of the subject as a whole. Fact entries giving technical, mathematical, or biographical details are included, where appropriate, at the end of the article to which they relate. There is also an alphabetical glossary of terms at the end of the book, so that the reader's memory can be refreshed and so that the book can be used for quick reference whenever necessary.

All articles are relatively short, but none has been condensed artificially. Most articles occupy two pages, some are four pages long, and few exceed six pages in length.

The sample two-page article *(right)* shows the important elements of this editorial plan and illustrates the way in which this organization permits maximum flexibility of use.

(A) **Article title** gives the reader an immediate reference point.

(B) **Section title** shows the part of the book in which a particular article falls.

(C) **Main text** consists of approximately 850 words of narrative information set out in a logical manner, avoiding biographical and technical details that might tend to interrupt the story line and hamper the reader's progress.

(D) **Illustrations** include specially commissioned drawings and diagrams and carefully selected photographs, which expand, clarify, and add to the main text.

(E) **Captions** explain the illustrations and make the connection between the textual and the visual elements of the article.

(F) **Annotation** of the drawings allows the reader to identify the various elements referred to in the captions.

(G) **Theme images,** where appropriate, are included in the top left-hand corner of the left-hand page, to emphasize a central element of information or to create a visual link between different but related articles.

(H) **Fact entries** are added at the foot of the last page of certain articles to give biographical details, chemical or mathematical formulas, or additional information relating to the article but not essential to an understanding of the main text itself.

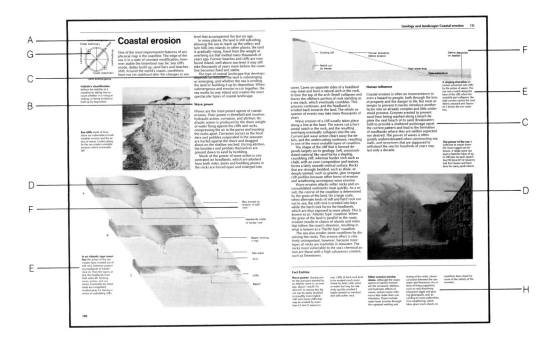

Introduction

Increasingly, the earth sciences have become more closely related to people's daily lives. From topics of little more than academic interest, they have developed to provide information of fundamental importance to many human activities—from agriculture to weather forecasting, for example. Perhaps more important, increasing knowledge has led to a better understanding of the complex interactions between the various earth processes and between human beings and their planet; in particular we have come to realize that, apart from the sun's radiation, all of our fuels and material resources are products of the earth and are, therefore, almost all finite.

The discovery and exploitation of natural resources is perhaps the strongest driving force in our attempt to understand the earth. But it is not all. Natural curiosity, which every-

one has to some degree, is aroused whenever we look around and contemplate our natural environment, and it reflects the inquiring minds of eighteenth century geologists. What makes hills and mountains? When were they formed? Why is our climate so different from that of the Sahara, and has it always been like this? Speculation on questions like these stretches back at least as far as the ancient Greeks, long before modern scientific study.

Early geology

For much of human history, notions of geology—where they existed at all—contained sizable elements of astronomy (whether the earth was a star or a planet) or of navigational controversy (whether the earth was round or flat). It must be remembered that at the time Columbus' crew set sail for India in the early 1490's, many people believed the ship would sail "over the edge." Nearly four centuries later, however, little was known about the earth's composition and geological history.

Toward the end of the eighteenth century, Abraham Gottlob Werner, a German geologist, formulated a theory on the origin of the earth that was widely accepted in his time. According to his theory the earth was created with primitive rocks and a primeval ocean. All the rocks now found at the surface were originally formed in this ocean, and because the formation of rocks and other processes was dominated by the ocean, the followers of Werner were called Neptunists (after the Roman god of the sea).

Through the first half of the nineteenth century the Neptunists were opposed by supporters of James Hutton, whose adherents were dubbed the Plutonists. Hutton published his book *A Theory of the Earth* in 1785 and introduced two startling concepts, both of which ran counter to Werner's theory. His first proposal was that igneous (including volcanic) activity had taken place spasmodically throughout geological time. Vulcanism was driven by the internal heat of the earth (hence the name Plutonists, Pluto being the Greek god of the underworld), which was also the main driving force behind the processes involved in Hut-

Ayers Rock, situated about 200 miles (322 kilometers) southwest of Alice Springs in central Australia, is one of the world's most impressive inselbergs (steep-sided mounds with rounded tops). Isolated in a large, almost barren plain, it rises about 1,000 feet (300 meters) above the surrounding land and has unusual vertical strata.

ton's second, even more startling concept. This was that, far from there having been one short episode of rock formation or one main creation followed by a small number of subsidiary rock formations, there had been numerous such episodes. Thus, according to Hutton, the earth's history consisted of repeated episodes of rock formation followed by periods of destruction or erosion, succeeded in turn by reformation. In so far as the earth's past consisted of repeated cycles, he could see "no vestige of a beginning, no prospect of an end." The same theme was taken up in the mid-nineteenth century by Charles Darwin and his supporters. If evolution had taken place in the way Darwin envisaged, changes in organisms were so slow, but also so profound, that the time required seemed to be much longer than some scientists of the day were willing to allow. The distinguished Lord Kelvin, assuming that the earth cooled from a molten condition, estimated its age to be between 20 million and 40 million years. Even Kelvin's figures seemed too small to many geologists trying to account for the immense thickness of slowly accumulated sedimentary rocks and to paleontologists and biologists at-

tempting to explain the fantastic variety of plants and animals.

During the middle and late years of the nineteenth century interest in geology and biology was intense. Geological books by Hugh Miller and Charles Lyell, for example, were best sellers and were reprinted in many editions. Throughout this time scientific data accumulated slowly, and this new information seemed to support Hutton's idea of the geological cycle and of the very great age of the earth.

Hutton's theory provided a paradigm as fundamental to the earth sciences as Newton's contributions to physics and Harvey's to medicine. It is no exaggeration to say that for 150 years scientists explored the framework provided by Hutton. There were, of course, modifications to his original ideas. The central role ascribed to igneous activity was diminished; an enormous amount of detail was added to the history of the earth; and novel concepts like continental drift were proposed. Nevertheless, many scientists believe Hutton's framework has retained much validity.

The South Orkney Islands are a group of uninhabited islands in the southern Atlantic Ocean. Although 370 miles (596 kilometers) from Antarctica, the islands may be surrounded by the thick, solid ice pack that extends from the Antarctic continent when the sea freezes in winter.

Human influence on the environment is vividly illustrated by the oil refinery standing amid cultivated wheat fields in Canada. In many parts of the world the amount of agricultural land is decreasing as urban areas expand into the surrounding countryside.

The beginnings of modern geology

Many, although not all, biologists, geologists, and physicists were reconciled following the Curies' discovery of radioactivity in the early years of this century. Minerals in the crust with radioactive elements are a source of heat undreamed of in Kelvin's calculations. Moreover, long-lived isotopes of uranium, for example, provide a means of estimating the age of the rocks in which they occur. Most scientists believe that the oldest rocks found on earth have ages measured at some 4.1 billion years. And the earth's age has been estimated at about 4.5 billion years. These scientists also believe that the vast periods indicated by some of the early results have been confirmed by continuing experimentation; and that there has been a resolution of the discrepancies between the age of the earth and the long time spans necessary for sediments to accumulate, for continents to drift and mountains to be squeezed up between continental masses and then to be eroded down again, and for living organisms to evolve and diversify.

Some problems remained, however. The basic mechanisms involved in mountain building remained obscure. Were they due to the earth contracting? Or was it, in fact, expanding? The oceans—which account for more than 70 per cent of the earth's surface—were virtually unexplored before the 1950's, and while such a large area of our world was unknown, any theories of the earth were bound to be inaccurate or incomplete. Post-World War II investigations of the oceans and developing technology produced masses of new data, and the stage was set for a new paradigm. It came in 1967 in the form of plate tectonics, a theory at once elegant in its simplicity and far-reaching in its ramifications. It will probably form the basis for continued investigations for many years to come.

Geological investigation

Methods of investigation in the earth sciences, whether in meteorology, oceanography, or geology, have traditionally been dominated by the collection of observed data in the field. Thus the discipline resembles astronomy in that the scientist has little control; in a sense, the "experiment" has already taken place, and conditions and processes have to be inferred from the results. The advances during the last two centuries are a tribute to the success of this method. Recently, however, inferences and speculation on natural processes and on the earth's history have been augmented in two important respects. On the one hand, increasingly powerful computers have allowed the development of models simulating natural conditions. Complicated phenomena, such as atmospheric and oceanic circulations, are being modeled with more and more accuracy by computers, thereby enhancing our understanding of nature. On the other hand, increasingly sophisticated techniques have enabled natural conditions to be reproduced in the laboratory. In this latter technique the earth sciences are using the methods of, and so becoming closer to, physics and chemistry. The growth of crystals in lava and other igneous rocks, for example, is understood much better now that the conditions of high temperature and pressures similar to those in the crust and mantle can be reproduced in the laboratory. Even so there is still a long way to go because both computer simulations and laboratory experimentation currently require considerable simplification compared with natural conditions.

Both of these approaches will be used increasingly to support field observations. In these studies the main concern is to understand the processes involved and to portray their action as rigorously as possible, employing, where feasible, mathematical formulations of the processes. The aim is to understand how the earth works. Perhaps most earth scientists would emphasize this aspect, and indeed, their work is directed toward this end.

In addition, the use of satellites to survey and map the Earth has revolutionized much of geophysical science. Photogrammetric techniques have enabled cartographers to produce maps and charts to an almost infinitesimal degree of accuracy. In a similar way, the sea floor is constantly being mapped and explored not only by means of satellites but also by seagoing hydrographic vessels. The resulting navigational aids, tide- and current-forecasting, and the detection of mineral and gas deposits, are useful to us all.

But the earth sciences are also intimately concerned with historical events. It is of intellectual interest to understand the processes involved in the evolution of any planet. It is also of economic and sociological importance to know what has happened on our planet. In the historical context we are involved in reconstructing the past, drawing maps of past geographies, and placing floras and faunas in their appropriate time slots. Whimsically, we can be intellectual time-travelers; in our imaginations we can travel back 350 million years to a "Europe" covered by vast swamps with tangled clumps of enormous trees, a dense undergrowth of ferns, numerous insects, such as giant dragonflies, and strange amphibians. Or we may go back 700 million years to an earth without vertebrates, inhabited only by invertebrate creatures without hard skeletons. Or more excitingly, we can go back 70 million years and roam around a land with dinosaurs and other creatures more bizarre than any science-fiction writer has ever imagined, perhaps even confront the fearsome tyrannosaurus rex.

Alternatively, we should look forward to a future landscape modified by what present generations of humankind are doing to their world now. Farming, mining, transportation, and urban development are all making an impact on the surface geography of our planet, an effect that may alter the earth forever. We must be careful, through land management and popular concern, not to make things worse for ourselves than we already have. As the human population grows, however, it is inevitable that more of us will knowingly or unknowingly take up residence in areas of danger—where earthquakes are likely, perhaps, or tidal waves common. Modern science may in the future help us in such situations by prediction and warning.

The earth sciences hold the intellect with challenging problems in the physics and chemistry of our planet and delight the imagination in recreating a past of seemingly limitless time and fantastic variety. Everyone may take part. It may require a rigorous training to work in the more sophisticated areas of the discipline, but any interested amateur may contribute something to the science and gain a personal satisfaction. For example, temperature and pressure readings linked with observations on the weather provide a continuing, absorbing occupation. Rocks give an insight into conditions in the distant past. The collection of fossils gives a never-ending thrill of discovery. Observations of rock types, local rivers, and the sea inform our appreciation of the landscape. In taking notice of our environment we feel closer to it, we use it more sensibly and sensitively, and we learn to listen to, understand, and be entranced by the "symphony of the earth."

Fumaroles, holes or vents in the ground that emit steam and other gases, are usually found in volcanic areas and dramatically demonstrate the existence of dynamic processes occurring below our planet's surface.

Earth from space

Viewed from Venus—our nearest planetary neighbor in the solar system—Earth would resemble a bright star, much as Venus appears to us. From the nearest star (not counting the sun), Earth would not be detectable at all by any means known to today's technology. Yet, for all its insignificance in the universe as a whole, Earth is the most dynamic and interesting planet known. Even from the moon, the patches of brown continents and blue oceans can be seen, often partly shrouded in a shifting veil of atmospheric cloud.

A combination of solid, liquid, and gas

The three classical elements of the earth—land, sea, and air—have their own properties, and each can move and change in response to the energy produced within the earth and by external sources, such as the sun.

The earth's crust, which forms the land masses and the beds of the oceans, is moved by convection currents that originate deep within the planet, produced by the heat of the earth itself. One result of these movements is the eruption of volcanoes, through which molten material from the earth's interior is ejected onto the surface.

The second major element—water—is unique to our planet. Nowhere else in the solar system are the influences of temperature and pressure currently balanced to allow water to exist in its three forms of ice, liquid, and vapor. It is the presence of water in the atmosphere, in the oceans, and in the icecaps that is largely responsible for many aspects of the world's climate; it also facilitates the variety and density of life that exists on our planet.

The third component of the elements, the atmosphere, is constantly circulating, heated from beneath by the earth's re-radiation and reflection of the sun's heat and from above, to a smaller extent, by the sun's radiation. The direction of movement of the atmosphere is modified by the turning of the earth on its axis (similar movements occur on any rotating planet with a dense enough atmosphere). Called the Coriolis effect, the result is the deflection of atmospheric movement to the right in the Northern Hemisphere and to the left in the Southern Hemisphere. The air in our atmosphere is a mixture of gases, consisting mainly of nitrogen (about four-fifths by volume) and oxygen (about one-fifth), with traces of carbon dioxide, inert rare gases, and water vapor. The ozone in the atmosphere reaches its highest concentration about 15 miles (24 kilometers) above the surface where it acts as a shield to protect the earth from dangerous ultraviolet radiation.

The earth is also unique (in the solar system) in having the right type of atmosphere for supporting life as we know it. Surrounding the sun there is a theoretical region called the eco-sphere in which the temperature of a planet would be suitable for the existence of life. It extends from within the orbit of Venus, about 67 million miles (108 million kilometers) from the sun, to just beyond the orbit of Mars, about 140 million miles (225 million kilometers). But Venus has an atmosphere that is rich in carbon dioxide, which tends to trap most of the heat that is reflected from the planet's surface, thereby maintaining the surface temperature at about 850° F. (454° C)—far too high for life as we understand it to exist. Mars, on the other hand, has too thin an atmosphere; without an adequately insulating cover the temperatures on the Martian surface vary widely.

The origin of Earth

Earth's beginnings have always been—and still are—a matter of debate. Many scientists currently believe that it formed at the same time as the rest of the solar system from a vast spinning disk of dust and gas. The disk began to condense into solid lumps about 5 billion years ago, with gravitational forces causing matter to coalesce at the center. The enormous convergent pressures made the temperature rise until eventually it was just enough to sustain atomic reactions that began to radiate heat, and the sun was born. Across the rest of the disk small concentrations of material began to attract additional matter to themselves, and these eventually gave rise to the planets.

As the earth formed, the heavier materials—particles of iron and nickel—sank to the center and became the core. Lighter silicate elements tended to remain on the outside, forming the stony mantle and crust. Finally the lightest substances—the gases—were attracted to the mass but remained as an external envelope and constituted the original atmosphere. By about 4.5 billion years ago Earth was in existence, and its long evolution had begun.

Statistics of Earth

Earth has a diameter of 7,926 miles (12,756 kilometers) and orbits the sun at a distance of 92,950,000 miles (149,589,000 kilometers). In more familiar terms, if the earth were a ball the size of a grapefruit the sun would be as big as a house, two-thirds of a mile (1.12 kilometers) away. The moon would be the size of a large marble orbiting the earth at a distance of about 10 feet (3 meters). Even on this tiny scale the analogous distance to the stars is astronomical; the nearest star (4.3 light-years away) would be at a distance of 236,000 miles (380,000 kilometers).

A full description of the earth as a planet includes information about orbital inclination, magnetic field, the effects of the sun's radiation, and gravity; these topics are dealt with in the articles that follow. It is interesting that much of the latest data has come not from earth-bound observations, which geologists and physicists have been making for a century or more, but from comparatively recent ventures into space.

High-altitude sounding rockets make measurements in the upper atmosphere and orbiting satellites photograph the earth, producing detailed "maps" that have many uses from monitoring crops to forecasting the weather. Details about the earth's magnetic field (such as the discovery of the Van Allen radiation belts girdling the equator) and the composition of the wide band of electromagnetic radiation reaching earth from the sun have been supplied by detectors on space probes. It is only since scientists have been able to send instruments and cameras into space and train them back at the earth that they have been able to view our planet as a whole.

The Grand Canyon holds much information about the evolution of the earth. The strata of the rock walls reveal details of the composition and age of the earth's crust as well as its movements. The walls are composed of layers of limestone, shale, and sandstone. The canyon was gouged by the river, cutting down into the rock because of uplift in the land. Wind and rain erosion also played a part in the canyon's creation. The rock layers contain fossils of animals and plants.

Seen from space the most striking feature of Earth is the predominance of white clouds in its atmosphere. At any one time about half of the planet is shrouded in these white vortices. The clouds indicate humidity in the troposphere up to about 10 miles (16 kilometers) above Earth's surface. The large amount of water covering the planet is also very much in evidence, giving it a blue appearance in the gaps of cloud. The only man-made features on Earth that are visible from space are the Great Wall of China and tracks cut through the forests of the northern continents.

Earth's attitude

Earth is the third of the nine known major planets of the solar system, in order of increasing distance from the sun. Among the planets there is a tremendous variation of surface temperature. Mercury, the nearest planet to the sun, is heated to about 650° F. (343° C). At the other extreme, Pluto, on the edge of the known solar system, has a surface temperature only about −369° F. (−187° C). The range of distance from the sun that is congenial to the existence of life is relatively narrow, and Earth, alone among the planets, is almost ideally situated within this.

Earth's orbit

Like all members of the solar system, the motion of Earth in space is dependent on the sun. Our planet is compelled by the powerful solar gravity to describe a slightly elliptical orbit, with a radius of approximately 93 million miles (150 million kilometers). One orbit takes approximately $365\frac{1}{4}$ days (more accurately 365 days, 6 hours, 9 minutes, and 9.54 seconds). To keep our calendar closely regulated by the sun, each 4-year interval has 3 "common" years of 365 days followed by a "leap" year of 366 days.

In the Northern Hemisphere winter, the distance from the sun is least—approximately 91.4 million miles (147.1 million kilometers). Six months later, the distance has increased to approximately 94.5 million miles (152.1 million kilometers). As a result of this ellipticity, the solar radiation falling on Earth in the Southern Hemisphere summer is about 7 per cent greater than in the northern summer. This has little effect on Earth's climate, however, because the major factor is the distribution of continents and oceans.

Earth's inclination and the seasons

Earth makes one complete rotation about its own axis each day, causing alternate daylight and darkness. Earth's axis of rotation may be imagined as a line through Earth's center that joins the North and South Poles. The northern direction of the axis points to within one degree of the bright star Polaris—the Pole Star. If this axis were exactly perpendicular to the flat plane in which Earth's orbit lies, there would be no seasons. The sun would be continually overhead at the equator, and at each pole it would skirt the horizon. The fact that the axis is tilted, with respect to a line at right angles to the plane of Earth's orbit (by 23° 25'), however, causes the sun's rays to strike a given latitude at different angles throughout the year.

As Earth journeys round the sun, the inclination of its axis remains fixed relative to its orbit, but the plane of Earth's orbit, because of the tilt, is not coincident with Earth's equator. Hence every six months alternate hemispheres are turned towards the sun. The extreme points of Earth's orbit (solstices) and the two midpoints between these (equinoxes) are particularly significant in the annual calendar. These occur on March 20 or 21 (vernal equinox), June 21 (summer solstice in the Northern Hemisphere), September 22 or 23 (autumnal equinox), and December 21 (winter solstice in the Northern Hemisphere). The climatic significance of these dates is that the hours of sunlight are maximal and minimal in summer and winter solstices, respectively. And at the equinoxes, day and night are of equal length. In the Southern Hemisphere the longest day is the December solstice, and the shortest the June solstice.

At the December solstice, the Northern Hemisphere reaches its greatest tilt away from the sun. Hence, north of the equator the sun is low in the sky, even at midday. The hours of daylight are short and, in general, temperatures are low. In contrast, the Southern Hemisphere at this time receives the maximum benefit from the sun's light and heat. Also, the sun is directly overhead well south of the equator—at the Tropic of Capricorn in latitude $23\frac{1}{2}°$ south. Six months later, conditions in the two hemispheres are reversed and the sun is overhead in the Northern Hemisphere at the Tropic of Cancer, at latitude $23\frac{1}{2}°$ north. The two equinoxes are almost exactly midway between the solstices; on these dates both hemispheres are equally illuminated, and on the equator the sun shines directly overhead.

The Arctic and Antarctic Circles

The Arctic and Antarctic Circles, which are situated at latitudes $66\frac{1}{2}°$ north and $66\frac{1}{2}°$ south of the equator, respectively, form the limits of the polar regions. As one moves north or south from the equator, the annual variability of hours of daylight and darkness increases, until

Earth is divided into five climatic zones: two Frigid Zones, two Temperate Zones, and one Torrid Zone. These zones have precise astronomical definitions based on the angle of tilt of Earth's axis ($23\frac{1}{2}°$) relative to the plane of Earth's orbit. Coldest are the North and South Frigid Zones, lying between the poles and the Arctic and Antarctic Circles (each of which is at an angle of $23\frac{1}{2}°$ to the Earth's axis). Between the Frigid Zones and the Tropics of Cancer and Capricorn (each of which is at an angle of $23\frac{1}{2}°$ to the plane of the equator) are the Temperate Zones. The hottest region, lying between the Tropics on both sides of the equator, is the Torrid Zone.

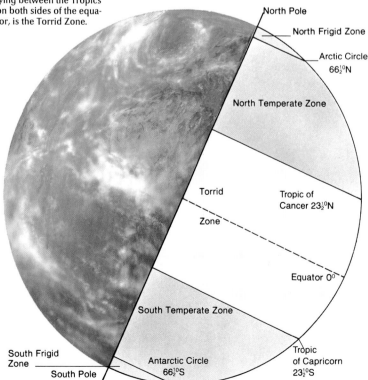

North Pole

North Frigid Zone

Arctic Circle $66\frac{1}{2}°$N

North Temperate Zone

Torrid

Zone

Tropic of Cancer $23\frac{1}{2}°$N

Equator 0°

South Temperate Zone

Tropic of Capricorn $23\frac{1}{2}°$S

South Frigid Zone

South Pole

Antarctic Circle $66\frac{1}{2}°$S

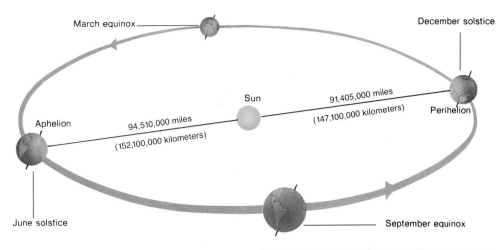

March equinox

December solstice

Aphelion

94,510,000 miles
(152,100,000 kilometers)

Sun

91,405,000 miles
(147,100,000 kilometers)

Perihelion

June solstice

September equinox

Earth's orbit is an ellipse with the sun at one focus. In the northern summer, therefore, when Earth is farthest from the sun (aphelion) it receives approximately 7 per cent less solar radiation than in the southern summer, when it is closest to the sun (perihelion).

at the poles this reaches its extreme. On the equatorial sides of the Arctic and Antarctic Circles, the sun rises and sets once every 24 hours throughout the year. On the polar sides, however, this is not the case: between the vernal and autumnal equinoxes the Northern Hemisphere points toward the sun, because of Earth's position on its orbit, and there is perpetual daylight at the North Pole, with the sun rising and falling towards the horizon but never sinking beneath it. At the summer solstice in the Northern Hemisphere, the sun is as far north as possible, and hence on this day all places within $23\frac{1}{2}$ degrees of the North Pole (and thus inside the Arctic Circle) have constant sunlight. At the South Pole, during this time, there is perpetual night. At the northern winter solstice, conversely, the North Pole, being tilted away from the sun, experiences perpetual night, while in the Southern Hemisphere the "midnight sun" is visible throughout the south polar region.

Midsummer (the summer solstice) is celebrated in Sweden and Finland with bonfires and open-air festivities.

The midnight sun remains visible within the Frigid Zones for a month at latitude 66°40', two months at latitude 69°, three months at latitude 72°30', and six months at the poles.

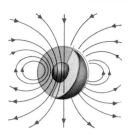

The earth's magnetic field is similar to that of a bar magnet placed at the center of the earth and inclined at a small angle to the axis of rotation.

Magnetic field

A compass points north because the earth's magnetic field is closely dipolar: that is, it has the shape of field that would result from a very strong bar magnet situated at the center of the earth aligned roughly along the axis of rotation. Normally a compass needle is mounted so that it can swing only horizontally, but a needle freely suspended would also tilt: down toward north in the Northern Hemisphere, up in the Southern Hemisphere. It would be horizontal, but pointing north, only at the equator.

The magnetic axis is inclined at about 11° to the axis of rotation, so a compass needle points only approximately north (to the magnetic pole) at most places. The magnetic north and south poles and equator are all somewhat different from the geographic ones.

The magnetic field in the past

The earth's magnetic field is not constant. When observations began in London in the sixteenth century a compass pointed 12° east of north. By 1820, it pointed 24° west of north, but since then it has been moving back eastward. This slow, or secular, variation has to be allowed for when comparing magnetic north with true north.

In order to investigate the magnetic field before the start of historical records it is necessary to make use of rocks, pottery, and other materials that have the property of becoming permanently magnetized when they form, because the magnetic materials they contain align with the earth's magnetic field at the moment of their formation. By using such materials of known age, it has been discovered that although the magnetic axis is at an angle to the geographic axis and wobbles round it, these

variations tend to cancel out when averaged over a few thousand years. One particular advantage of this is that it allows us to discover how continents have moved over hundreds of millions of years.

The earth's magnetic field also inverts at irregular intervals, which range from a fraction of a million to several million years. The time it takes to complete the inversion is far less, being several thousand years, than the time between inversions. During inversion the field seems to weaken as well as change in direction.

It is also possible to measure how the magnetic field has changed in strength as well as direction, particularly over the past few thousand years, by measuring the residual magnetization of pottery or other materials such as mud bricks. Such investigations reveal, for instance, that in Egypt at the time of the pharaohs the strength of the magnetic field varied considerably—even to the extent of doubling or halving—within the space of one or two centuries.

The source of the magnetic field

The primary source of the magnetic field lies deep within the earth. Surface rocks, which contain varying amounts of iron oxides, sometimes produce a limited magnetic field, but this has only a local effect. An additional contribution comes from electric currents in the upper atmosphere, but these too are limited, normally producing less than 1 per cent of the total field.

About halfway to the center of the earth the rocklike silicate minerals of the mantle give way abruptly to the iron alloys of the core. Although this might suggest that the core is a huge permanent magnet, this cannot be so as it is far too hot for any material to retain its magnetism; indeed, the outer core is liquid.

Mud bricks in Egypt have survived from the time of Ramses II, about 1280 B.C., because of the exceptionally dry climate, and have recorded the strength of the magnetic field at the instant the mud was thrown into the mold.

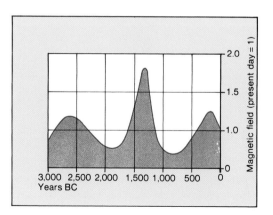

Variations of the strength of the earth's magnetic field in Egypt can be detected in bricks and pottery from different periods to give a picture of the way the magnetic field's strength has fluctuated.

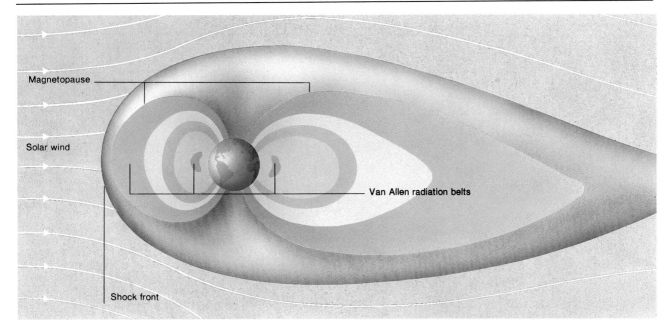

Magnetopause

Solar wind

Van Allen radiation belts

Shock front

Moreover, a permanent magnet could not produce a changing or inverting field. Instead, the field is produced by electric currents, and it follows, therefore, that there must be some kind of dynamo to generate them. A dynamo consists of an electrical conductor moving relative to a magnetic field, and it is believed these are provided by complex patterns of both liquid flow and electric current in the liquid iron of the outer core. The electric currents produce a magnetic field that, passing through the flowing liquid, generates more electric current. This reinforces the original current in a self-exciting manner. Self-exciting dynamos can be made in the laboratory. Some even show a tendency to invert. But so far one has not been made that realistically represents the earth's core or reproduces the behavior of the earth's magnetic field.

The energy to generate the field

Any dynamo requires energy to drive it, as is obvious to anyone who has experienced the effort needed to turn a small bicycle dynamo. In the earth's outer core, the flows of liquid may be driven by thermal convection arising from the heat released by radioactive elements, just as water in a heated saucepan stirs itself. But it is not certain that there is enough radioactivity in the core to produce this energy; a more promising theory is that the outer core is slowly cooling, and that the solid inner core is growing correspondingly. As material solidifies it releases latent heat of fusion, which is removed by convection. This thermal convection may be enhanced by a second process: because the core probably contains some nickel (and other elements) in addition to iron, the material solidifying out on the surface of the inner core is enriched in nickel, which is denser than iron. This leaves the bottom layer of the liquid outer core depleted in nickel, and consequently less dense than the liquid above, so it tends to rise.

Both this mechanism and radioactive heating would have the potential to drive such a dynamo mechanism throughout the 4.5 billion years of the existence of the earth, and it is known from magnetization in rocks that there has been a magnetic field for at least 3.5 billion years.

Other aspects of the earth's magnetic field

There is evidence that changes in the weather are associated with variations in the earth's magnetic field, on a relatively short time scale of years, as well as on a longer scale of decades and centuries. It is also believed that the earth's magnetic field may be used as an aid to natural navigation—by migrating birds, for example—although the mechanism enabling this to occur is not known.

The magnetosphere is formed by the interaction between the earth's magnetic field and the ionized matter of the solar wind, which cannot cross magnetic field lines and so "flows" round the earth's magnetosphere, distorting it into its characteristic teardrop shape. The earth's magnetosphere contains the Van Allen radiation belts, regions with a relatively high density of charged particles. The boundary of the magnetosphere is the magnetopause. The region between this and the shock front is the magnetosheath.

Magnetic compasses have been used for navigation for nearly 1,000 years. This sailor's compass dates from the 1500's.

The sun's radiation

Our planet depends almost entirely on the sun for light and heat. The occurrence of volcanoes and hot springs in a variety of places is proof that the earth does have some heat of its own, but without the continuous stream of radiation from the sun, the earth would be a dark, frozen world having an average surface temperature not much above absolute zero.

The sun behaves as a giant nuclear reactor, producing energy by gradually converting its resources of hydrogen into helium by nuclear fusion. So vast are these resources that although astronomers estimate the present age of the sun to be about 4.6 billion years, it is expected to continue shining for a similar length of time in the future.

Solar radiation is emitted into space as electromagnetic waves, which vary in size from very short-wave radiation, such as X rays, to very long wavelength radio waves. Visible light and infrared radiation or heat lie roughly in the middle of the solar spectrum.

The solar constant

Much of the sun's radiation is either reflected (for instance by clouds) or absorbed by our atmosphere. The solar constant is the energy that crosses each square meter at the top of the atmosphere per second. Measurements made by instruments carried on artificial satellites give a value for the solar constant close to 1.35 kilowatts per square meter (about 0.125 kilowatts per square foot). Even on the earth's surface, at the base of the atmosphere, about one kilowatt of power per second can be streaming through each square yard of a sunward-facing open window. A variation of approximately 3.5 per cent above or below the average occurs because of the earth's slightly elliptical orbit.

The solar constant does, in fact, vary, however, as a result of changes in the solar output of energy. These are of great concern to scientists, because large changes might have serious effects on the earth's climate. Experiments to measure these variations are performed from rockets and artificial satellites above the level of the atmosphere. The Solar Maximum Mission satellite, launched in 1980, made very accurate observations and monitored continual changes in the solar constant by 0.1 to 0.2 per cent. So far, however, no change of as much as 0.5 per cent has been detected, and effects on the earth's climate of small variations such as these are probably negligible; at present there is no evidence to link climatic change with alterations in the solar output.

Although the solar constant itself does not change appreciably, the amount of energy received in particular wavelength bands, for example, ultraviolet radiation and X rays, varies over the 11-year solar activity cycle. Whether much larger variations do occur, perhaps over long periods, with corresponding effects on climate, is a matter for future research.

Evidence from fossils reveals that the sun has shone at a remarkably steady rate for many millions of years. What we may call advanced life forms (from fish to man on the evolutionary sequence) have existed on the earth for about 600 million years, and a fairly stable climate is required for such complex creatures to have been able to thrive over much of the earth's surface. It is likely, therefore, that the average global temperature has remained within about a few degrees of the present value of 57° F. (14° C) throughout the whole of this vast length of time. It can be calculated from this that the solar output has varied by less than 25 per cent in this time.

Measurements of the solar constant recorded by the Solar Maximum Mission in 1980 showed small, frequent, and relatively regular variations. These are too small, however, to affect the global climate.

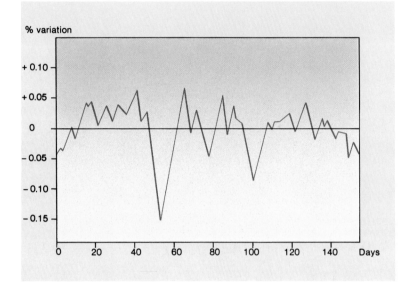

% variation

Vegetation on earth converts the sun's radiation into the essential elements of life.

Absorption in the earth's atmosphere

Absorption of the sun's radiation by our atmosphere is most effective for short wavelengths. As a result, harmful X rays and ultraviolet rays are filtered out at high altitudes, which is fortunate, because protection from these rays is vital to the existence of life on earth. At the other end of the spectrum, solar radio waves pass through the atmosphere unhindered. These are of little importance, however, because the sun is a very feeble radio emitter compared to certain radio stars.

Atmospheric absorption of infrared radiation actually improves the heat balance of the earth, because the small amount of carbon dioxide in the atmosphere (approximately 0.035 per cent by volume) produces an important "greenhouse effect." Much of the solar radiation that reaches the earth's surface is absorbed in the ground, warming it and causing it to emit its own radiation, which has very long wavelengths. Atmospheric carbon dioxide is relatively opaque to these wavelengths so that some of the outgoing radiation is trapped, causing the earth's surface to be heated further. It has been calculated that the greenhouse effect warms the earth's surface by as much as 59° F. (15° C).

Ultimately, however, all of the radiation the earth receives from the sun is sent back into space. If this were not so, the surface temperature would continue to rise indefinitely. As it is, our planet is in a state of thermal equilibrium; or so it is believed to be, unless the balance has been upset by the gradual increase of atmospheric carbon dioxide that has occurred since the Industrial Revolution. Whether or not this has had a noticeable effect on climate is still a matter of debate. Its potential to do so, however, should not be underestimated. Scientists estimate that the thick blanket of carbon dioxide on Venus increases the surface temperature by as much as 750° F. (399° C).

Visible light is only slightly dimmed by the atmosphere except when the sun is low in the sky or when clouds get in the way. When cloud cover is at its most dense, for instance, only about 1 per cent of the available sunlight actually reaches the ground. Over the earth as a whole, about 34 per cent of the light from the sun is reflected back into space, mainly by clouds. Seen from a nearby planet, such as Mars or Venus, Earth would, therefore, appear as a rather bright object, much as Venus appears to us. The ratio between the total amount of light reflected from an object in space and the total amount of light falling on the object is the albedo. A perfect reflector has an albedo of 1, and Earth has an albedo of 0.34. The moon, in contrast, has an albedo of 0.07, indicating minimal reflection.

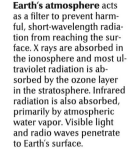

Earth's atmosphere acts as a filter to prevent harmful, short-wavelength radiation from reaching the surface. X rays are absorbed in the ionosphere and most ultraviolet radiation is absorbed by the ozone layer in the stratosphere. Infrared radiation is also absorbed, primarily by atmospheric water vapor. Visible light and radio waves penetrate to Earth's surface.

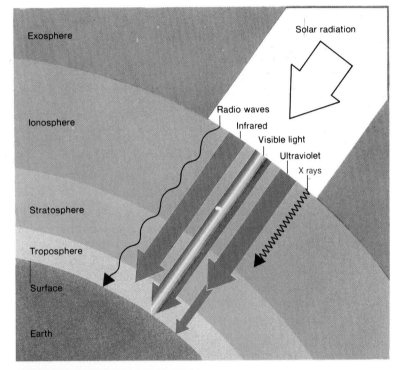

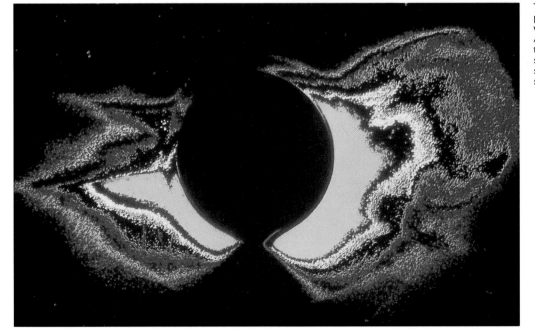

The solar corona is the primary source of short-wavelength solar radiation. A computer-enhanced photograph taken by *Skylab 3* shows the corona in the sun's magnetic field. The sun itself is obscured.

Gravity

Because of its substantial mass, the earth exerts a considerable force of gravitational attraction on objects close to it. As yet, there is still no fully satisfactory theory to explain exactly how gravity acts. However, even in such a complex task as the navigation of a space probe, the laws of gravitational attraction formulated by Isaac Newton more than three centuries ago are still relevant. Since the force with which the earth attracts an object depends on the mass of the object (and the square of its distance from the earth), it is more useful to think in terms of the object's acceleration due to gravity. Near the earth's surface, a falling object increases its speed by about 32 feet per second (9.75 meters per second) in every second of its fall, if air resistance is ignored.

The gravity field of Earth in space approximates fairly well to that of a uniform nonrotating sphere. It is, however, complicated by a variety of factors, for instance the overall shape of Earth and the presence of irregular features on its surface. On the surface itself, gravity is also affected by the daily rotation of our planet. These factors are only significant in precise measurements, however, and if Earth were to cease rotating, people would not experience any change.

Gravity and Earth's rotation

The rotation of Earth affects gravity in two quite distinct ways. First, the spin produces a centrifugal acceleration that tends to oppose gravity. This effect is strongest at the equator and diminishes to zero at the poles where there is no movement of rotation. From this cause alone, the value of g (the acceleration due to gravity) at the equator is about 0.35 per cent less than at the poles.

Second, the rotation of Earth distorts its spherical figure, giving it a slightly flattened shape. As a result, the polar diameter of 7,899.83 miles (12,713.54 kilometers) is about 26.5 miles (42.7 meters) less than the equatorial diameter. This flattened shape has the effect of still further reducing g at the equator while the value at the poles increases slightly. Ignoring local effects, the value of g varies from about 32 feet/second^2 (9.780 meters/second^2) at the equator to about 32 ft. 3 in./sec^2 (9.830m/sec^2) at the poles, giving a maximum variation of a little more than 0.5 per cent.

Gravity above and below Earth's surface

Earth's gravitational field can be detected far out into space—as far as 1 million miles. It is strong enough to produce measureable irregularities, or perturbations, in the orbital motions of Venus and Mars. And it is the gravitational attraction between Earth and the moon that maintains the latter in its elliptical orbit and causes it to always present the same side toward Earth. The lunar orbit is also affected by the tremendous gravitational pull of the sun. It was his studies of lunar motion that first led Newton to formulate the inverse square law for gravitational attraction.

The flattening of Earth also distorts its gravitational field, and this has a noticeable effect on the orbital motion of the moon. Closer to Earth, the orbits of artificial satellites are strongly influenced by irregularities in Earth's gravitational field, with the result that the whole orbit spins, or precesses, in space. Because of this phenomenon, the precise flatten-

An astronaut (or a satellite, or any other object) beyond the attraction of earth's gravitational force is said to be in a state of zero gravity, or weightlessness.

ing of Earth is best calculated from studies of the motion of artificial satellites. Such studies also enable anomalies over Earth's surface to be mapped in detail from the minor perturbations caused in a satellite's orbit by local variations in the gravity field.

If the earth were of uniform density throughout, gravity would gradually decrease below ground level towards the center of the earth. However, studies of the passage of earthquake waves through the earth's interior show that the density of the rocks increases rapidly with depth. This is partly because of the pressure of the material above, but is also due to the presence of heavy minerals, such as compounds of iron. The value of g reaches a maximum of about 34 feet/second² (10.4 meters/sec²) at the boundary of the liquid core—some 1,800 miles (2,900 kilometers) down. At the earth's center, g is zero.

Gravity anomalies

Below the earth's surface, the characteristics of the gravitational field resemble those of a point the same mass of the earth, located at the precise center of the planet. This is because, in the earth's interior, density of rock is principally a function of depth. The diminution of gravity with height above sea level can thus be calculated in terms of the actual distance from the earth's center. Near the surface, therefore, g diminishes by about 0.01 feet/second² (0.003 meters/sec²) per 0.6 mile of distance above sea level.

Accurate surveys using gravimeters reveal local variations in g—or gravity anomalies—of up to 100mgal, due to the attraction of mountains or areas of dense rock. But it has been known for over 200 years that even such mountain ranges as the Himalayas produce much smaller anomalies than expected, sometimes even negative anomalies. It is inferred from this that the rock beneath a mountain range is of lower density than the rock surrounding it.

This inference led to the theory of isostasy, which maintains that the continental masses are composed of lighter rock "floating" on the denser rock of the earth's mantle. The two principal theories both assume that adjacent blocks of the earth's crust move independently on the mantle, that the latter exhibits the properties of a fluid, and, therefore, that a constant pressure is achieved at a given depth within the mantle. One, proposed by G. B. Airy in 1851, suggested that the crust is of constant density but variable depth and is thickest under the most elevated ground. The other, proposed by J. H. Pratt in 1856, suggested that the crust rests on the mantle at a constant depth but that the density of different blocks varies. Although the premises of each hypothesis may be questioned, both offer remarkably accurate models for the gravity anomalies observed over much of the earth.

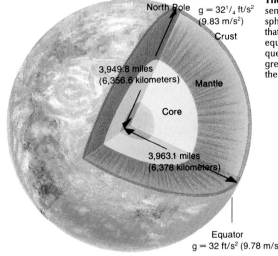

The shape of the earth resembles a slightly flattened sphere, with a polar radius that is smaller than the equatorial radius. In consequence gravity is slightly greater at the poles than at the equator.

North Pole g = 32¼ ft/s²
(9.83 m/s²)
Crust
3,949.8 miles
(6,356.6 kilometers)
Mantle
Core
3,963.1 miles
(6,378 kilometers)
Equator
g = 32 ft/s² (9.78 m/s²)

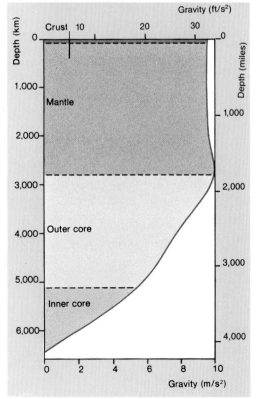

A gravimeter is used by geologists to measure variations in the earth's gravitational field. The resulting survey assists prospectors in their search for mineral resources—in this instance, oil.

Gravity beneath the earth's surface remains approximately constant through the mantle; it increases at the mantle-core boundary, then decreases steadily to zero at the center of the core, where the gravitational force is equal in all directions.

Gravity (ft/s²)
Crust 10   20   30
Depth (km)
Depth (miles)
Mantle
Outer core
Inner core
Gravity (m/s²)

Earth's atmosphere and climate

Soon after its formation (about 4,500 million years ago) Earth may have resembled present-day Jupiter or one of the other giant planets, with a thick layer of gases surrounding a very dense core. In Earth's past much of this original atmosphere was eventually lost, possibly having been burned off during a period of intense solar activity. This theory is supported by the fact that, compared to their cosmic abundance, the rare gases (neon and xenon, for example) are found in only infinitesimal amounts in the modern atmosphere.

The secondary atmosphere

In place of the cosmic gases a secondary atmosphere developed, deriving from the earth itself. For many millions of years after its formation, the earth's surface was probably molten and, even after a thin outer crust had solidified, there was incessant volcanic action. During this period of great activity, the rocks gave off large quantities of gases, including nitrogen, ammonia, carbon monoxide, methane, and probably carbon dioxide and water vapor as well—a mixture similar to that given off by volcanoes and fumaroles today. Like modern volcanic gases, the primeval atmosphere is thought to have contained only the slightest trace of oxygen, and so it would have been poisonous to almost all modern life forms.

Photosynthesis and oxygen

The earth gradually cooled, and after its surface temperature had fallen to below 212° F. (100° C), water vapor in the atmosphere condensed and fell as rain, which filled hollows and created shallow lakes and seas. In these waters, at depths of more than 33 feet (10 meters), the limit of penetration by lethal ultraviolet radiation, the first primitive plants evolved. They were probably algae and, according to the fossil record, appeared approximately 3,000 million years ago. They produced their own food by photosynthesis (a form of metabolism in which light is used to convert inorganic molecules such as carbon dioxide and water into more complex organic molecules, such as sugar), and released oxygen—a by-product of photosynthesis—into the atmosphere.

In the air molecules of oxygen (O_2) were broken down by ultraviolet radiation into single atoms (O), and some of these atoms combined with oxygen molecules to form ozone (O_3). Ozone is an unstable gas, the molecules of which absorb ultraviolet radiation. In doing so, they are often broken down and turned back into oxygen molecules and single atoms. Hence ozone forms and reforms continuously in the atmosphere at a rate that varies according to the amount of ultraviolet light, which itself depends on such factors as sunspot activity, the season, and even whether it is day or night.

Because of the photosynthetic activity of the early plants, the concentration of oxygen and ozone in the primeval atmosphere steadily increased, thereby providing more and more protection from harmful ultraviolet radiation. Eventually, the amount of this radiation reaching the earth's surface had diminished to such an extent that it penetrated only the top few inches of the oceans. As a result, marine organisms could begin to develop more fully.

Despite the continuing evolution of oxygen-producing plants, the amount of ultraviolet radiation reaching the Earth's surface remained comparatively high. Plant life did not spread

The earth's atmosphere has changed throughout its history. It is generally thought that shortly after the earth's formation (about 4.5 billion years ago), the atmosphere consisted mainly of carbon dioxide, with some nitrogen and hydrogen. Initially our planet was volcanically highly active, and large amounts of gas (especially nitrogen) were given off by the rocks; as this activity gradually decreased, the rate of increase of nitrogen in the atmosphere also slowed down. About 3 billion years ago the first plants developed and began to give off oxygen; as a result, the amount of oxygen increased, reaching a plateau when oxygen-breathing animals became numerous.

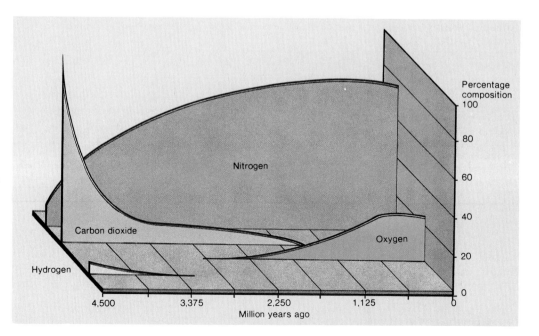

Percentage composition
100
80
60
40
20
0

Nitrogen

Carbon dioxide

Oxygen

Hydrogen

4,500   3,375   2,250   1,125   0
Million years ago

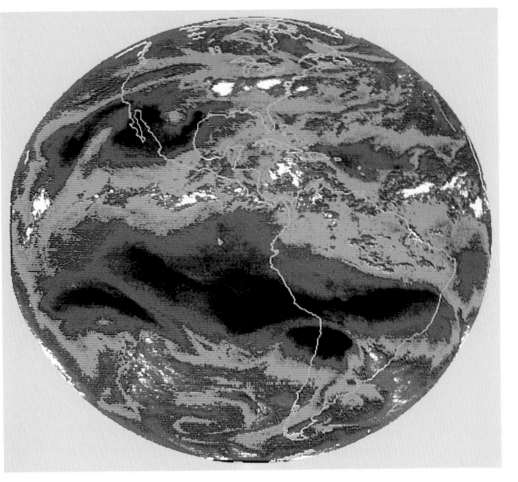

beyond the safety of lakes and seas until the late Silurian period (about 420 million years ago), when the atmosphere contained more ultraviolet-blocking oxygen/ozone—although still probably less than about 10 per cent of its present concentration. But this amount was sufficient to enable plants to grow on land, and within 30 million years (in the early Devonian period), extensive forests had developed. The amount of oxygen in the air then began to increase even more quickly, thus preparing the way for the emergence of the first land animals—the oxygen-breathing amphibians of the late Devonian period.

The modern atmosphere

The chief gases in the atmosphere today are nitrogen (78.09 per cent), oxygen (20.95 per cent), and argon (0.93 per cent). The remaining 0.03 per cent is made up of carbon dioxide (which is photosynthesized by plants), very small quantities of neon, helium, ozone, and hydrogen, and minute traces of krypton, methane, xenon, and other gases. Another important constituent of the atmosphere is water vapor, which makes up 4 per cent of the atmosphere by volume and 3 per cent by weight. The atmosphere also contains tiny particles of salt, smoke, dust, and man-made pollution. Volcanic dust erupted into the lower stratosphere—well above the various weather processes that would return it to the surface—may remain there for several years.

The composition of the atmosphere is relatively constant up to about 30 miles (48 kilometers) above the earth's surface, with the exceptions of ozone—which is concentrated in the stratosphere, between 27 and 33 miles (44 and 56 kilometers) above the earth—and water vapor. Water vapor originates on the earth's surface, and so its concentration decreases with height; it is almost completely absent beyond about 7 miles (11.3 kilometers) above the surface.

Fumaroles give off a mixture of gases—including nitrogen, ammonia, carbon monoxide, and methane—similar to that believed to have been released by rocks and volcanic activity early in the earth's history.

Clouds are classified according to their altitude and shape into four main groups: high, middle, and low clouds, and clouds of vertical development. High clouds (cirrus, cirrostratus—often with a halo—and cirrocumulus) occur above 20,000 feet (6,100 meters). Middle clouds (altostratus and altocumulus) are found between 6,000 and 20,000 feet (1,800 and 6,100 meters). Low clouds (nimbostratus, stratus, and stratocumulus) are situated below 6,000 feet (1,800 meters). Cumulonimbus and cumulus are clouds of vertical development.

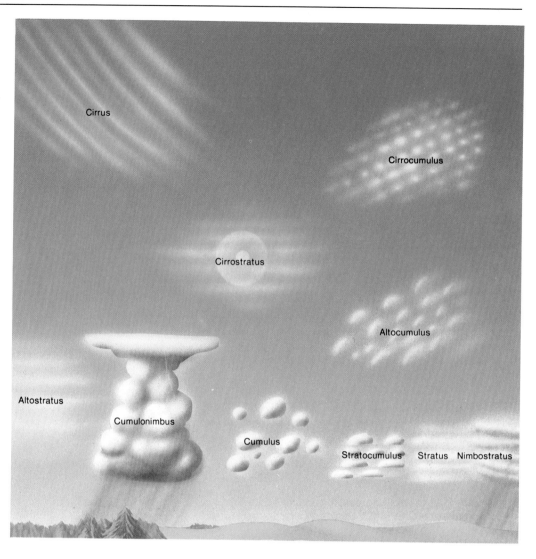

Carbon dioxide

In one respect, the composition of the atmosphere has been changing in the last 200 years. Scientists have estimated that the concentration of carbon dioxide in the atmosphere before the Industrial Revolution was between 275 and 285 parts per million (ppm); by 1958 it had risen to 315ppm, and by 1980 it had increased still further, to 338ppm. This increase is a result of human disturbance of the carbon cycle by the burning of fossil fuels and the destruction of forests.

Moreover, the proportion of carbon dioxide in the air is continuing to increase. This continual increase has become a matter of concern because although carbon dioxide allows short-wavelength radiation from the sun through to the earth's surface, it absorbs some of the longer wavelength radiation that is re-radiated by the surface (water vapor and clouds also have this absorptive effect), giving rise to the "greenhouse effect." Thus carbon dioxide prevents the loss of radiation from the earth, and the greater the amount of this gas the warmer it will become. An extreme example of the greenhouse effect occurs on Venus, where carbon dioxide makes up 95 per cent of the atmosphere, and the average surface temperature is about 850° F. (454° C). On earth, an increase of the carbon dioxide concentration

to 570ppm could, according to one calculation, raise global temperatures by an average of 5° F. (3° C), which could have unforeseen and possibly disastrous ecological consequences.

Water vapor

About 0.001 per cent of the world's total water supply is in the form of vapor in the atmosphere. The amount of atmospheric water vapor varies according to the temperature, because warm air can hold more vapor than can cold air. Absolute humidity is a measure of the actual amount of water vapor in a given volume of air (usually expressed in terms of grams of water vapor per cubic meter of air). Relative humidity, on the other hand, is a measure of the amount of water vapor in a given volume of air expressed as a percentage of the amount that volume of air could hold at that temperature if it were saturated. Air that is saturated—with a relative humidity of 100 per cent—is said to be at dew point, because any cooling causes condensation.

Water vapor comes from the evaporation of water in the sea, lakes, and moist ground; most plants and animals also give off water vapor as a natural by-product of their metabolic processes. The water vapor is transported upward by atmospheric turbulence, another consequence of the heating of the ground by solar radiation. As the rising air cools, its capacity to hold water vapor diminishes until it reaches dew point. The water vapor then condenses around minute particles in the air to form tiny water droplets that are so light that they remain suspended in the atmosphere. In condensing, heat is released from the vapor; the movement of water vapor through the atmosphere is, therefore, one of the ways in which heat is redistributed between the hot tropics, where evaporation is greatest, and the cooler, temperate regions to the north and south, where the condensation may occur.

Clouds

Clouds are formed of masses of water droplets (which may remain in a liquid state as supercooled droplets at temperatures as low as −40° F. (−5° C) and ice crystals. They are classified according to their shape and height above ground level. Generally, there are two main cloud shapes. Cumuliform, or heap, clouds have considerable vertical depth. They form in air that is rising fairly quickly and steeply. The highest cumuliform cloud, the cumulonimbus, or thunderstorm cloud, may measure more than 60,000 feet (18,000 meters) between its dark, heavy base and its often anvil-shaped top. Stratiform, or layer, clouds are thin sheets spread across the sky. They generally form when air rises slowly and at relatively gradual gradients.

Temperatures fall at a fairly constant rate up to about 6 miles (10 kilometers) of about 3.5° F. for every 1,000 feet (6.5° C for every 1,000 meters). But in fast-rising air, the release of heat associated with condensation may make the rising air much warmer than the surrounding air. This effect reinforces the upward movement, heightening the cloud and creating unstable conditions that lead to precipitation from the clouds.

Precipitation

The term precipitation includes all forms of condensation—dew, mist, fog, smog, frost, rain, hail, sleet, and snow. In the turbulent warm air of tropical regions clouds may consist almost entirely of water droplets, and raindrops heavy enough to overcome air resistance form as the water droplets merge. But in temperate regions the temperature in the clouds is often well below freezing point. In this case, the supercooled droplets freeze on contact with the ice crystals in the clouds. The ice crystals eventually become so heavy that they fall toward the ground. If the air near the ground is warmer than about 39° F. (4° C), the ice crystals melt and become raindrops; if the air is colder, some crystals may melt to form sleet, or none may melt and all reach the ground as snow.

Artificial rainmaking is carried out by "seeding" a cloud from above or below with ice or certain other crystals (silver iodide, for example). Like naturally formed ice crystals, the introduced crystals also become larger when they collide with super-cooled droplets in a cloud, and so rain may be artificially induced.

Precipitation occurs in three main ways. Convectional rain is produced when intense heating of the air near the ground causes fast-moving, warm, and moisture-laden air to rise in strong currents, only to sink again after it has cooled, so setting up convection currents. In tropical regions, this may occur in a daily cycle. Near large expanses of water convection currents are often set up in the morning, cumulonimbus clouds form in the late morning and afternoon, and thunderstorms occur in the late afternoon.

Orographic rain occurs when moist winds from the oceans are forced to rise up mountain slopes. This air cools as it rises, resulting in precipitation on the windward slopes.

Cyclonic rain occurs when warm air rises above cold air along fronts in the low-pressure regions that form in the middle latitudes.

Every year approximately 10,000 cubic miles (42,000 cubic kilometers) of ocean water evaporates, and about 11 per cent of this eventually

Rainbows occur because raindrops act like small prisms and split the sun's light into constituent colors.

The beautiful colors of a sunset (and sunrise) are caused by refraction of the sun's light by the atmosphere. Large amounts of dust and other small particles in the air increase the light-scattering effect, giving rise to abnormally colorful morning and evening skies.

falls on the continents as rain or snow. The water cycle, of which this is a part, enables life forms to live on land by supplying a constant source of fresh water.

Pressure and temperature

The atmosphere weighs an estimated 5,700 million million short tons (5,200 million million metric tons). About half of this total mass is in the lower layers, within about 3 miles (5 kilometers) of the earth's surface. At sea level, the average atmospheric pressure is 14 pounds per square inch or 1,013 millibars. The pressure (and density) of the atmosphere decreases with increasing altitude; at a height of

3.5 miles (5.6 kilometers), the average pressure is 500 millibars—about half that at sea level—and at 10 miles (16 kilometers), it is only 100 millibars.

Variations in pressure are also caused by temperature changes. The chief source of heat is solar radiation, although little heat comes directly from the sun's short wavelength radiation. Of the radiation that reaches the outer atmosphere, only about 46 per cent reaches the earth's surface, most of the rest having been scattered or reflected back into space. At the surface, however, solar radiation is absorbed (thereby heating the surface) then reradiated in the form of longer wavelength radiation. It is this long-wavelength radiation that is absorbed by the carbon dioxide, water vapor, and clouds in the lower atmosphere, creating the greenhouse effect. Hence the atmosphere is heated principally from below, and as a result, temperatures decrease with increasing altitude in the lower part of the atmosphere.

Heating by long-wavelength radiation near ground level makes the air expand so that it becomes less dense than the overlying cold air. As a result, the warm air tends to rise, leaving behind an area of comparatively low pressure. This contrasts with cold, dense air, which tends to sink, creating relatively high air pressure.

The troposphere

The depth of the atmosphere is difficult to define because it has no clear outer boundary; the top-most layer—the exosphere—becomes increasingly rarefied, gradually merging into outer space. The troposhere, the lowest layer, contains about 75 per cent of the total mass of the atmosphere. It extends up to about 6 miles (10 kilometers) over the poles and 10 miles (16 kilometers) over the equator, where the greatest heating takes place.

The troposphere is the atmospheric zone of most interest to meteorologists, because it contains almost all of the water vapor and because most of the various weather phenomena occur in it. In the troposphere temperatures generally fall with increasing altitude, near the upper boundary (the tropopause), however, they stabilize at about −67° F. (−20° C), although this may vary by as much as 68° F. (20° C). Above the tropopause is the stratosphere.

In the middle latitudes, strong winds rotate around the earth in shifting bands from west to east. These winds are concentrated in the upper troposphere and lower stratosphere. Called the circumpolar vortex, or jet streams, these winds blow between the permanent areas of high pressure over the poles (caused by the sinking of cold air) and permanent areas of low pressure over the tropics (caused by ascending warm air).

These high-level jet streams are fairly regular, because they are not subject to friction with land surfaces nor are they affected by various other factors that complicate wind flows near the earth's surface. The jet streams often move as fast as 200 miles per hour (322 kilometers per hour) and so they are of great importance to aircraft. On long flights, a subsonic jet plane can save up to one hour and ten tons of fuel if it uses routes with the

The atmosphere comprises four main layers: the troposphere, stratosphere, ionosphere (subdivided into the mesosphere and thermosphere), and the exosphere, which gradually diffuses into space. Atmospheric pressure decreases continuously with increasing altitude but the temperature (the colored band in the chart below) fluctuates.

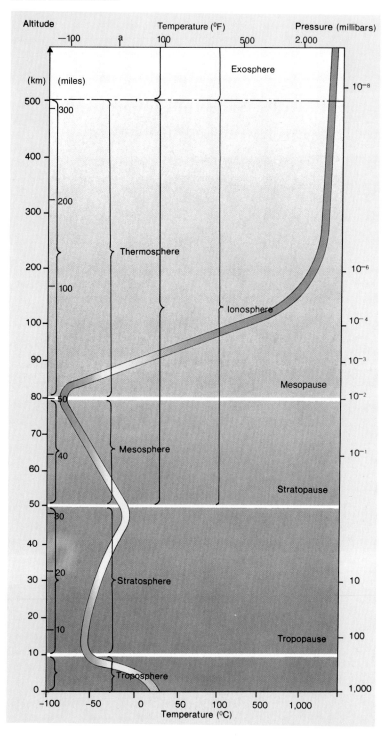

strongest tail winds. First discovered by high-flying aircraft during World War II, the jet streams are now known to have a considerable influence on the weather at ground level.

Above the troposphere

The stratosphere extends from the tropopause to about 30 miles (48 kilometers) above ground level. In this zone is the important ozone layer, where heat is generated by the absorption of ultraviolet radiation. Hence, although temperatures are stable in the lower stratosphere, they increase steadily at higher levels, reaching about 28° F. (−2° C) at the stratopause.

Between about 30 and 190 miles (48 and 306 kilometers) above the surface is the rarefied ionosphere, which is often divided into the mesosphere and the thermosphere. In the mesosphere temperatures fall again, reaching about −150° F. (−101° C) at the mesopause (the boundary between the mesophere and the thermosphere). But in the thermosphere, they increase steadily with height. This phenomenon occurs because at an altitude of about 125 miles (201 kilometers) a layer of atomic oxygen (O) absorbs ultraviolet radiation. In addition to ultraviolet radiation, the ionosphere is also bombarded by cosmic radiation and solar X rays, which cause the gases in the ionosphere to ionize (that is, the gas molecules are changed into electrically-charged particles called ions). Brilliant displays of colored lights in the sky—called the Aurora Borealis in the Northern Hemisphere and the Aurora Australis in the Southern Hemisphere—occur when streams of electrically-charged particles from the sun (the solar wind) ionize the atmospheric gases. Aurorae are normally visible only relatively near the poles and are usually accompanied by magnetic storms.

Beyond 300 miles (483 kilometers) is the very rarefied exosphere, which consists only of scattered atoms of oxygen, hydrogen, and helium.

The atmosphere as a natural resource

The atmosphere is a valuable natural source of many gases that are widely used in industry—argon for welding, for example. Most of these commercially important gases are obtained by compressing and liquefying air, then separating each of the air's constituent gases by fractional distillation.

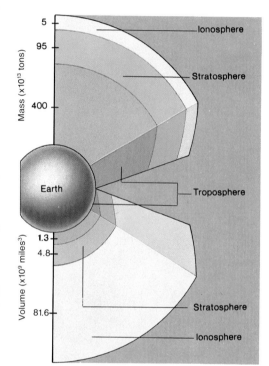

The masses and volumes of the inner atmospheric layers are compared in this diagram. With increasing altitude, the volume of air increases but the mass decreases; for example, the ionosphere occupies about 60 times the volume but has only $\frac{1}{80}$th the mass of the innermost layer, the troposphere.

The path of a jet stream is revealed by the line of clouds in this satellite photograph. Jet streams are cold, high-level winds that blow in shifting circular paths.

The weather

The circulation of the atmosphere is essentially a gigantic heat-exchange system, a consequence of the unequal heating of the earth's surface by the sun. The intensity of solar radiation is greatest around the equator and least near the poles. Thus, the equator is the hottest region and, to balance the unequal heating, heat flows from the tropics to the poles.

Prevailing winds

Around the equator, radiation from the earth's surface heats the lower layers of the atmosphere, causing them to expand and rise. This effect creates a permanent low-pressure zone (called the doldrums) of either calms, light breezes, or sudden squalls.

The light warm air rises and eventually cools, spreading north and south to form convection currents. At around latitudes 30° North and 30° South the air in these currents sinks, creating two belts of high pressure, called the horse latitudes. Like the doldrums, the horse latitudes are regions of light winds and calms. The dry, subsiding air and therefore stable atmospheric conditions of the horse latitudes tend to give rise to huge deserts on the earth's surface—the Sahara, for example.

From the horse latitudes, air currents (winds) flow outwards across the earth's surface. Those that flow toward the equator are the Trade Winds, and those moving toward the poles are the Westerlies. The Westerlies eventually meet cold air currents (the Polar Easterlies) flowing from the poles—areas of high atmospheric pressure caused by the sinking of cold, dense air. The regions between 30° and 65° North and South are transition zones with changeable weather, contrasting with the stable conditions in the tropics. The weather in these transition zones is influenced by the formation of large fronts, or cyclones, which result from the intermingling of polar and subtropical air.

Complicating factors

Although there is a continual heat exchange between the tropics and the poles, winds do not blow directly north-south. The Coriolis effect, caused by the rotation of the earth on its axis, deflects winds to the right of their natural direction in the Northern Hemisphere, and to the left in the Southern Hemisphere. (The Coriolis effect also deflects ocean currents in a similar way.)

The paths of winds and the positions of the dominant low- and high-pressure systems also undergo seasonal changes. These result from the 23.5° tilt of the earth's axis, which causes the sun to move northward and southward (as seen from the earth) during the year. At the equinoxes (on about March 21 and September 23) the sun is overhead at the equator, and solar radiation is equally balanced between the two hemispheres. But on about June 21, the summer solstice in the Northern Hemisphere, the sun is overhead at the Tropic of Cancer (23.5° North), and on December 21, the winter solstice in the Northern Hemisphere, the sun is overhead at the Tropic of Capricorn (23.5° South).

The overall effect of these changes in heating is that the wind and pressure belts move north and south throughout the year. For example, Mediterranean regions come under the influence of the stable atmospheric conditions of the horse latitudes in summer, giving them hot, dry weather, but in winter the southward shift of wind belts brings cooler weather and cyclonic rain to Mediterranean lands. The astronomical dates pertaining to seasons do not coincide exactly with the actual seasons, however, because the earth's surface is slow to warm up and cool down. As a result, the summer months in the middle latitudes are June, July, and August. Similarly winter in the Northern Hemisphere occurs in December, January, and February.

Winds are also affected by the fact that land heats up and cools faster than does water. Rapid heating of coastal regions during the day creates an area of relatively low air pressure on land, into which cooler air from the sea is drawn. At night, the land cools rapidly and cold air flows from the land toward the relatively warmer sea.

Differential heating of the land and sea also leads to the development of huge air masses over the continents and oceans. There are four main types of air masses. Polar maritime air is relatively warm and moist, because it is heated from below by the water. Polar continental air, by contrast, is cold and mainly dry in winter, but warm in summer when the land heats quickly. Tropical maritime air is warm and moist, whereas tropical continental air, such as that over the Sahara Desert, is warm and dry. The movements of these air masses and their interaction with adjacent masses along boundaries called fronts have important effects on the weather in transitional areas.

The atmosphere circulates because of unequal heating of the earth by the sun. At the equator air is heated, rises, and then flows toward the poles, creating a permanent low-pressure area (the doldrums) around the equator. At about 30° N and 30° S some of the air sinks, giving rise to the zones of high pressure called the horse latitudes. Continuing to move away from the equator, the air cools and sinks (creating high pressure) over the poles. It then flows back toward the equator. The overall effect of the atmosphere's circulation is to create a pattern of prevailing winds (gray arrows in the illustration) that blow from high- to low-pressure areas.

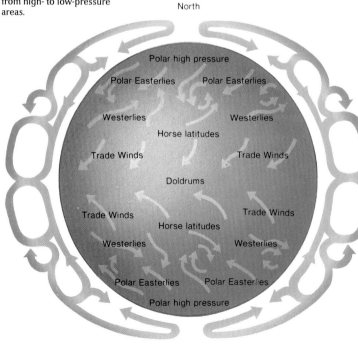

North

Polar high pressure

Polar Easterlies · Polar Easterlies

Westerlies · Westerlies

Horse latitudes

Trade Winds · Trade Winds

Doldrums

Trade Winds · Trade Winds

Horse latitudes

Westerlies · Westerlies

Polar Easterlies · Polar Easterlies

Polar high pressure

South

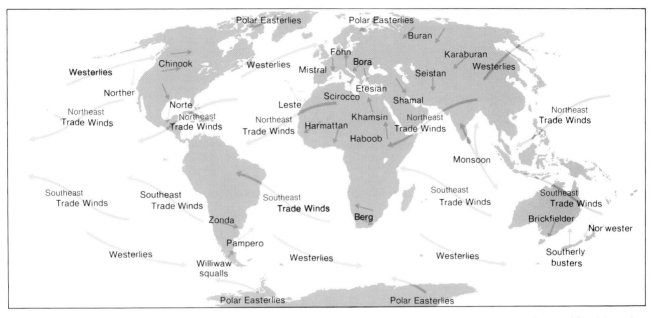

Fronts

Fronts form along the boundary between the polar and tropical air masses in the middle latitudes. They begin when undulations or waves develop; warm air then flows into pronounced undulations, thereby forming fronts. The forward arc of the undulation is called the warm front, and the following arc is the cold front. Fronts are low-pressure air systems, and winds are therefore drawn towards their centers. But the deflection caused by the Coriolis effect makes winds circulate around rather than blow directly into the center of a front. The wind circulation in fronts (cyclones) is in an anticlockwise direction in the Northern Hemisphere and clockwise in the Southern Hemisphere.

On weather maps, fronts appear as a series of concentric isobars (lines joining places with equal atmospheric pressure—analogous to contour lines of height on land maps), with the lowest pressure at the center. When the isobars are closer together the pressure gradient is steep, and the steeper the pressure gradient, the stronger are the winds, which tend to blow parallel to the isobars.

The formation of fronts is closely related to the paths of the jet streams in the upper atmosphere. On charts of the higher atmospheric layers, a poleward ripple in the westward-flowing jet stream usually indicates a front below. The flow of the jet streams affects the development of fronts. When a jet stream broadens, it tends to suck air upward, intensifying the low pressure below and causing wet, windy weather. When a jet stream narrows, it tends to push air down, thereby raising the pressure below. The jet streams are strongest in winter, when the temperature difference between polar and tropical regions is greatest; therefore the pressure gradient between these two regions is also steepest in winter. When a jet stream becomes strongly twisted, waves may break away. The jet stream soon connects up again, however, cutting off blocks of cold or warm air from the main flow. Such stationary blocks can bring spells of un-

The map *(above)* shows the principal prevailing winds (large arrows) and various local winds (small arrows).

The effect of a prevailing wind is dramatically exemplified by the tree *(left)* that, in growing away from the direction of the wind, has become contorted.

The wind was used as a source of power for centuries but, with the development of electricity generating stations, windmills generally fell into disuse. Recently, however, there has been renewed interest in wind power, and many new, more efficient windmills have been designed, such as the one shown on the left.

A front consists of a wedge of warm air between masses of cold air. At the front edge of a front is a warm air mass; a cold air mass marks the back edge. The approach of a front is usually indicated by the appearance of high cirrus clouds, followed successively by cirrostratus, altostratus, nimbostratus, and stratus clouds, these last often bringing rain. When the warm air mass has passed, temperatures increase but thunderstorms often occur. The cold air mass is frequently marked by rain-bearing cumulonimbus clouds.

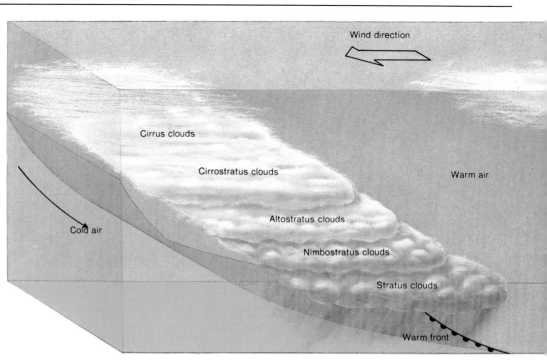

Air pressure is represented on weather maps by isobars—lines joining points of equal pressure. Cyclones are fronts of extreme low pressure, whereas anticyclones are high-pressure areas—as can be seen below where, on the graphical representation above the conventional isobar chart, cyclones appear as troughs and anticyclones as mounds.

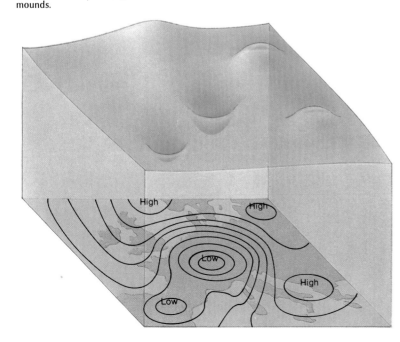

seasonal weather, such as the so-called "Indian summer."

Within a front, warm air flows upwards over cold air along the warm air mass. Because the gradient is gradual, the clouds ahead of the warm air mass are usually stratiform in type. Along the cold air mass, cold air undercuts the warm air, causing it to rise steeply; as a result, towering cumulonimbus clouds often form behind. Because the cold front moves faster than the warm front, the warm air is gradually pushed upward, or occluded. Bands of cloud linger for some time above occluded fronts, but the front soon weakens or is replaced by another.

Weather conditions in fronts

No two fronts bring exactly the same weather, but a knowledge of the general sequence of weather associated with these phenomena is an aid to forecasting. A front is often heralded by the appearance of high cirrus clouds, usually drawn into long, hooked bands by the jet stream. As the warm air mass approaches, cloud cover increases as progressively lower clouds arrive: cirrostratus, altostratus, nimbostratus, and stratus. The advance of the warm air mass is usually marked by increasingly heavy rain. After it has passed, air pressure stops falling and temperatures increase. After a few hours, however, thunderstorms often occur, associated with a narrow belt of squally weather along the cold front. After this belt has passed, the skies clear, pressure rises, and humidity diminishes.

Anticyclones

Adding to the variety of weather conditions in the middle latitudes are anticyclones, or high-pressure air systems. Anticyclones appear on weather maps as a series of concentric isobars with the highest pressure at the center. Winds tend to blow outward from the center of anticyclones (although not as strongly as winds blow into fronts) but are deflected by the Coriolis effect. As a result, the winds circulate around the center of an anticyclone in a clockwise direction in the Northern Hemisphere and in an anticlockwise direction in the Southern Hemisphere.

Anticyclones generally bring settled weather; warm weather with clear skies is typical in summer, whereas cold weather, frost, and fogs are associated with anticyclones in winter.

Storms

It has been estimated that severe storms (notably hurricanes and tornadoes) account for about 20 per cent of the huge annual cost of the damage caused by natural disasters. The most common storms, however, are thunderstorms, about 50,000 of which occur every day.

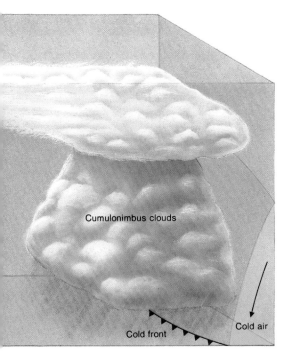

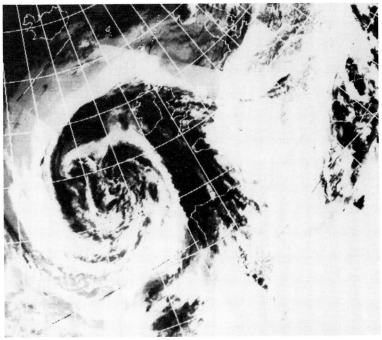

Cumulonimbus clouds

Cold front

Cold air

Thunderstorms, which are associated with cumulonimbus clouds formed in fast-rising air, are commonly accompanied by lightning, caused by the sudden release of accumulated static electricity in the clouds. The mechanisms by which static electricity forms in clouds is not known, but according to one popular theory, electrical charge is produced as a result of the freezing of super-cooled droplets in clouds. The outer layers of these droplets freeze first and, in so doing, become positively charged (a phenomenon that has been observed in laboratory conditions); the warmer, still unfrozen cores acquire a negative charge. A fraction of a second later the cores freeze and expand, thus shattering the outer layers. Positively-charged fragments of the outer layers are then swept upward to the top of the cloud while the still intact, negatively-charged cores remain in the cloud's lower levels. Eventually the total amount of charge in the cloud builds up sufficiently to overcome the electrical resistance of the air between the cloud and the ground, and the charge in the cloud is discharged as a huge electric spark—a flash of lightning. The violent expansion of the air molecules along the path of the lightning generates an intense sound wave, which is heard as thunder. Lightning is seen before thunder is heard because light travels faster than does sound.

Hurricanes

Hurricanes, which are also called tropical cyclones or typhoons, are intense, circular low-pressure systems that develop between latitudes 5° and 25° North and South over seas whose surface temperature is higher than about 82° F. (28° C). Around a central core of ex-

An occluded front is marked by the spiral cloud formation towards the left of the satellite photograph above. An occluded front is formed when a cold front reaches a warm front.

Lightning occurs in several types, of which forked lightning *(left)* is the most common. A lightning flash is a discharge of electrical charge that has accumulated in a cloud. The flash, with a current of some 10,000 amps, travels at 186,282 miles (299,792 kilometers) per second. The enormous amount of energy in the flash heats the air along its path to more than 60,000° F. (33,316° C) and generates an intense sound wave, thunder.

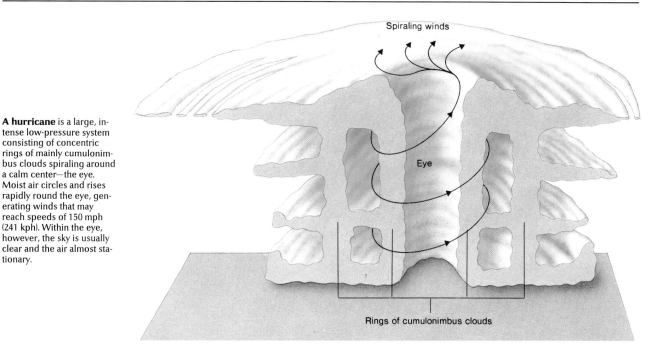

Spiraling winds

Eye

Rings of cumulonimbus clouds

A hurricane is a large, intense low-pressure system consisting of concentric rings of mainly cumulonimbus clouds spiraling around a calm center—the eye. Moist air circles and rises rapidly round the eye, generating winds that may reach speeds of 150 mph (241 kph). Within the eye, however, the sky is usually clear and the air almost stationary.

The spiral structure of a hurricane is clearly visible in this satellite photograph. Hurricanes may be more than 400 miles (644 km) across and extend from just above ground level to altitudes of 30,000 feet (9,144 m) or higher. The calm central eye is relatively small—typically between 4 and 30 miles (6 and 48 km) in diameter.

tremely low pressure (the eye of a hurricane) the moist air spins and rises swiftly to form spiraling belts of clouds, which, seen from above, resemble a whirlpool. The storm is maintained by the vast amount of energy released by rapid condensation in the rising air.

Hurricanes drift generally westward in both hemispheres. When they strike land, the winds, which may reach speeds of 150 miles per hour (241 kilometers per hour), can do tremendous damage. Hurricanes are recognizable on radar screens and satellite photographs, and so it is possible to issue storm warnings. Over land hurricanes are deprived of their moisture, and they gradually die out as air fills the low-pressure storm center.

Tornadoes

Tornadoes are whirlwinds that are up to 1.5 miles (2.4 kilometers) across. They are common in the American Midwest, where warm, moist air from the Gulf of Mexico underlies cold, dry air from the north.

The exact cause of tornadoes is not known, but they form when a long funnel of cloud

sinks from a turbulent cumulus cloud. Warm air is sucked upward around the strong downcurrent in a powerful spiral. Wind speeds may reach 380 miles per hour (612 kilometers per hour) although no instruments have survived to prove this. It is not only the winds that cause devastation, but also the great difference in pressure between the air inside buildings and the extremely low pressures outside; this difference can make buildings collapse. Tornadoes travel up to 200 miles (322 kilometers). Similar features at sea are called waterspouts.

Measuring the weather

Meteorology developed as a science in the seventeenth century with the invention of the barometer to measure atmospheric pressure, an accurate thermometer to measure air temperatures, and the hygrometer (using a human hair, which lengthens with increasing moisture) to measure humidity. The first known weather map, a generalized wind chart, appeared by 1686, but weather forecasting did not become feasible until 1844, when the American Samuel Morse perfected the electric telegraph, which made possible the rapid reporting of weather data.

Today about 10,000 weather stations are situated around the world on land and on ships at sea. Observations are usually made every three hours and include measurements of air pressure, temperature, humidity, wind speed and direction (using anemometers and wind vanes), and precipitation (using rain gauges). Other information collected includes the amount of cloud cover and types of clouds involved, hours of sunshine, and visibility. All the information collected at a weather station is translated into an international code and transmitted to a weather center.

Another important set of observations is concerned with the upper air. These are made by releasing a radiosonde, a hydrogen-filled balloon that carries various automatic instruments and a radio transmitter. As the balloon floats upward—reaching a height of about 90,000 feet (27,432 meters) before it bursts—its instruments take measurements of temperature, pressure, and humidity at various heights, and this information is transmitted to a recorder on the ground. When the balloon bursts, the instruments are parachuted down and are usually safely recovered.

Weather forecasting

Until recently the information received at weather centers was decoded and used with other information, such as photographs and other data from weather satellites, to plot synoptic charts. These hand-drawn maps showed isobars and other categories of information in conventional symbols, giving a complete picture of the weather at a particular time.

A team of meteorologists then analyzed the chart and compared it with perhaps six or more charts that depicted conditions over the past day. Air systems and the conditions associated with them were studied to see how they had developed and whether there were signs of any new systems. From this analysis, the meteorologists prepared a prognostic chart that summarized their view of future weather conditions. From this chart written forecasts were prepared and issued to the various news media.

The procedures have been modified to some extent because of the availability of large computers. Today, when the information reaches a weather center, it is fed into the computer. (Because the weather data is in the form of an internationally accepted code, information from any part of the world can be used without having to be translated.) The computer then produces synoptic charts that not only describe conditions at ground level but also those at several levels (sometimes as many as 15) of the upper air.

Large computers can also produce prognostic charts by applying the measured quantities of various weather factors (temperatures, air densities, wind velocities, and humidities, for example) to formulae based on the physical laws that describe the interaction of these factors. Computer forecasts are reasonably accurate in predicting the behavior of the atmosphere, but are less successful in predicting the weather. This is chiefly because of the fact that the interactions between air, land, and sea are extremely complex, and judgments based on long experience of local peculiarities are still needed for accurate short-term forecasting. For this reason prognostic charts and forecasts are still produced by human hands.

Short-range and long-range forecasting

The most familiar weather forecasts are short-range, covering an 18- to 36-hour period plus a "further outlook." The accuracy of such forecasts has increased greatly in recent years and, in the early 1980's, the U.S. National Weather Service claimed an accuracy of more than 85 per cent.

Long-range forecasts (a month ahead) are prepared in two ways. One way involves an

analysis of the previous month's daily charts, showing atmospheric pressures but omitting all minor complications; they thus give a broad view of changing conditions over the previous month and provide a basis for prediction. The other method is based on the assumption that previous weather patterns are likely to recur. The present conditions are "matched" to similar conditions in the past, and the weather that followed then is used to predict what is likely to follow now. Long-range forecasting is, however, still in its infancy.

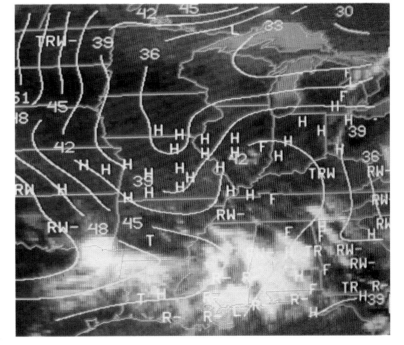

The computer-plotted chart of air humidity over part of North America (above) was based on data from meteorological satellites. As a result of the increasing use of satellite data and of computers to analyze weather information, forecasts have become more accurate, although they are still far from perfect.

"Dust devils," which resemble tornadoes, are rapidly spinning vortices of air. Although they are usually relatively small—often less than 160 feet (49 m) across—dust devils can cause considerable damage because of their high wind speeds and very low air pressures.

World climate

Weather is the condition of the atmosphere at a particular time or over a short period. Climate, on the other hand, is often described as the average, or the usual weather that an area experiences over a long period of time.

This definition of climate has, however, encouraged the belief that whereas the weather is changeable, the climate is fixed and predictable. This, however, is a false assumption because any period that is used to assess climatic averages may turn out to be abnormal. For instance, many parts of the world experienced considerably higher average temperatures in the period 1945-1960 than they had probably had for hundreds of years.

Any definition of climate should allow for long-term changes. It should, therefore, be a statement of the total weather of a place over a specific period of time. Furthermore, any description of climate should take account not only of average values, but also of extremes, including the reliability and frequencies of particular climatic features.

Factors influencing climate

Various factors prevent climatic regions from occurring in simple latitudinal bands; one such factor is the nature of the terrain. Mountains, for example, have a considerable influence on climate because they act as barriers to the wind and also because temperatures decrease with increasing altitude by about 3.5° F. for every 1,000-foot increase in height (6.5° C for every 1,000 meters). The windward sides of many mountains are rainy, whereas the leeward sides are in a rain shadow and are relatively dry. The highest mountains also affect movements of air in the upper troposphere; for example, the westward-flowing jet stream rises and veers northward over the Rocky Mountains, but turns southward again on the far side. The effect is to maintain relatively warm air over the Rockies at a high level.

The configuration of the continents and proximity to the sea are also important, because large expanses of water (including lakes) tend to moderate the climate; thus lakeside and coastal locations usually have less extreme climates than do places in the center of a continent. This moderating influence of water is generally greatest near the sea, which not only retains heat more readily than does land, but also transports it. Hence warm and cold ocean currents play a major part in determining the climates of coastlands.

The development of maritime and continental air masses is another factor that influences climate dramatically—exemplified when seasonal changes cause reversals of wind directions, or monsoons. Monsoon climates are most marked in southern Asia, where rapid cooling in winter causes the development of a high-pressure air mass over the land. From this air mass blow the dry northeastern Trade Winds. In spring, the northward movement of the sun causes northern India to be heated and, as a result, a marked low-pressure system develops into which southeastern Trade Winds are sucked across the equator, changing direction as they do so to become moist Westerlies.

Local climatic factors

Local climates are influenced by special factors that operate within comparatively small areas—for example, various local winds. The Föehn winds of the northern foothills of the Alps blow when low-pressure systems over northern Europe suck in winds from the south. As they descend, the Föehn winds become warm, causing rapid temperature increases in the areas through which they pass. The Chinook, a similar wind that occurs in late winter and early spring on the eastern slopes of the Rockies, can raise air temperature by 77° F. (25° C) in three hours.

Vegetation flourishes in the hot, wet tropics, where both temperature and rainfall are high throughout the year.

Rice-growing in India and much of southern Asia depends on the summer monsoon rains brought by warm, moist winds (which alternate seasonally with warm, dry winds blowing from the opposite direction).

Another local influence is the percentage of solar radiation reflected by the surface, or the albedo. Newly-fallen snow has an albedo of about 90 per cent, which explains why it may not melt in bright sunlight. Dry, sandy soils have a higher albedo than dark, clayey soils. Forests have low albedos, but forest floors tend to remain cool even on hot days because much of the sun's radiation is absorbed by the trees and comparatively little penetrates to ground level.

Some local climatic factors are man-made. For example, air pollution over cities reduces the sunshine and, therefore, the heat that reaches the ground. But this effect is counteracted by the warm air that blankets many urban areas. Furthermore, the presence in cities of many buildings of different heights tends to reduce wind speeds but also increases turbulence, resulting in comparatively light but gusty winds. This effect is often most noticeable at the intersections of streets lined by tall buildings.

Classification of climates

Climate has a great influence on soils and vegetation, but climatic regions, like soil and vegetation zones, seldom have precise boundaries on the ground; instead, one climatic type usually merges imperceptibly into another. Nevertheless, various attempts have been made to produce world climatic classifications, the most widely used being those of the Soviet meteorologist Vladimir Köppen, who between 1900 and 1936 published a series of classifications of varying degrees of complexity. Essentially he sought to relate climatic and vegetation features by using two basic criteria: temperature and rainfall. On this basis he divided the world into five main regions, designated *A, B, C, D,* and *E.*

Type *A* is the tropical rainy climate in which the average temperature in the coldest month is more than 64° F. (18° C). Type *B* is the dry climate in which the average annual rainfall is less than 10 inches (250 millimeters), although it could be greater if the average annual tem-

The Köppen classification is one of the most widely used climate categorizations. Based on temperature and rainfall, it divides the world into five principal climatic zones *(A, B, C, D,* and *E),* the distribution of which is shown below.

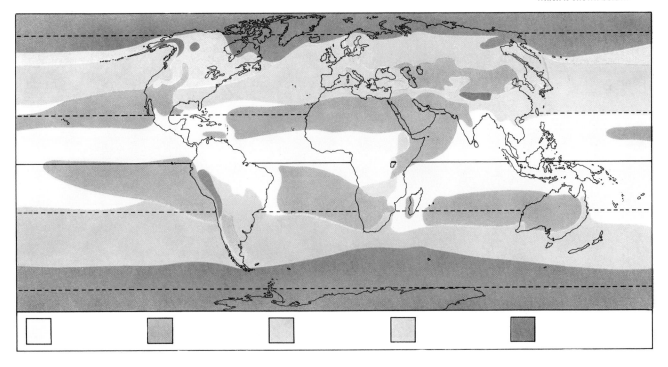

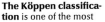

Estimations of temperature trends in temperate regions over the last 15,000 years indicate that, apart from minor fluctuations, the climate has become warmer. Some scientists believe that the temperature curve has reached a plateau and that the earth will enter another ice age similar to that of the Pleistocene epoch (which ended about 11,000 years ago).

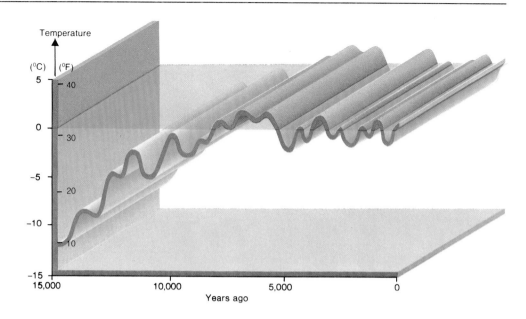

Ancient rock paintings found in regions that are now arid—such as the picture of horses *(below)*, which was found in Algeria—indicate that these areas were previously wetter and more fertile than they are today.

perature is high enough to ensure that evaporation exceeds precipitation.

Type *C* is the warm temperature climate, with an average temperature in the coldest month of between 26° F. and 65° F. (−3° C and 18° C), and an average temperature in the warmest month of more than 50° F. (10° C). Type *D* is the cold boreal forest climate, where the average temperature in the coldest month is below 26° F. (−3° C), but the average temperature in the warmest month is more than 50° F. (10° C). Type *E* is the polar climate, in which the average temperature in the warmest month is less than 50° F. (10° C).

Köppen's isothermal boundaries delineated a series of regions between the tropics and the poles. But he later found it convenient to add a sixth main type, *H,* to incorporate mountains, because the climates of high mountains reflect the various latitudinal vegetation zones that occur at sea level between the equator and the poles.

Köppen's simple classification was further subdivided. Temperature features were designated *a,* representing a hot summer; *b,* a warm summer; *c,* a cool summer; *d,* an extremely cold winter; *h,* a dry and hot climate; and *k,* a dry but cold climate. Rainfall features were assigned other codes: *S* for dry steppeland; *W* for deserts; *f* for places with ample precipitation all the year round; *m* for tropical regions with a marked rainy or monsoon season; *s* for places with a dry summer season; and *w* for places with a dry winter. Hence *Csa* denotes a warm temperature climate with a dry summer and a warm winter, a description corresponding to the climate of Mediterranean regions. Similarly, *Af* signifies a tropical rainy climate with precipitation all the year round, as opposed to an *Am* climate, which has a marked monsoon season.

Changing climates

The existence of coal seams in Antarctica and of dinosaur fossils in Spitsbergen (which is within the Arctic Circle) demonstrates that climates have changed radically during the millions of years of the earth's history. We also know that the positions of the continents have changed, and are still changing, as a result of movements of the earth's crustal plates. Hence we can postulate, for example, that during the Cretaceous period (which lasted from about 130 to 65 million years ago), when fossil evidence shows that breadfruit, fig trees, and luxurious ferns grew on Disko Island off Greenland, this island must have been much closer to the equator than it is today.

But plate movements are slow, averaging little more than 1 inch (2.5 centimeter) per year. Hence the advances and retreats of the huge ice sheets during the recent Pleistocene Ice Age (from about 1,800,000 to 11,000 years ago) and the even more recent climatic fluctuations experienced in the last 1,000 years cannot be explained by plate tectonics.

Evidence of climatic fluctuations

Evidence has been accumulating of frequent climatic cycles, with alternating warm or wet periods and cold or dry ones. During the Pleistocene Ice Age, for example, there were from 6 to 20 major periods in Europe when the ice advanced, and these glacial ages were punctuated by interglacial phases (also called interstadials). Some scientists believe that we are now in a fifth interstadial, although they have not been able to predict the date of onset of the sixth glacial age.

The evidence comes from several sources, including rock cores drilled from the sea bed. In these core samples the abundance of fossils of certain marine organisms that proliferate during warm conditions and become scarcer in cold periods shows cyclic variations, which indicates that the climate also varied periodically. Further evidence has been obtained from analyses of cores of ice from the ice sheets, soil samples, and tree rings.

According to recent findings it appears that the Northern Hemisphere had a warmer climate between A.D. 900 and 1300 than it does today. It was in the tenth century that Norsemen founded a settlement in Greenland, where average temperatures were estimated to be 1-7° F. (1-4° C) higher than they are today, but this settlement had disappeared by the end of the fifteenth century, probably because of the gradually worsening climate. In Europe the period 1450-1850 is often called the Little Ice Age. Although no precise figures exist before the invention of meteorological instruments, there is much evidence for the Little Ice Age from historical documents (including records of crop failures and paintings of frozen rivers that never freeze today), and from modern analyses of such factors as seed and pollen counts in soils and deposits dating from that period. From 1850 the climate became warmer, although recently there seems to have been a certain amount of cooling—as evidenced by the fact that in 1968 Arctic ice reached as far south as northeastern Iceland, the first time this had occurred for 40 years.

The causes of climatic change

The causes of climatic fluctuations have not yet been fully elucidated, although many different theories have been proposed. Some scientists believe that small variations in the earth's orbit around the sun (which would af-

fect the intensity of solar radiation reaching the earth) are the principal cause. But others have hypothesized that minute alterations in the earth's tilt on its axis may cause the climatic belts to shift, thus changing the climate as a whole. It has also been suggested that long- and short-term fluctuations in the sun's activity—those caused by the 11-year sunspot cycles, for example—may affect the climate.

Changes may also occur following prolonged volcanic activity. Volcanic dust can reduce the amount of solar radiation reaching the surface, causing changes in the weather. After the eruption of Krakatoa in 1883, for example, dust stayed in the atmosphere for a year; during this period a 10 per cent fall in solar radiation was recorded in southern France. There is also some concern that major climatic changes may result from human activities, such as deforestation and pollution of the atmosphere.

The fossils of small marine animals *(above)* are used by scientists to help determine past climates. Different species of these animals (called foraminifera) flourish in different water temperatures, therefore by dating and counting the various species, a guide to past water temperatures can be obtained.

The world climate is influenced by many factors, including pollution of the atmosphere. Some scientists have postulated that an increase in air pollution will cause global temperatures to increase because the pollutants help to retain the earth's heat. Others believe that the main effect of air contamination is to block the sun's rays, as a result of which temperatures will eventually fall. As yet, however, neither prediction can be confirmed.

Earth's oceans

More than 70 per cent of the earth's surface is covered by water, and of this amount 97 per cent is made up by the oceans. The largest is the Pacific Ocean, which covers an area of 63,800,000 million square miles (166,000,000 million square kilometers) and has a volume of 167.023 million cubic miles (696.182 million cubic kilometers).

The composition of seawater

The water in the oceans differs from pure water in that seawater has substances dissolved in it. The two most abundant elements in seawater are sodium and chlorine, mostly combined in the form of sodium chloride (common salt); the presence of these elements is the reason for the salty taste of the sea. Sodium and chlorine, together with four other elements—magnesium, sulfur, calcium, and potassium—make up about 95 per cent in weight of the substances dissolved in seawater. Many other elements also occur in the sea, but are present in very low concentrations. The total volume of seawater is enormous, however, so there is a large total quantity of each element in it. For example, there are about 10 million tons of gold in the sea, but in very small concentrations; only about one part of gold is found in each million million parts of the water, and it cannot be removed easily.

The concentrations of some of the less abundant elements in the sea vary because they are removed locally by plants and animals. Carbon and oxygen (as carbon dioxide) are two elements that are taken out by green plants because they are necessary for photosynthesis and plant growth. Other elements in the ocean, such as nitrogen and phosphorus, are essential for plant nutrition. These nutrients are also present in only very small amounts.

The salinity of seawater depends on the amount of substances dissolved in it. Salinity is usually expressed as the weight of the dissolved substances in a thousand parts of water. The ocean has an average salinity of 34.5 parts per thousand (about 3.5 per cent), but this figure varies between 33 and 38 parts per thousand in the open ocean. Water from rivers or melting ice dilutes seawater, and reduces its salinity. For this reason the water in the Arctic Ocean has a comparatively low salinity, less than 33 parts per thousand. The evaporation of seawater, however, increases its salinity, especially in tropical regions and in seas that are almost enclosed, such as the Mediterranean Sea and the Red Sea, where salinity can be as high as 41 parts per thousand.

The temperature of seawater

Seawater freezes at a lower temperature than pure water because of the dissolved substances in it. Pure water freezes at 32° F. (0° C),

whereas the temperature of seawater must drop to 28.6° F. (−1.9° C) before it will freeze. (Salt is put on roads in winter for this reason, to stop the water on them from freezing.) The temperature of the sea ranges from freezing point to about 86° F. (30° C) at the surface in tropical seas. Below the surface the temperature of the water declines rapidly until it levels out at a few degrees celsius at a depth of about 1,800 feet (547 meters). This middle region is sometimes known as the thermocline. Below it there is uniform salinity. More than 75 per cent of the water in the oceans has a temperature of less than 41° F. (5° C).

Light and sound in the sea

A few hundred feet below the ocean's surface it is dark because light cannot penetrate to those depths. Blue light penetrates water farther than red or violet light, and because more blue light is returned to the surface without

being absorbed, the open ocean usually looks blue in color. Seawater may look blue-green when it contains a large amount of phytoplankton—tiny, plantlike organisms that contain chlorophyll. The yellow-brown sea found in coastal regions probably gets its coloring from mud, sand, or pollution.

Sound—particularly high-frequency sound—penetrates much further than light does in the ocean. This property has led to the development of echo-sounders that are used to construct pictures of the ocean floor. Sound can also be used to locate shoals of fish. At a depth of between about 1,650 and 5,000 feet (503 and 1,524 meters) a sound channel exists where sound waves can be trapped and along which they travel for large distances. Whales have been known to use the sound channel to communicate with each other when they are thousands of miles apart; zoologists believe that their long-distance "songs" may attract others to new hunting or breeding grounds. The sound channel has also been used by submarines when hiding in the ocean. A submarine floating in or below the sound channel is difficult to detect because most of the noise it makes travels horizontally and cannot be picked up by ships at the surface.

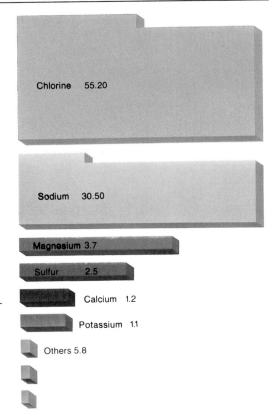

Chlorine	55.20
Sodium	30.50
Magnesium	3.7
Sulfur	2.5
Calcium	1.2
Potassium	1.1
Others	5.8

The composition of seawater is dominated by the presence of chlorine and sodium. This diagram shows the concentrations, in parts per thousand, of the major constituents of seawater. How it acquired most of these elements is not known, although it is thought that the water from rivers is the source of the sodium chloride in seawater.

The oceans covering the earth are rich in animal and plant life, but neither of these communities could survive without the chemical or gaseous constituents of seawater. To phytoplankton, for instance, the silicates, nitrates, and phosphates found in this water are essential. Oxygen, also necessary for marine life, is found in abundance in the sea—an average of six parts per thousand in volume. The dependence on the salinity of water is also reflected in the movement of marine communities around its increase and reduction. Light also affects them in this way. The blueness of the sea depends on the depth of penetration of blue light, which, in turn, depends on the smoothness of the waters. In clear waters, such as the Caribbean, light may reach depths of 525 feet (160 meters); on rough coasts it may go down to only 50 feet (15 meters).

Ocean currents

The main patterns of water movement in the oceans result from the earth's rotation and the gravitational interaction between the earth, moon, and sun. The ocean's surface currents are created and driven by the winds on the earth's surface, which themselves result from differences in the temperature of the air between the equator and the poles. The earth's rotation subjects the movements of air and water on its surface to a force that causes them to move in a clockwise fashion in the Northern Hemisphere, and in an anticlockwise motion in the Southern Hemisphere. This is known as the Coriolis effect.

Currents at the surface

Surface currents move slower than the prevailing winds that create them. The faster ocean currents travel at up to 5.75 miles per hour (9.22 kilometers per hour) and the slower ones at about 1.16 miles per hour (1.87 kilometers per hour). The currents do not move in the same direction as the winds because of the Coriolis effect.

Land masses also deflect currents and cause water to travel in large circular paths called gyres. The principal gyres move in a clockwise direction in the North Atlantic and North Pacific oceans and anticlockwise in the South Atlantic and South Pacific oceans, following the Coriolis effect. The North Atlantic gyre is composed of three major currents—the Gulf Stream, the Canary Current, and the North Equatorial Current. The gyre in the northern Indian Ocean changes direction with the seasons because of the seasonal change of the monsoon winds. In winter the wind blows from the northeast, causing an anticlockwise

circulation in the ocean; in the summer it blows from the southwest, creating a clockwise current. This is known as the Monsoon effect.

The currents on the western sides of gyres move water away from the equator, as do the Gulf Stream and the Brazil Current in the Atlantic, and they are warm. They gradually lose their heat and those currents that return water to the equator, such as the Canary and Benguela currents, are cooler.

Water in the center of gyres is almost stationary. The warm currents on their western sides are narrow and flow quite quickly, whereas the cold currents on the eastern sides are much slower and occur in broad bands. Surface currents extend to less than 1,150 feet (350 meters) deep, but they still transport large volumes of water. The Gulf Stream, for example, probably contains 100 times as much water as all the earth's rivers.

When water is turned away from land masses, a phenomenon called upwelling occurs. To replace the surface water blown away from the coastline, water moves up from deeper, colder layers and decreases the temperature of the surface water. Ocean currents can thus moderate climate by cooling hot regions and, sometimes, by warming cool ones. Nearly all the harbors of Norway, for example, are kept ice-free by the North Atlantic Drift, which is warmed by the Gulf Stream.

In addition to their climatic influences, ocean currents have a profound effect on marine plants and animals—and, indirectly, on some terrestrial forms of life. All marine animals ultimately depend for food on small photosynthetic plankton, which, in the relatively light upper layers of the oceans, use sunlight to convert inorganic substances into food, giving off oxygen as a byproduct. Slightly denser than seawater, the plankton slowly sink but are brought back to the surface by turbulent up-

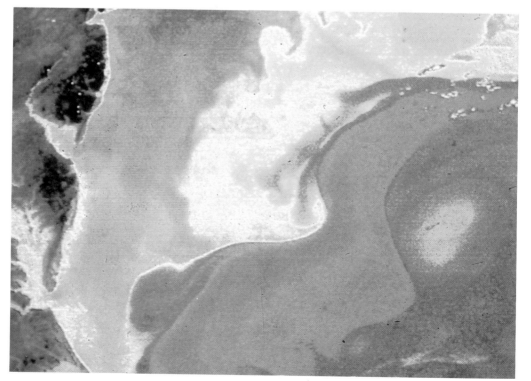

The Gulf Stream is shown here rounding the northeastern coast of North America. The computer-enhanced image was assembled from infrared data and shows the temperature range of the current and the surrounding area. White signifies clouds and represents a temperature of less than 38° F. (3° C). Blue, indicating a temperature between 38° and 57° F. (3° and 13° C), marks the coastal waters and the continental shelf. Orange, red, and yellow are the outer margins of the current, between 57° and 63° F. (13° and 17° C), and pink through black represent land and the center of the current at 66° to 80° F. (19° to 27° C).

welling; they can also be carried long distances by ocean currents. Many marine animals feed on plankton and, therefore, tend to follow their food source as it is moved by the sea which, in turn, determines the movements of those animals that eat the plankton-feeders. This interdependence of predator and prey continues through numerous marine species and may eventually involve terrestrial forms of life that feed on marine creatures.

Unlike most ocean currents, there is one that flows all the way around the world—the Antarctic Circumpolar Current. Just north of the Antarctic land mass there are no land barriers, and so the Westerlies can drive the current eastward without being obstructed. Near the equator, the winds are not very strong, and a narrow weak current—the Equatorial Counter Current—flows eastward between the westward flowing North and South Equatorial Currents.

Deepwater currents

Currents also exist in ocean waters deep below the surface. These are not caused by the wind but by differences in density of the water. Denser water flows over the ocean floor beneath warmer, less dense water. The density of water depends, in turn, on its temperature and salinity; cold water has greater salinity and is denser than warmer water.

Deeper currents often flow in the opposite direction to the surface currents, and they usually travel more slowly. The layer of water below the surface current moves with the top layer because of the friction between the two, but because its speed is slightly slower than the layer above, the Coriolis force moves it farther to the right or left of the wind's direction. This process continues down through successive layers, in what is known as the Ekman spiral, each layer decreasing in velocity until, at a

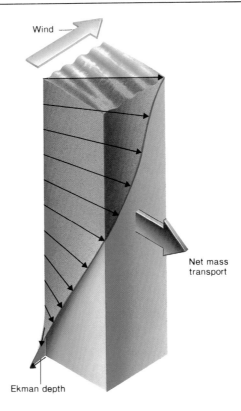

Wind

Net mass transport

Ekman depth

depth of about 330 feet (100 meters), the water flows at 180° to the wind's direction and at about 4 per cent of the speed of the surface current. In the Straits of Gibraltar, for example, the surface current flows eastward into the Mediterranean Sea, but a more saline current flows beneath it, out into the Atlantic Ocean. A deep current also exists below the Gulf Stream, which flows southward along the sea bed in the opposite direction to the surface current.

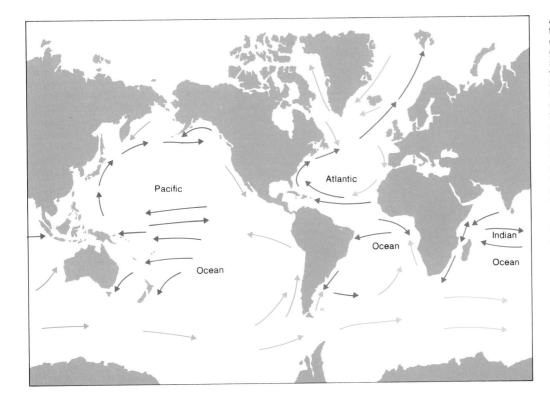

Pacific

Ocean

Atlantic

Ocean

Indian

Ocean

A map of the ocean's surface currents shows the clockwise rotation of the gyres in the Northern Hemisphere and the anticlockwise movement in the Southern Hemisphere. Every gyre has an area in its center that is higher than the water level at its edges—the North Atlantic gyre is about 500 feet (152 meters) higher at its center than at the edge of the warm Gulf Stream. The water at the center of the gyres is also still because virtually no surface currents exist there. Some places are so stagnant that fish travel to them to spawn, such as the area between the Bahamas and the Azores.

Ocean waves

When we see waves rolling into and breaking on a shore, it seems as if all the water is moving horizontally. But it is mainly energy and not water that is being moved. Waves possess kinetic energy. This energy in waves derives from the orbital movement of water molecules, which move up and down and in small circles—but not horizontally because most of the water is not being moved along. The energy of a wave can be quite substantial; for instance, when a wave 4 feet high breaks on the shore it releases the equivalent of about 25 megawatts of power per mile of shoreline.

The wind and water movement

The greatest amount of wave energy in ocean waters is derived from small wind-generated waves. Like the currents on the surface of the ocean, most waves are caused by wind blowing over the water. A gentle breeze can create ripples, or capillary waves; but because the ripples present a greater surface area to the wind, there is additional friction and pressure, which increase the length of the waves. This, in turn, results in a greater velocity, so that eventually the waves may reach the same speed as the wind.

Waves usually reach about 10 feet (3 meters) in height, but can range from mere ripples to about 50 feet (15 meters) high; the highest wave height ever measured was 112 feet (34 meters). The height of waves increases with the speed of the wind, the length of time it has been blowing, and the distance the wind has traveled over the ocean—called the fetch. The wind speed in metric knots (1 knot = 1.166 miles per hour or 1.876 kilometers per hour) is about twice the wave height in meters. Waves with a short wavelength tend to disperse because they lose height when they collide with each other.

Most wind-driven waves start as deepwater waves, where the depth of the water is more than half their wavelength. Waves in the ocean consist of different wave-trains of varying wave height and length, each wave-train moving at its own speed. When the wave in front of the train moves into still water, some of its energy is transferred to the water molecules in the undisturbed water, which starts their orbital motion. In this way the leading wave is perpetually losing its energy and dispersing, and it is replaced by the next wave, which undergoes the same process. The water molecules continue their motion after the train has passed and a new wave is created at the end of the train.

Breaking waves

The wind-generated waves that reach a shore change in nature and gradually become shallow-water waves. The orbital motion of the water particles differs in shallow water, whereas in deep water the movement is circular; each circle decreases in size with increased depth, shallow-water particles move in an increasingly elliptical motion with increasing depth until their movement is linear, and they move back and forth.

When a deepwater wave comes within a depth that is half its wavelength, it is bent, or refracted. At this depth the wave slows down, which causes its length to decrease, and the leading part of the wave moves slower than the rest of the wave. The effect of refraction can be seen as a wave approaches the shore and seems to bend around so that it breaks almost parallel with the shore. At this stage it also differs from a deepwater wave in that all the waves in a train in shallow water have the same velocity for a particular depth.

As the wave reduces its speed the waves behind it, which are moving faster, start to pile up. The result is an increase in the height of the wave and a compression of the motion of the water particles. The orbital speed of the particles decreases in the trough of the wave but not at the crest, making the wave increasingly less stable. By the time the angle from

A surfer makes use of what is termed a spilling wave—one that rolls gently over a gradually sloping shore before breaking. The other main type of wave dumps water after breaking violently over a steeply sloping shore.

A wave approaching the shore decreases in length and velocity while pressure from the waves behind it builds up, causing it to increase in height. The circular motion of the water particles becomes increasingly compressed and elliptical. They slow down in the trough but not in the crest, so that the crest overtakes the rest of the wave and spills over.

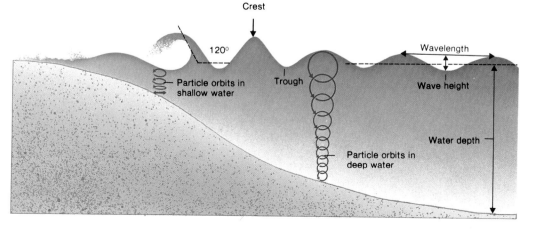

Crest

Wavelength

120°

Particle orbits in shallow water

Trough

Wave height

Particle orbits in deep water

Water depth

the inside center of the base of the wave to the crest is more than 120°, and the ratio of the wave's height to its length exceeds 1:7, the crest is moving at a greater speed than the rest of the wave; it overshoots the rest of the wave, and the water breaks. At this point, the crest is sometimes moving at double the speed of the wave. Waves break on the shore when the water depth below them is about 1.3 times the wave height; a 6-foot wave, for example, breaks in 8 feet of water.

Tsunamis

The most destructive waves in the ocean are tsunamis, often wrongly called tidal waves. They are not caused by tides, but by underwater earthquakes, landslides, volcanic eruptions, or by hurricanes. These disturbances cause the sea bed to move very quickly, which shifts a large amount of water and disrupts the sea surface. A train of waves is set in motion and travels away from the source of disturbance.

Tsunamis travel extremely fast—up to 500 miles per hour (805 kilometers per hour). They have a long wavelength, their crests often being 93 miles (150 kilometers) apart, so that a crest passes only every 15 minutes or so. In the open ocean they are very low and usually pass ships unnoticed. In shallow water, however, tsunamis change and as each wave reduces its velocity, the wave height builds up to tens of feet until it breaks. Where the shape of the sea floor concentrates the energy of the wave, tsunamis can cause devastation on the shore.

The eruption of a volcano in 1883 on the island of Krakatoa caused destructive tsunamis. Waves 130 feet (40 meters) high crashed into

the nearby islands and even swept a boat far inland. The shores of the Pacific more than those of any other ocean have been damaged by tsunamis because volcanic eruptions and earthquakes occur frequently in that area. The time tsunamis take to travel from a submarine disturbance to the nearer coasts and islands can be calculated from seismic readings, however, and adequate warning can usually be given.

Waves in the ocean derive most of their energy from the wind. Even a slight breeze can start ripples that, because they present a greater surface area to the wind, are exposed to more friction and grow in length. The waves in this photograph are probably caused by a wind blowing at about 28 miles per hour (45 kilometers per hour).

Breakers on the shore may be the end of a wave that was started by storm winds in the middle of an ocean thousands of miles away. Their nature depends not only on the slope of the shore but also on its composition; plunging, or dumping, waves occur mostly on a smooth, steep sea floor, whereas spilling waves are more likely on a gently sloping shore with rocky outcrops.

Tides

Tides result from the regular rise and fall of the water level in the oceans. This phenomenon is caused by the gravitational pull of the moon and sun on the earth, and by the centrifugal force generated by the rotation of the moon-earth system as a whole. These two forces act in opposite directions. The bulge of the water surface caused by the gravitational pull of the sun and moon is repeated on the opposite side of the earth, where the bulge is due to the centrifugal force. The sun, although much more massive than the moon, is also much farther from the earth. As a result, the sun's effect on the earth's tides is only half that of the moon.

Spring and neap tides

Tides occur every day, and their timing and position depend on the earth's rotation on its axis related to the position of the moon. If the moon were stationary, each point on the earth would have two high and two low tides every day. But because the moon orbits the earth every 27.33 days and because the earth takes just more than a day (25.02 hours) to rotate once in relation to the moon, the positions of the high tides on the earth change. At any one location they occur about an hour later each day.

When the moon and sun are aligned on the same side of the earth, the tide caused by their combined action is higher than normal and is called a spring tide. This event recurs every 14 days, at new moon or full moon. When the sun and moon form a right angle with the earth, the gravitational pulls of the moon and sun are in opposition and result in weaker, intermediate tides called neap tides. These also take place every two weeks, at the first and third quarters of the moon.

Because tides depend on the rotation of the earth and that of the moon and the earth around their common center of mass, the time of high and low tide at any point on the earth can be predicted. The solar tide has a period of 12.41 hours (because of the monthly rotation of the moon around the earth). The moon's closest approach to the earth is at perigee, and the farthest point of its orbit is at apogee, the mean between the two being about 238,857 miles (384,403 kilometers). When perigee coincides with the spring tides, they rise about 20 per cent higher than normal.

Tidal range

Other variations in tidal height and occurrence can arise depending on the size, depth, and shape of the ocean, the shape of the coastline, the latitude, and the angles of the moon and sun relative to the equator. Spring tides have a larger tidal range than do neap tides. Most parts of the ocean have two high and low tides a day, but a few areas have only one high and one low tide. In some areas of the Pacific Ocean,

The tidal bulges on the earth's surface (A) are caused by the gravitational force of the sun and moon, and by the centrifugal force that results from the rotation of the earth-moon system. As the moon orbits the earth (B), the time of high tide changes from day to day, recurring approximately every fortnight when the moon has completed half of its orbit (1 to 5). When the moon and sun are in line on the same side of the earth, their combined gravitational pull results in a higher tide than normal, called a spring tide (C). A neap tide (D) occurs when the moon and sun are at right angles to each other. They cause an intermediate tidal level, which is slightly more pronounced in the line of the moon because its gravitational pull is stronger than the sun's.

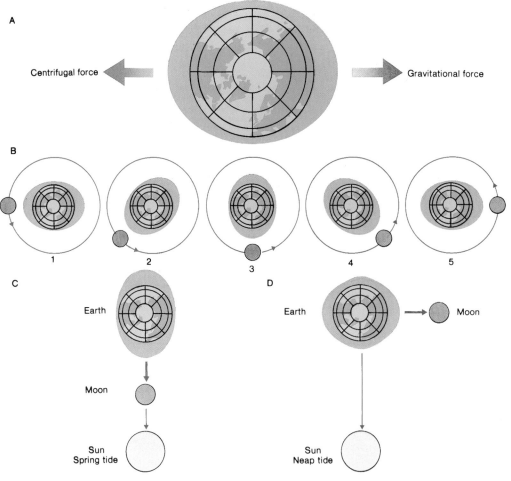

A

Centrifugal force   Gravitational force

B

1   2   3   4   5

C

Earth

Moon

Sun
Spring tide

D

Earth   Moon

Sun
Neap tide

the high tides differ in height from each other, and so do the low tides.

The tidal range in the open ocean is usually quite small—only a foot or so in amplitude—but toward the coasts waves increase in height and velocity. The English Channel, for example, has a daily tidal range of about 6.5 feet (2 meters). In narrow bays the tidal range can be greater. One of the world's largest tidal ranges is in the Bay of Fundy, on the eastern coast of Canada, where it can reach 60 feet (18 meters). Estuaries or seas that are almost enclosed, such as the Mediterranean Sea, often have their own tides that are small in range. When these cycles coincide with the earth's tidal period, such relatively small bodies of water can experience large tidal ranges.

Attempts have been made in areas with large tidal ranges to use the regular rise and fall of water to generate electricity, such as the tidal power station in the Rance estuary in Brittany, France, where the average height range of the tide is 28 feet (8.5 meters). Energy from tides was used as early as 1650 in New England, when tidal power was harnessed to run grist mills. Today, tidal energy is converted into electrical power by making the tidal waters drive reversible turbines. These machines extract the potential energy from the water that flows in and then ebbs away.

Tidal bores

When an incoming mass of water flows into a narrowing channel, such as a bay or an estuary, the funneling process causes the water to flow much quicker than it would were it allowed to spread. The water at the front of the tide tends to slow down because of the narrowing, but the water behind it rushes up at normal speed, so that the water increases in height and velocity, resulting in a wall of water that surges up the channel. This happens particularly in Asia, the best-known example being that of the Tsientang Kiang River estuary in northern China, where the tidal bore reaches a height of 25 feet (7.6 meters) and moves at about 14 miles per hour (23 kilometers per hour). Tidal bores occur mainly during spring tides.

Tidal currents

Changing tides can also create tidal currents, particularly in areas that are almost enclosed. The typical speed of these currents in most channels and straits is about 7 miles per hour (11 kilometers per hour), but in some regions it may reach 11 miles per hour (18 kilometers per hour), such as the Straits of Georgia, which lie between Vancouver Island and British Columbia. Tidal currents are most powerful in deep waters and weakest in shallow areas. They change position and direction with the earth's rotation, just as the tides do. These currents sometimes run at right angles to the tide, in the opposite direction or even in the same direction.

Local climate can also affect the level of coastal waters to an even greater degree than the tides. The surging water is then known as a meteorological tide. A storm surge, for example, is the result of a climatic effect on water.

The tidal bore on the Tsientang Kiang River, China, reaches a height of 25 feet (7.6 meters). The waves flood in at intervals of 15 minutes, each rising higher than its predecessor.

The tidal range around St. Michael's Mount in Cornwall, England, is such that at low tide it is possible to walk across the causeway, whereas at high tide a boat would be needed. The tidal range in the English Channel is about 6.5 feet (2 meters).

Sea ice

Two main types of ice occur in the sea: pack ice, which is formed by the freezing of seawater, and icebergs, which break off from glaciers or other accumulations of snow on land.

Pure water freezes at 32° F. (0° C), but seawater does not freeze until the temperature drops to about 28.6° F. (−1.9° C) because of the dissolved salts in it. In polar regions cold winds from the icecaps cool the ocean until the top layer reaches freezing point; at this stage, ice crystals start to form on the surface of the sea. Ice requires a larger volume than a similar mass of water. It is therefore less dense than water and so floats on the surface of the sea. Salts from the seawater are not included in the hexagonal ice crystals but are trapped in the liquid between them. The salt solution moves slowly downwards out of the ice, so that five or six years after its formation the ice looks like a honeycomb. Newly formed ice has a salinity of anything between five and ten parts per thousand, whereas old ice has a salinity of less than two parts per thousand.

Ice packs

Ice packs develop from the accretion of small ice crystals. To begin with the crystals coalesce into small thin platelets, known as frazil ice. As the ice thickens, the frazil ice platelets freeze together into a continuous skin of ice, which in a rough sea may break up into individual disks up to 3 feet (1 meter) across. The plates collide with each other, which often causes their edges to turn up and form what is known as pancake ice.

As the sea freezes still further, the ice thickens and the pancake ice joins together to form an ice floe which may be as small as 30 feet (9 meters), or as large as 5 miles (8 kilometers). The seawater underneath the ice is insulated by it against the cold air, so the ice floe thickens only slowly, reaching a thickness of about 6.5 feet (2 meters) in the Arctic and 10 feet (3 meters) in the Antarctic at the end of the winter of the first year. In the summer, the sun melts the surface of the ice floe, which forms pools of fresh water. The ice melts through completely in places, but if the floe survives the summer, an even thicker floe is formed when the water refreezes.

The wind and tides can change smooth ice floes into bumpy packs of ice by moving them together, crushing and deforming them. In addition, these forces can cause the ice to crack along lines of weakness. The movement of ice packs can also cause cracks in the ice that open into long, narrow channels or into patches of open water, called polynyas. The water in polynyas usually freezes quickly, forming a thin sheet of ice, which may be crushed if the sides of the polynya start to close together.

The Arctic Ocean has a large area of permanent pack ice, which is even more extensive in winter, when it reaches Alaska, the Soviet Union, northern Canada, and Greenland. Ordi-

Pancake ice forms when wind or water motion disturbs thin sheet ice or frozen slush ice and breaks it up. The fragments are then ground together until they are shaped into disks with upturned edges. The disks can form in only a few hours.

Arctic icebergs often calve from glaciers. The snout of the glacier from which these icebergs have broken can be seen behind them. The varying shapes of Arctic glacial icebergs usually result from the melting of a glacier's surface near its snout at a faster rate than the erosion of the bottom layers, which produces an underwater shelf that eventually breaks off and bobs up to the surface. Icebergs can be black, brown, or green in color, due to the amount of sediment they contain as well as the plankton that they carry from under the ice shelf.

nary ships cannot cross the Arctic because of this ice, and even icebreakers cannot force their way through the thicker areas. But submarines can travel below the ice pack, using sonar to detect the thickness of the ice above. The Antarctic has a smaller area of pack ice that consists of large floating ice shelves that join onto the land mass.

Icebergs

Icebergs are chunks of ice that have broken from an icecap on land; they therefore contain no salt. In the north polar regions, glaciers flow down to the sea from the icecaps. When a glacier reaches the water, the front slides in and breaks into large pieces of ice—a process that is called calving. The icebergs then float in the sea and are carried away from the land by currents, or they remain frozen in the pack ice for a year or so. Arctic icebergs drift southwards along the western side of the North Atlantic Ocean and travel as far south as Newfoundland before melting completely. Once in the open ocean they last for less than three months, but they can become a hazard to shipping because of their size.

Antarctic bergs differ from those of the Arctic in that they are formed from the ice shelf that surrounds Antarctica. Every year the shelf moves northward about 300 feet (91 meters), and during this movement, ice breaks off. The bergs may drift as far north as latitude 40° S before melting. Arctic bergs may reach up to 300 feet (91 meters) out of the water and extend to depths of 1,300 feet (396 meters) below the surface, whereas the longer, tabular Antarctic bergs rise to only about 160 feet (49 meters) above the water and reach only 500 feet (152 meters) below it, but they can be as large as 60 miles (96 kilometers) wide and 200 miles (322 kilometers) long. Several thousand icebergs break off from Greenland and Antarctica each year.

Icebergs have caused ships to sink, the most famous example being the *Titanic,* which sank in 1912 after hitting a relatively small iceberg. In North Atlantic shipping lanes, icebergs are now tracked by an International Ice Patrol. They do not show up well on radar, but they drift quite slowly and if the location of one is known, ships can alter course around it. Icebergs are an even greater danger to oil rigs at sea. Oil rigs cannot be moved and can be severely damaged or destroyed if an iceberg drifts into one. Icebergs have been towed away from rigs to prevent collisions. But this is often a difficult operation because of the size of the icebergs.

Icebergs could, however, be put to use. They are composed of fresh water, and so they would be a useful source of water if it were possible to tow them to arid areas of the world (such as the Middle East) without melting. Unfortunately they can only be towed very slowly, and it takes several months to reach a dry area—during which time much of the ice melts.

Icebergs in the Antarctic are more abundant and much larger than those of the Arctic. They are usually tabular, about 5 miles (8 kilometers) long, and project at least 150 feet (46 meters) out of the water. A tabular iceberg can be seen in the background on the right.

Ice packs vary in thickness; for example, the weight of accumulated blocks of ice can force down parts of the ice pack far below the surface to form roots of ice that descend as deep as 160 feet (49 meters). In thinner parts, however, cracks and polynias appear, particularly in summer.

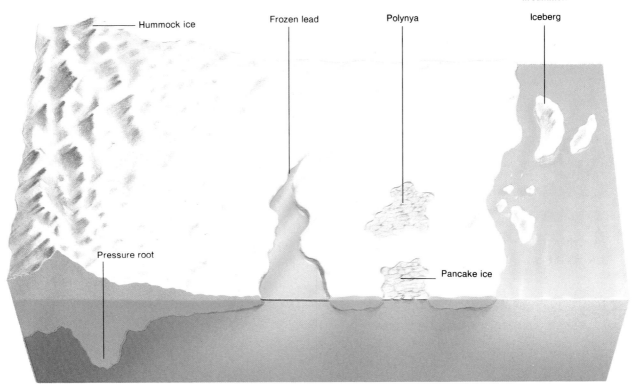

Hummock ice

Frozen lead

Polynya

Iceberg

Pressure root

Pancake ice

Structure and surface of the earth

The earth has four main structural components: the crust, the mantle, the outer core, and inner core. The crust extends down to about 25 miles (40 kilometers) and consists of rocks with a density of less than 188 pounds per cubic foot (3,000kg/m³). The mantle, divided by a transition zone, is made up of denser rocks than is the crust. The temperature in this region rises rapidly, particularly between 60 and 125 miles (96 and 201 kilometers) below the surface, where it reaches 1,600° F. (871° C). At the core-mantle boundary (the Gutenberg discontinuity), 1,800 miles (2,897 kilometers) below the surface, the pressure suddenly increases, as does the density from 345 to 620 pounds per cubic foot (5,500 to 9,900 kg/m³). The outer core is believed to be completely liquid, while the inner core is believed to be solid; it has an average density of 690 pounds per cubic foot (11,000kg/m³).

The crust, the uppermost layer of the solid earth, is a region of interaction between surface processes brought about by the heat of radioactive reactions deep in the earth. It is the most complex layer of the lithosphere in its physical and chemical nature. The earth's crust contains a wide variety of rock types, ranging from sedimentary rocks dominated by single minerals, such as sandstone (which is mainly silica) and limestone (which is mainly calcite), to the mineral-chemical mixtures of igneous rocks, such as basalt lavas and granite intrusions.

The crust is divided into ocean crust and continental crust. The average height of the two differs by about 2.8 miles (4.5 kilometers), but the difference in their average total thickness is more exaggerated. Continental crust is about 25 miles (40 kilometers) thick, and oceanic crust about 5 miles (8 kilometers). The boundary between the crusts and the mantle is almost everywhere defined sharply by the Mohorovičić seismic discontinuity. They contrast strongly in structure, composition, average age, origin, and evolution. Vertical sections of both types of crust have been studied in zones of uplift caused by colliding tectonic plates. Combined with seismic evidence, these sections provide a unified view of crustal structure and composition.

Oceanic crust

Seismic studies of the ocean crust and upper mantle have identified four separate layers characterized by downward increases in wave propagation velocity, density, and thickness. The upper two layers were studied by the Deep Sea Drilling Project in 1968, whereas all that is known about the third and fourth layers has come only from ophiolites—uplifted ocean crust sections that are exposed on the earth's surface. The top layer of the ocean crust, with an average thickness of 2,650 feet (808 meters) comprises sedimentary muds (pelagic clays). They include the finest particles that were eroded from continents, and biochemically precipitated carbonate and siliceous deposits.

The bottom three layers are made up of igneous materials formed during ocean-ridge processes. The chemical composition of these layers is that of basic igneous rocks, but their physical characteristics vary. The second layer, with an average thickness of 1 mile (1.6 kilometers) consists of basalt pillow lavas that were originally quenched by seawater when they erupted onto the sea floor. At the boundary between the second and third layers, the lavas give way to sheeted complexes of almost vertical dikes. These features, which have an average vertical thickness of 1.1 miles (1.8 kilometers), are followed by a thick sequence of

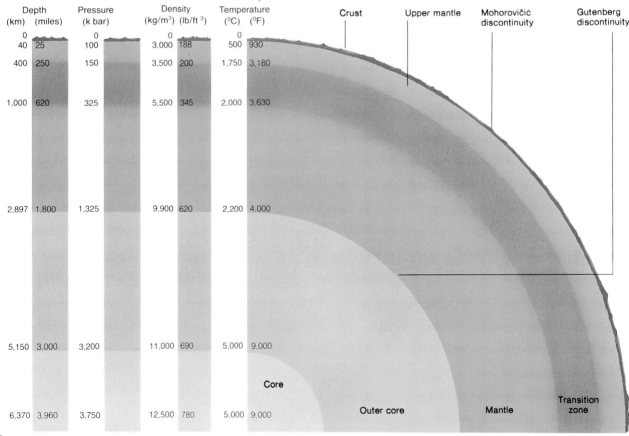

Depth (km)	(miles)	Pressure (k bar)	Density (kg/m³)	(lb/ft³)	Temperature (°C)	(°F)
0		0	0		0	
40	25	100	3,000	188	500	930
400	250	150	3,500	200	1,750	3,180
1,000	620	325	5,500	345	2,000	3,630
2,897	1,800	1,325	9,900	620	2,200	4,000
5,150	3,000	3,200	11,000	690	5,000	9,000
6,370	3,960	3,750	12,500	780	5,000	9,000

Crust — Upper mantle — Mohorovičić discontinuity — Gutenberg discontinuity

Core

Outer core — Mantle — Transition zone

layered, coarse-grained, intrusive gabbros almost 2 miles (3 kilometers) thick that must have cooled and crystallized slowly at a depth, with early formed crystals segregating into layers. The bottom layer includes layered peridotite, which grades downward into unlayered mantle peridotite.

Both layered peridotites and gabbros probably represent a fossilized magma chamber, which was originally created by the partial melting of the mantle beneath an ocean ridge. Molten material was probably ejected from the chamber roof, forming dikes that fed the pillow lava eruptions of the second layer. The Mohorovičić discontinuity lies between the two deepest layers.

Continental crust

In terms of seismic structure, the earth's continental crust is much less regular than the ocean crust. A diffuse boundary called the Conrad discontinuity occurs between the upper and lower continental crusts at a depth of between 9 and 15 miles (14.5 and 24 kilometers). The upper continental crust has a highly variable topmost layer that is a few miles thick and comprises relatively unmetamorphosed volcanic and sedimentary rocks. Most of the sedimentary rocks were laid down in shallow marine conditions and subsequently uplifted. Beneath this superficial layer of the upper crust, most of the rock is similar in composition to granodiorite or diorite and is made up of intermediate, coarse-grained intrusive, igneous rocks. The total thickness of the upper continental crust reaches a maximum of about 20 miles (32 kilometers) in zones of recent crustal thickening caused by igneous activity (such as the Andes mountain range in South America) and by tectonic overthrusting during collision (such as the Alps in Europe). This crust is of minimum thickness in the ancient continental cratonic shield areas, where igneous rocks have been metamorphosed to granite gneisses.

The lower continental crust extends down to the Mohorovičić discontinuity and comprises denser rocks that may otherwise have a similar composition to those of the upper crust. They include intermediate igneous rocks that have suffered intense metamorphism at high pressures, resulting in the growth of dense minerals and basic igneous rocks at lower degrees of metamorphism. This region is the least well-known, most inaccessible part of the earth's crust.

Age and evolution

All of the ocean crust is approximately the same age (less than 180 million years) because it is continuously created at ocean ridges and destroyed at destructive plate margins. In contrast, continental crust yields a spectrum of ages, ranging back over most of the earth's history. Ancient Precambrian igneous and sedimentary rocks occur, frequently in a strongly metamorphosed and deformed state, in stable ancient cratons such as the Canadian and Baltic shields. Cratons are large masses of Precambrian rock that have been unaffected by later mountain-building. Younger rocks surround them, developed around the cratons by

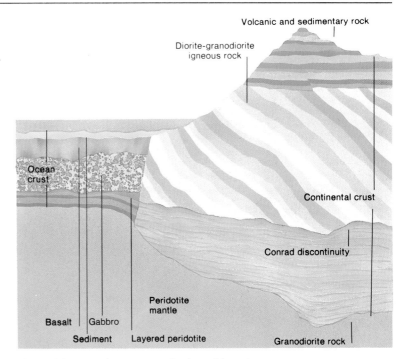

The earth's crust is divided into oceanic and continental crust. Oceanic crust is about 2.5 miles (4 kilometers) lower than continental crust and is about 20 per cent of its thickness. The structure of oceanic crust is uniform: a layer of sediment covers three layers of igneous rock of which the thickest is the layer of gabbro. These layers form from the partial melting of the underlying peridotite mantle. In contrast to the uniformity of oceanic crust, the structure of continental crust is varied and changes over short distances.

Gneiss, visible in the foreground and in the middle distance bordering the bay, is a metamorphic rock that is formed under intense pressure deep in the crust. It is exposed over time by uplift and erosion.

A seismic wave moving through the crust arrives at a point on the surface later than a wave that has traveled farther but that has been refracted into the denser mantle and then refracted back to the surface. This phenomenon occurs because the denser the rock the faster the wave travels.

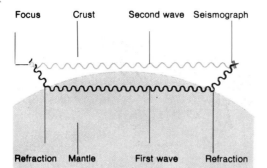

Gabbro, a coarse-grained, basic, igneous rock, is found at the bottom of continental and oceanic crust. This photomicrograph is of a sliver of olivine gabbro. Olivine, a silicate mineral with a dense structure, is one of the essential components of gabbro.

The Alps are a typical example of a mountain chain formed by tectonic overthrusting. At some stage the strata of the Alpine region were subjected to compressive deformation from opposing plates, which resulted in extensive faulting and elevation.

processes analogous to those at modern active plate margins in which partial melting of the sinking ocean plate yields magmas that rise to build mountain ranges like the Andes. Continents may be considered to grow by a two stage partial melting process: when the mantle beneath ocean ridges melts to form ocean crust, and when oceanic crust beneath destructive plate margins melts to form continental crust. Such processes have probably occurred throughout the earth's history but at a declining rate, because the vigor of mantle convection and plate motions depends on the output of radioactive heat sources, which is declining.

The earth's interior

Despite the information available about the surface of our planet, little is known about the state and composition of its interior. The deepest boreholes—about 7.5 miles (12 kilometers)—hardly scratch the earth's outer skin. The deepest known samples of rock, nodules of unmolten material brought up in volcanic lavas, come from a depth of only about 60 miles (97 kilometers), just 1.5 per cent of the distance to the center.

Our knowledge of the deeper interior relies on indirect evidence from physical measurements of the earth's mass, volume, and mean density, observations of seismic waves that have passed through the deep interior, observations of meteorites and other bodies in the Solar System, experimental studies of natural materials at the high pressures and temperatures of the earth's interior, and studies of the earth's magnetic field.

Internal structure

The earth's mean density is 345 pounds per cubic foot (5,520kg/m³), whereas the densities of surface rocks lie in the range 155 to 185 pounds per cubic foot (2,500-3,000kg/m³). Density obviously increases with depth, but this increase alone need not imply changes in state or composition because the density of any material increases under compression.

Seismic waves passing through the earth's interior have revealed two major and three relatively minor discontinuities where changes in chemical and physical state occur. This data also helps to determine the density and elastic properties of the materials through which the waves pass, properties that govern wave velocities.

The seismic discontinuities are broadly concentric with the earth's surface; they therefore mark the boundaries of spherical shells with successively greater density—the major subdivisions into crust, mantle, and core occur at the Mohorovičić and Gutenberg discontinuities.

The crust varies in thickness from about 5 miles (8 kilometers) in oceanic areas to about 25 miles (40 kilometers) under the continents, and the mantle extends down to 1,800 miles (2,900 kilometers). It contains a low-velocity layer that lies between 30 and 125 miles (48 and 201 kilometers) below the surface, where seismic wave velocities are reduced by a few per cent, and it is most prominent and shallow beneath oceanic areas. The mantle also has a transition zone from 250 to about 600 miles (402 to 966 kilometers) deep, which is characterized by several sharp increases in wave velocity and density with depth. The earth's core is subdivided into outer and inner regions by a minor discontinuity at a depth of about 3,200 miles (5,150 kilometers); the outer core is believed to be the only totally fluid layer in the earth.

The mantle

The combined evidence from volcanic nodules, exposed thrust slices of possible mantle rocks, physical data, and meteorite studies indicates that the upper mantle is made of silicate minerals. Among these minerals, dark green olivine predominates, together with lesser amounts of black pyroxene, iron silicates, and calcium aluminum silicates in a rock type known as peridotite.

Because temperature increases rapidly with depth in the outer 125 miles (201 kilometers) of the earth, there comes a point (at about 2,700° F.) at which peridotite starts to melt. The presence of partial melt accounts for the low-velocity layer and basalt magmas that erupt from oceanic volcanoes. Because olivine has the highest melting temperature of the silicate minerals in peridotite, it remains solid while other, less abundant, minerals contribute preferentially to the melt.

Temperature increases less rapidly with greater depth than does the melting point, so no further melting occurs at extreme depth although the hot, solid material is susceptible to plastic deformation and convects very slowly. This part of the mantle is the asthenosphere, or weak layer, which is distinct from the rigid uppermost mantle and crust, or lithosphere.

Increasing pressure is responsible for the transition zone where several rapid increases in density are probably caused by changes in the structure of the solids. In this zone, the atomic structures of the compressed silicate minerals change to new forms in which the atoms are packed together more closely to occupy less volume. These new forms are thought to persist down to 1,800 miles (2,900 kilometers).

The core

A marked physical and chemical change occurs across the core-mantle boundary—from solid to liquid, from a density of 345 pounds per cubic foot to one of 620 (5,500 to 9,900kg/m³), and from silicate to iron and nickle. Evidence of an iron-rich core is substantiated by iron meteorites and by observa-

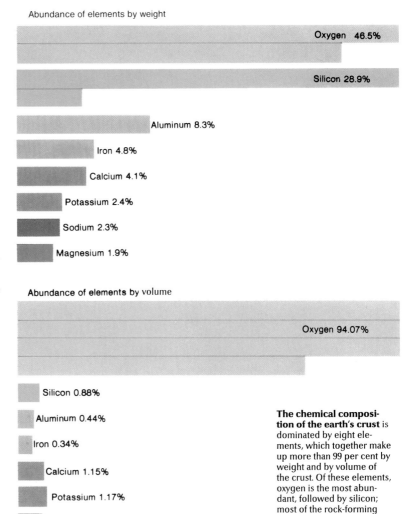

Abundance of elements by weight

Oxygen 46.5%
Silicon 28.9%
Aluminum 8.3%
Iron 4.8%
Calcium 4.1%
Potassium 2.4%
Sodium 2.3%
Magnesium 1.9%

Abundance of elements by volume

Oxygen 94.07%
Silicon 0.88%
Aluminum 0.44%
Iron 0.34%
Calcium 1.15%
Potassium 1.17%
Sodium 1.07%
Magnesium 0.26%

The chemical composition of the earth's crust is dominated by eight elements, which together make up more than 99 per cent by weight and by volume of the crust. Of these elements, oxygen is the most abundant, followed by silicon; most of the rock-forming minerals of the crust are therefore silicates.

tions of rapid variations of the earth's magnetic field.

The observed outer core density is slightly too low for pure iron, however, and is thought to comprise a mixture of melted iron and nickel. In the inner core, this situation is reversed and because a heavy element must accompany iron, the mixture is thought to be 15 per cent nickel and 85 per cent iron alloy. Because iron-sulfur mixtures melt at lower temperatures than do iron-nickel alloys, these compositions are consistent with the transition from liquid to solid across the outer-inner core boundary.

Fact Entries

Ophiolites are rock sequences formed when oceanic crust rides over continental crust during island or continent collision and is broken up and exposed on the earth's surface.

The upper continental crust consists of igneous rocks, such as diorite, granodiorite, and granite, which have a high silica content (about 60-65 per cent). These are less dense than lower crustal rocks.

The Gutenberg discontinuity, named after the American seismologist Beno Gutenberg, who discovered it in 1914, separates the mantle from the core at a depth of about 1,800 miles (2,900 kilometers).

Andrija Mohorovičić recorded two groups of seismic waves a few hundred miles from their source and found that one arrived later than the other. In 1909, he proposed that the second group had traveled directly through the crust, whereas the first had moved through a deeper zone at a higher velocity, and was then refracted to the surface. In this way he discovered the crust-mantle boundary, the Mohorovičić discontinuity.

Crustal movements

The outermost part of the earth consists of a fairly rigid layer called the lithosphere, which consists of the crust and the top layers of the mantle. It floats on a yielding layer beneath it, termed the asthenosphere. The height of the surface of the lithosphere (measured relative to sea level) varies in response to various factors, such as changes in mass caused by the addition or removal of rock and changes in density due to heating and cooling. These balancing movements of the lithosphere and asthenosphere are known as isostasy and have provided geologists with much information about the composition of the interior of the earth.

Consequences of isostasy

Various general features of the earth's surface result from isostasy. For example, continents are higher than ocean floors not because they have more volume but because their constituent rocks are less dense than those of the seabed. A similar effect can be seen with wood floating in water; the heights of the blocks above water level depend on their thickness and density. Mountains are usually higher than plains because they are underlain by a thick layer of the relatively low-density continental rock. In contrast, the weight of Greenland's great ice sheet has depressed the land mass beneath it and caused rock surface to become saucer-shaped, with its center below sea level.

The asthenosphere is viscous, much like extremely thick molasses, and it therefore does not respond rapidly once a constraint is removed. Full isostatic readjustment may take many thousands of years. For this reason, depressions in North America that were caused by the weight of ice during the last ice age remained after the ice melted; they filled with water, creating the Great Lakes.

Another consequence of isostasy is that as erosion wears away land and makes it less massive, the land rises up to maintain the equilibrium, and so compensates for the imbalance caused by erosion. As erosion cuts deep valleys into a mountain chain, individual peaks may simultaneously rise even though the average surface height as a whole decreases. Conversely, as a large basin fills with sediment it sinks and effectively deepens so that eventually the sedimentary layer may become thicker than the original depth of water.

Gravity and isostasy

The force of gravity arises from the pull of the whole earth, but it varies slightly from place to place because of the unequal local distribution of mass in the earth's surface layer. If a mountain were simply extra rocky material rising above the surrounding plain, the force of gravity would be greater on the mountain by an amount that depends on the size of the mountain, its density, and the slightly greater distance to the mountain top from the center of the earth. An increase in the acceleration due to gravity occurs across mountain ranges, but not as much as would be expected because the extra mass rising up is largely compensated for by the greater depth to which the base of the mountains extends down into the denser supporting medium (the asthenosphere).

Some mountains, such as the Andes and the Himalayas, are still being formed, and because isostasy takes time to come into effect their "growth" downwards into the asthenosphere is not complete. Isostasy was originally discovered through its effect on gravity, and variations in gravity are still used to measure the degree of isostatic compensation.

Ocean-spreading ridges

Isostasy also helps to explain the shapes of submarine "mountain ranges," such as the Mid-Atlantic Ridge. Such oceanic ridges form where two crustal plates are moving apart and

Blocks of wood floating in water show that those blocks that are thickest and least dense will protrude the most. Similarly, continents are higher than the ocean floor because their underlying rocks are less dense than those of oceans.

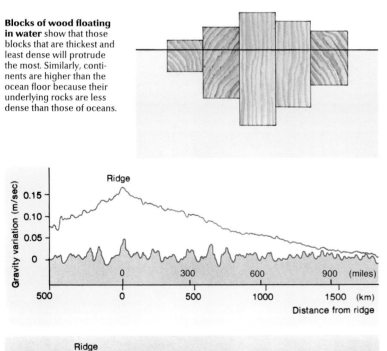

Gravity along the ocean floor is fairly constant, represented *(above left)* by the lower line. But across a ridge the acceleration due to gravity increases and reaches a peak at the top of the ridge after which point it drops to its normal level.

A mid-ocean ridge *(far left)* forms from the upwelling of molten material from the asthenosphere where two crustal plates pull apart. The ridge is higher than the surrounding plates because due to its heat it is less dense.

molten rock wells up from the mantle to fill the gap. These ridges are high because they are less dense than the surrounding material. Over the surface of the ocean gravitational attraction varies very little, despite the varying depth of water below, demonstrating nearly perfect isostatic compensation. The ridges must, therefore, be supported on rock that is less dense, although this has much the same chemical composition as the rock on either side, which the ridges continually replace as the plates move apart. The ridges are probably less dense also because they are hotter due to their upwelling activity.

An oceanic plate is formed from the rigid, relatively cool topmost part of the mantle. As a plate moves away from a mid-ocean ridge, it cools, thickens, and settles downwards. The thickness of the ocean floor beyond a ridge crest should increase with its age. Areas of similar age in different spreading ridges have a similar profile regardless of the rate of spreading. If it were possible to reheat the plates, they would expand and rise again to their original heights.

Composition of lithosphere and asthenosphere

For ocean plates, the chief difference between the lithosphere and the asthenosphere is one of temperature, although chemical processes below a spreading ridge (where magma forms) cause the upper few miles of the lithosphere (the crust) to be of lighter material. The continental lithosphere is more complex. Much of its lightness is due to a crustal layer, which is less dense than the oceanic crust. Most continental crust is between 18 and 25 miles (30 and 40 kilometers) thick, but can be twice as thick beneath great mountain ranges. It is this thickness that provides much of the buoyancy that supports the mountains. The nature of the material below the continental crust is not known with certainty, but the thickness of the continental lithosphere ranges between 45 and 95 miles (72 and 153 kilometers).

The Great Lakes are an example of the time it takes for isostatic readjustment to occur. Initially weighted down by the North American ice sheet, when the ice melted the land remained in its depressed state.

Mount Everest was named after George Everest, who discovered that the extent of the gravitational pull of the Himalayas is less than would be expected. The discrepancy was explained by the proposal that mountains extend to great depths.

Plate tectonics

On the human time scale most of the earth seems passive and unchanging. But in some places—California, Italy, Turkey, and Japan, for example—the earth's crust is active and liable to move, producing earthquakes or volcanic eruptions. These and other dynamic areas lie on the major earthquake belts, most of which run along the middle of the ocean basins, although some are situated on the edges of oceans (around the Pacific Ocean, for instance) or pass across continental land masses (as along the Alpine-Himalayan belt).

It is this observation, that there are several relatively well-defined dynamic zones in the earth's crust, that forms the basis of plate tectonics. According to this theory, the crust consists of several large, rigid plates, and the movements of the plates produce the earth's major structural features, such as mountain ranges, mid-ocean ridges, ocean trenches, and large faults. Stable areas with few or no earthquakes or active volcanoes lie in the middle of a plate, whereas active areas—where major structures are constantly being destroyed or created—are situated along the plate boundaries.

The extent and nature of crustal plates

The positions and sizes of the crustal plates can be determined by studying the paths of seismic waves (shock waves produced by earthquakes). Such studies have also made it possible to estimate the thickness of the plates. Geologists have found that seismic waves tend to slow down and become less intense between about 60 and 250 miles (97 and 402 kilometers) below the surface. From this observation, they suggest that the solid lithosphere (which consists of the earth's outermost layer, the crust, and the top part of the mantle, the layer below the crust) "floats" on a less rigid layer (the asthenosphere), which, because it is plastic, allows vertical and horizontal movements of the rigid lithospheric plates.

By collating the findings from various seismological studies, geologists have discovered that the lithosphere is divided into a relatively small number of plates. Most of them are very large—covering millions of square miles—but are only between 45 and 95 miles (72 and 153 kilometers) thick.

Plate movements

The landforms, earthquake activity, and vulcanism that characterize plate boundaries are caused by movements of the plates. There are three principal motions: the plates may move apart, collide, or slide past each other.

Plate separation entails the formation of new lithosphere between the plates involved. This process occurs at constructive plate boundaries along the crests of mid-ocean

The Pyrenees extend along the border between France and Spain. They were formed as a result of tectonic movements (which produced folding of the rock strata) during the Eocene and Oligocene epochs (which together lasted from 54 to 26 million years ago).

A spectacular demonstration of the activity at a constructive plate boundary occurred in November, 1963, when the volcanic island of Surtsey emerged from the sea, erupting lava and emitting large amounts of gas and dust. Situated off southern Iceland, Surtsey stands on the Mid-Atlantic Ridge, which marks the boundary between the slowly-separating Eurasian and American plates.

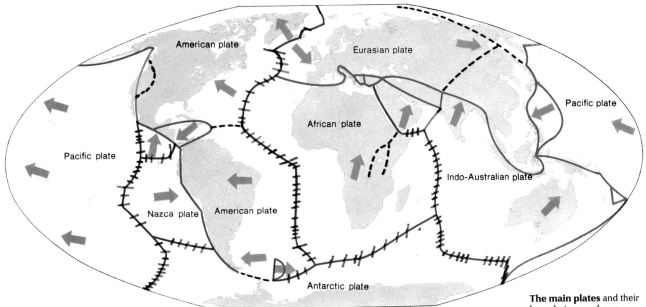

The main plates and their boundaries are shown above: constructive boundaries in dark purple, destructive boundaries in red, and transform faults in green; broken black lines mark uncertain boundaries. Plate movements are shown with blue arrows.

ridges (and is therefore termed sea-floor spreading), where material from the mantle wells up to create the new crust.

Plate collision, on the other hand, necessitates the destruction of lithosphere at a plate boundary. Ocean trenches mark destructive plate boundaries, and at these sites the lithosphere of one plate is thrust beneath an overriding plate and resorbed into the mantle; this process is called subduction. Ultimately, continued subduction of an ocean basin can lead to the complete disappearance of the basin and collision of the continents at its edges. In such collisions, mountain belts may be formed as the continents push against each other and force upwards the intervening land—as occurred when India collided with Asia some 50 million years ago, creating the Himalayas.

After a continental collision, the momentum of the plates is initially absorbed by thickening and overthrusting of the continental crust. But there is a limit to which this process can occur and, because the continental crust is too buoyant to be subducted, the momentum must be dissipated in other ways—by the sideways movements of small plates that form within the newly-created mountain belt or by a more general, probably world-wide, change in the boundaries and movements of the plates.

The other principal type of plate movement occurs when plates slide past each other (at what are called sites of transform faulting) which, unlike the first two types of movement, involves neither creation nor destruction of the intervening lithosphere. Often major faults, such as the San Andreas fault in California, mark these plate boundaries (which are called conservative plate boundaries).

Rates of plate movements

Most of our knowledge about the very slow rates of plate movements has come from studies of the earth's magnetic field. In the past, the magnetic field has repeatedly reversed direction (a phenomenon called polarity reversal). A record of the changing mag-

netic field has been preserved in the permanent "fossil" magnetism of the basalt rocks that form the ocean floor.

Around sites of sea-floor spreading, bands of rocks with normal polarity alternate with bands having a reversed polarity. By dating these different bands, the rate of spreading can be deduced. Using this method it has been found that the rates of plate separation vary from about .5 inch (.8 centimeter) a year in the northern Atlantic Ocean to 4 inches (6.4 centimeters) a year in the Pacific Ocean. From these determinations of separation rates, geologists have calculated the relative motions of plates that are moving together or sliding past each other. They have, thus, determined the movements of almost all the plates.

The Sinai Peninsula (in the center of the photograph below) is receding from Africa because of sea-floor spreading in the Gulf of Suez (left).

The ocean floor

About three-quarters of our planet's surface is covered with water, and the deep basins of the ocean floor account for approximately nine-tenths of this water-covered area, that is, some two-thirds of the earth's surface. (The rest of the water-covered area comprises mainly shallow seas, the continental shelves, and lakes.) The ocean basins are characterized not only by lying in deep water (the ocean floor averages about 2.5 miles [4 kilometers] below sea level) but also by being underlain by a thin layer of crust; on average, oceanic crust is only 4 miles (6.4 kilometers) thick, compared to 25 miles (40 kilometers) for continental crust.

Mid-ocean ridges

The mid-ocean ridges are the most extensive features of the earth's surface. Consisting of a narrow, continuous belt of submarine mountains, each ocean ridge extends along virtually the entire length of its ocean. The crests of the ridges rise to about 2.4 miles (3.8 kilometers) of the sea surface.

New oceanic crust is created at the ridge crests by sea-floor spreading. Thus the crests mark constructive plate boundaries where the earth's lithospheric plates are moving apart. As a result of this separation, hot material from the asthenosphere (the layer below the lithosphere, itself comprised of the crust and the top part of the mantle) wells up at the ridge crests and partly melts to form pockets of magma. The magma is lighter (of lower density) than the surrounding mantle and, therefore, rises into the relatively thin crustal layer. The molten material may then slowly crystallize in the lower crust; or it may rise to the middle of the crust and solidify in fissures, thereby forming dikes; or it may be extruded as lava onto the ocean floor.

As sea-floor spreading continues, newly-created crust moves away from the mid-ocean ridge crest and gradually becomes cooler, thicker, and denser, with the result that it subsides. Geologists have discovered that the amount by which the oceanic crust subsides is related to its age only (if the crust is not overlain with—and therefore depressed by—sediments). Thus, the fact that the East Pacific Ocean Ridge is much wider than is the mid-ocean ridge in the Atlantic Ocean reflects the markedly faster rate of crust creation at the East Pacific Ridge. Moreover, because of the greater rate of formation, crust of the same age (and, therefore, thickness) is farther from the ridge crest in the Pacific Ocean than in the Atlantic. So although the Pacific Ocean is much wider than the Atlantic, the oldest crust in the Pacific (found near the Mariana Trench) is about the same age (approximately 180 million years old) as the oldest crust in the Atlantic (which occurs near the eastern coast of the United States).

Ocean trenches

Not only is oceanic crust continually created at mid-ocean ridges, but it is also continually re-sorbed into the mantle at subduction zones, which are marked by deep ocean trenches. The Mariana Trench, the world's deepest, is more than 36,000 feet (11,000 meters) below sea level in some parts—about 23,000 feet (7,000 meters) below the mean depth of the ocean floor.

The trenches around the edges of the eastern Pacific Ocean are shallower than are those of the western Pacific. This phenomenon reflects the fact that younger (and, therefore, thinner) oceanic crust is being subducted at the eastern margin of the Pacific, which in turn results from the East Pacific Ridge being considerably nearer the eastern than the western ocean margin.

Fracture zones

Another major structural feature of deep ocean basins are large fractures in the sea bed. These fractures cut across mid-ocean ridges, usually offsetting the ridge crests. The fractures on the slowly-spreading ridges of the Atlantic and Indian Oceans tend to be closer together and to cause less offsetting than those of the faster-spreading Pacific ridges.

Submarine sulfide springs, such as the one shown below (situated off the western coast of the United States), are thought to be the source of the large deposits of iron and other metal sulfides that have been discovered in steep-sided depressions on the ocean floor.

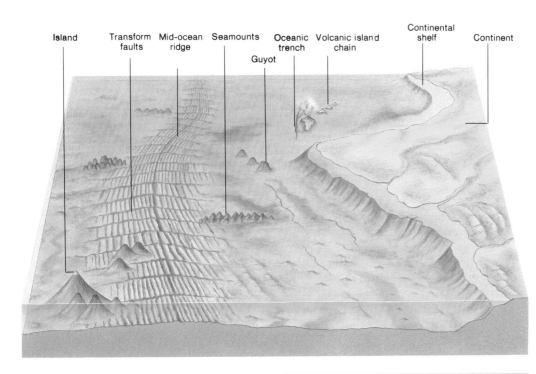

Island   Transform   Mid-ocean   Seamounts   Oceanic   Volcanic island   Continental   Continent
          faults   ridge   trench   chain   shelf
                                     Guyot

The ocean floor has a varied topography, although its features may be obscured by sediments. The principal features are illustrated on the left, and of these the most important are the mid-ocean ridges (where new crust is created) and the peripheral ocean trenches (where oceanic crust is subducted back into the mantle).

Fracture zones are seismically inactive along most of their lengths but represent the sites of previous active transform faulting (faulting caused by sideways plate movements).

Other features of the ocean floor

Most of the remaining features of the ocean floor result from large outpourings of magma, which typically form submarine volcanoes. Occasionally, so much magma is extruded that a rise or plateau with unusally thick crust forms; perhaps the most conspicuous example is the Icelandic Plateau, which protrudes above sea level.

Some marine volcanoes also rise above the sea surface, forming volcanic islands. Others are submerged but are flat on top (in which case they are called guyots) or have coral atolls associated with them—evidence that they previously protruded above the sea. The submergence of an oceanic volcano indicates that it was formed in relatively shallow water near an active ridge crest but has since been moved into deeper water (as a result of movement of the plate on which it stands) away from the active area (called a "hot spot"). If this movement continues, it may give rise to a chain of volcanic islands, atolls, and guyots stretching away from the hot spot; the Hawaiian Islands and Emperor Seamounts chain are examples.

The ocean floor is covered by a layer of sediments, the thickness of which depends on the age, the local topography, and on the abundance of the sediment supply. Submarine sediments are of two main types: those consisting of material washed from the land; and those comprising the skeletal remains of marine plankton. In the Pacific Ocean, where the marginal trenches trap land-derived sediments, the sedimentary covering on the ocean bed is less than about 330 feet (100 meters) thick, whereas in the Indian and Atlantic Oceans it may exceed 3,300 feet (1,000 meters).

Manganese nodules occur on the ocean floor at depths of more than 6,500 feet (1,981 meters) and are particularly common in the Pacific Ocean. About the size of a potato, they contain cobalt, copper, and nickel in addition to manganese.

The skeletons of foraminiferan plankton make up calcareous ooze, one of the main types of deep-sea sediment.

Structure of continents

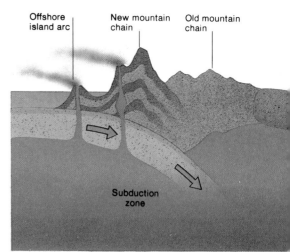

Offshore island arc   New mountain chain   Old mountain chain

Subduction zone

The continents are large areas of crust that make up the solid surface of the earth. They consist of the comparatively low-density material called sial and, thus, tend to float above other crustal material—the sima—in which they are embedded.

On a map of the globe, each continent has a very different shape and appearance from the others, and each has its own climate zones and animal life. The geological structure of each one is, however, very much the same.

The simple continent

In its simplest form, a continent is older at the center than at the edges. The old center is known as a craton, and it is made up of rocks that were formed several thousand million years ago, when the earth's crust was thinner than it is now. The craton is not involved in any mountain building activity because it is already compact and tightly deformed by ancient mountain building, although the mountains that had been formed on it have long since been worn away by the processes of erosion. Typical cratons include the Canadian Shield, covering northern and central North America, the Baltic Shield in northern Europe, and the Siberian Shield in northern Asia. Several smaller cratons exist in South America, India, Africa, Antarctica, and Australia.

The craton is the nucleus of the continent. It is flanked by belts of fold mountains, the oldest nearer the craton and the youngest farther away. North America provides an excellent example, consisting of the Canadian Shield flanked in the east by the Appalachians and in the west by the Rockies. Close to the shield, the Appalachians were formed nearly 230 million years ago. The same is true of the mountains to the west; the main part of the Rockies are about 100 million years old, whereas the coastal ranges are still geologically active.

The reason for this structure is that when a continent lies at a subduction zone at the boundary between two crustal plates, its mass cannot be drawn down into the higher-density mantle. Instead it crumples up at the edge, the sedimentary areas around the coast being forced up into mountain chains, which may be laced through with volcanic material from the plate tectonic activity. These movements may take place several times during a continent's history, with each subsequent mountain chain being attached to the one that was formed previously.

Supercontinents

In reality, the situation is much more complicated. As the continents move about on the earth's surface, two may collide with each other and become welded into a single mass. The result is a supercontinent, which has two or more cratons. The weld line between the two original continents is marked by a mountain range that was formed as their coastal ranges came together and crushed up any sediments that may have been between them. Europe and Asia together constitute such a supercontinent, the Urals having been formed when the two main masses came together about 230 million years ago.

On the other hand, a single continental mass may split, becoming two or more smaller continents. This has happened on a grand scale within the last 200 million years. Just before that time all the continents of the earth's crust had come together, forming one vast temporary supercontinent, known to geologists as Pangaea. Since then the single mass has fragmented into the distribution of continents we know today. Indeed the process is still continuing. The great Rift Valley of eastern Africa represents the first stage of a movement in which eastern Africa is breaking away from the main African land mass. The slumping structures found at the sides of a rift valley are also seen at the margins of continents that are known to have split away and have not yet been subjected to any marginal mountain-building activity. The eastern coast of South

The continents—the land areas of the world—cover only about 30 per cent of the earth's surface, and little of it rises to more than about 3,300 feet (1,000 meters) above sea level.

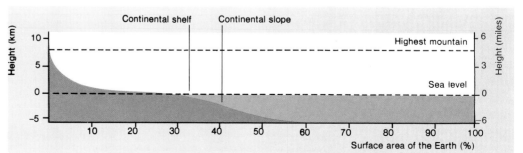

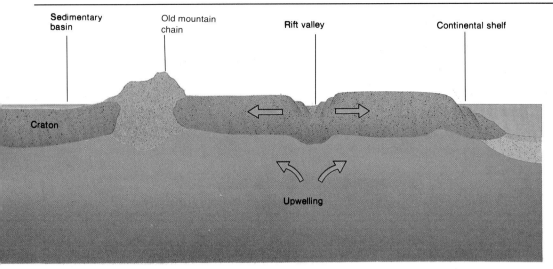

Sedimentary basin | Old mountain chain | Rift valley | Continental shelf

Craton

Upwelling

At the edge of a continent *(far left),* where the continental crustal plate is riding over an oceanic plate, typical features include offshore island arcs (such as the Japanese islands) and relatively young mountain chains (such as the Andes). Farther inland a sedimentary basin (such as the North Sea) may form on top of the older rocks of a crater. Rift valleys form in mid-continent.

America and the western coast of Africa show such features.

Not all continental masses are above sea level. The Indian Ocean contains many small continental fragments that have sheared off, just as India and Antarctica split away from Africa 200 million years ago. Such fragments include the Agulhas Plateau, off South Africa, and the Seychelles and Kerguelen plateaus, each with islands representing their highest portions.

Areas of sedimentation

The other significant feature around the continents are their depositional basins. These are areas that have subsided and may even be below sea level. Because rivers tend to flow into such areas, the basins soon become thickly covered by sediments. The North Sea is an example of a sedimentary basin in northern Europe.

In some areas of the continental margin, a large river may flow over the continental shelf and deposit its sediments in the ocean beyond. In such areas the edge of the continental shelf becomes extended beyond that of the rest of the area. The rivers Indus and Ganges produce shelf sediments in the Indian Ocean, and the Amazon and Zaire do the same on opposite sides of the Atlantic.

The actual land area of a continent may also be increased by these means, if the river builds up an extensive delta at its mouth. Considerable land areas have been built up in this way at the mouths of the rivers Mississippi and Niger.

The Pamir range, in the southern Soviet Union, consists of fairly old fold mountains, many of which rise to more than 20,000 feet (6,100 meters). They converge toward a central "knot," as revealed in this satellite photograph taken from an orbiting *Soyuz 22* spacecraft.

The Alps are comparatively young mountains, in geological terms, in which the rock strata form complex patterns because of the folding and faulting that accompanied their formation.

Fact Entries

The earth's oldest known rocks are about 4.1 billion years old and are found on the Canadian Shield in Greenland. The continental crust covers 77 million square miles (200 million square kilometers) or about 40 per cent of the surface area of the earth. Of this, 21 million square miles (54 million square kilometers) lie beneath the sea and can be regarded as part of the continental shelf. About 8 million square miles (21 million square kilometers) consist of depositional basins, which are filling up with the debris that has been eroded from the remainder. Continents are becoming larger all the time, due to the accretion of new mountain chains where a continent's edge lies on a destructive plate margin. The new mountains are made of sediment and volcanic material. Continents are growing at a rate of 0.1 cubic mile (0.5 cubic kilometer) per year. Extrapolated back through geological time this figure would produce only half the volume of continental material that exists today. There must have been a period of more active continent formation in the past.

Continental drift

The continental masses that stand proud of their surrounding oceanic crust have, according to a widely accepted theory, never occupied fixed positions on the earth's surface. They are constantly carried around on the tectonic plates rather like logs embedded in the ice floes of a partly frozen river. The movement is going on at the present day, with North America moving away from Europe at a rate of one inch or two to three centimeters per year, and the movement of Africa against Europe made evident by the earthquake activity and the presence of active volcanoes in the Mediterranean area.

The theoretical proof that this has been happening throughout geological time takes a number of forms.

Physical proof

The first line of evidence—in fact the first observation that suggested that the continents are in motion—is the apparent fit of one continental coastline with another. The eastern coast of South America and the western coast of Africa are so similar in shape that it seems quite obvious that the two once fitted together like the pieces of a jigsaw. The other continents can also be pieced together in a similar way, although the fit is not quite so obvious; for example, Africa, India, Antarctica, and Australia would also mate together. It is the edges of the continental shelves, rather than the actual coastlines, that provide the neat fit.

If the continents were placed together, certain physical features could be seen to be continuous from one to another across the joins. Mountains that formed 400 million years ago and now found in southeastern Canada and eastern Greenland would be continuous with those of the same age now found in Scotland and Norway, if North America and Europe were placed together. Mountain ranges in Brazil would be continuous with those in Nigeria if South America and Africa were brought together.

Evidence for ancient climates is also a good indicator of continental drift. Northern Europe went through a phase of desert conditions about 400 million years ago, followed by a phase of tropical forest 300 million years ago, and then another desert phase 200 million years ago. This is consistent with the movement of that area from the southern desert climate zone of the earth, through the equatorial forest zone, and into the northern desert zone.

About 280 million years ago an ice age gripped the Southern Hemisphere. The evidence for this includes ice-formed deposits and glacier marks from that period found in South America, southern Africa, Australia, and significantly, India—which is now in the Northern Hemisphere. If the continents were reassembled and the directions of ice movement analyzed, they would point to an icecap with its center in Antarctica.

Biological proof

The evidence from fossils is just as spectacular. Fossils of the same land animals and plants have been found on all the southern continents in rocks dating from about 250 million years ago. These are creatures that could not have evolved independently on separate continents. *Mesosaurus* was a freshwater reptile, resembling a small crocodile, and its remains have been found both in South America and South Africa. *Lystrosaurus* was like a reptilian hippopotamus, and its remains have been found in India, Africa, and Antarctica. The fern-like plant *Glossopteris* is typical of the plants that lived at the same time as these creatures,

Fossils of the late Paleozoic plant *Glossopteris (right)* have been found in South America, southern Africa, India, and Antarctica, providing evidence that all these land masses were once joined in the supercontinent of Pangaea. The mountains of the Himalayan range *(far right)* were uplifted as a result of the impact between the Indian subcontinent and the Asian crustal plate about 50 million years ago.

and its remains have been found in South America, Africa, India, and Australia.

Similar biological evidence is found in the Northern Hemisphere where European dinosaurs of 150 million years ago were quite similar to those of North America.

The mammals that developed in various parts of the world during the last 65 million years also reveal evidence of the movements of the continents. Up to about 10 million years ago the dominant mammals of South America were the pouched marsupials, similar to those of Australia today. This suggests that their origin lies in a single southern continent. Later, most of the South American marsupials became extinct after a sudden influx of more advanced placental mammals from North America, suggesting that South and North America became attached to one another about 10 million years ago. India was a similar isolated continent, broken away from the southern land mass, until it collided with Asia about 50 million years ago. It would be interesting to see if the mammals of India before this date were marsupials but no Indian mammal fossils have been found for the relevant period. In 1980 a fossil marsupial was found in Antarctica, helping to substantiate the theories.

Magnetic proof

The positions of the earth's magnetic poles change over a long period of time. Clues as to their location in any particular geological period lie in the way in which particles in the rocks that formed in that period have been magnetized. As rocks are formed, the magnetic particles in them line up with the magnetic field of the earth at that time and are then locked in position when the rock solidifies. This phenomenon is sometimes known as re-manent magnetism, and it has been actively studied since the 1950's. It has been found that the remanent magnetism for different periods in each of the continents point to a single north pole only if the continents are "moved" in relation to each other.

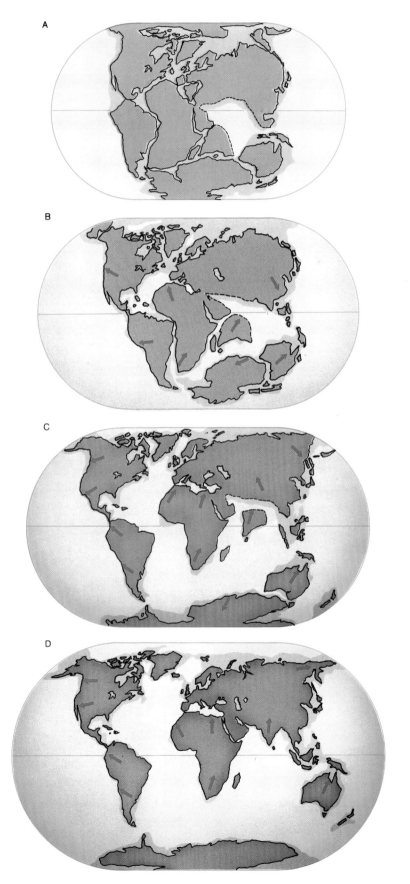

Nearly 200 million years ago, the land masses of the earth were, according to a widely accepted theory, concentrated into one supercontinent, called Pangaea (A, *top right*). Some geologists propose that, at that time, the earth was only four-fifths its present size, and computer-plotted maps seem to support this view. Then, as Pangaea broke up and the continents began to move apart, the earth as a whole gradually became larger. Map B is a reconstruction of the earth of about 120 million years ago. By about 55 million years ago (C), the Atlantic Ocean had widened, India was on a collision course with Asia, and Australia was beginning to become detached from Antarctica. Map D shows the earth as it is now, but even today the crustal plates are not static. Sea-floor spreading will continue to widen the Atlantic and Indian Oceans, and Australia will continue on its northeasterly course. Seismic and volcanic activity, as along the eastern seaboard of the Pacific Ocean, result from subduction of the Pacific plate as it is being overridden by the westward-moving Americas. In northeastern Africa, there is evidence that Arabia is splitting off from the rest of the continent.

Minerals

A mineral is a substance with a specific chemical composition that occurs naturally in rocks. Minerals are inorganic, being produced by the physical forces of the earth rather than by living organisms, and are always in the form of crystals. Their importance lies in the fact that they are the basic units from which rocks are composed; every rock can be considered as an accumulation of minerals.

Most rocks consist of at least two different minerals and may contain five or six. The proportions of the constituent minerals vary—both among different general types of rocks and among samples of the same type of rock. For this reason geologists do not classify rocks principally according to their compositions but by the way in which they were formed. There are three broad categories of rocks: igneous, sedimentary, and metamorphic. Igneous rocks are formed when molten magma cools and solidifies. Sedimentary rocks originate from deposits of material worn away from pre-existing rocks, as well as of plant and animal materials. And metamorphic rocks are formed by the alteration of pre-existing rocks by great heat or pressure. On the earth's surface, sedimentary rocks are the most common, covering about 75 per cent of the total land area. Below the surface they are much rarer, making up only about 5 per cent of the uppermost 10 miles (16 kilometers) of the crust; igneous and metamorphic rocks together account for the rest.

Rock-forming minerals

The proportions of minerals in the crust reflect the relative abundance of elements in the earth. Oxygen is one of the most abundant elements, hence many common minerals are in the form of oxides—compounds of oxygen and another element. Silicon is another very abundant element, and so the mineral silica (the compound of silicon and oxygen) is very common.

Most of the rock-forming, or essential, minerals are silicates, in which silica is combined with one or more of the other common elements, such as aluminum, calcium, iron, magnesium, potassium, or sodium. The essential minerals include feldspars (e.g., orthoclase), micas (e.g., muscovite), amphiboles (e.g., hornblende), pyroxenes (e.g., augite), olivines (e.g., chrysolite), and quartz. Of these, quartz is unusual in that it consists of only silicon and oxygen. Moreover, it is found only in rocks that have a far greater amount of silicon and oxygen than other elements, so that after these other elements have combined with silicon and oxygen to form complex silicate minerals there remains an excess of silica (in the form of quartz).

Crystals

Minerals are formed as crystals, the shape of which depends on the arrangement of their constituent atoms. But it is only rarely that a mineral's true crystalline shape can be seen by normal methods, although it is nearly always visible using X-ray crystallography. A mineral can usually be identified once its crystal structure has been determined.

When a molten mass cools and solidifies, the first minerals to crystallize out may form good crystal shapes, with straight edges and well-defined angles, because they have room to grow unimpeded in the surrounding fluid. The minerals that crystallize later fill the spaces left between the crystals already formed and so tend to be distorted.

The best-shaped crystals are usually those

Hematite (ferric oxide—Fe_2O_3) is an important ore mineral; it is the most abundant form of iron ore and also has a high iron content. It occurs in various forms, including kidney ore *(shown right)*; specular ore, which is speckled with bright, steellike crystals; and red ocher, which is fine-grained, soft, and earthy in texture and is used in some red pigments. Magnetite (ferrous oxide—Fe_3O_4), the other principal iron ore, is less abundant and, therefore, economically less important than is hematite. Lodestone, a naturally magnetic substance, is a form of magnetite.

that grow early in the formation of an igneous rock, when there is still sufficient space in the fluid magma to enable their full development. Good crystal shapes may also form in metamorphic rocks, but often the crystals grow under such high pressures that they become distorted. In general, sedimentary rocks tend not to have good crystal shapes because the rocks are formed by the compression and solidification of fragments from other rocks and new minerals develop in the small spaces between these fragments. Sandstones—one of the most common types of sedimentary rock—consist mainly of quartz grains cemented together by calcite (calcium carbonate) or by oxides of iron. These cementing agents, which are dissolved in the ground water that percolates through the sediments, form tiny crystals between the grains, binding them together. The minerals in extremely fine-grained sedimentary rocks consist of complex silicates called clay minerals; these are the weathered products of minerals, such as feldspars and micas. Chemical sedimentary rocks—rock salt, for example—are formed from substances that were originally dissolved in water and later precipitated as a sediment that was then compressed and cemented together into rock. In these conditions well-defined crystals may form.

Ore minerals

Minerals that are commercially valuable are known as ore minerals. Compared with rock-forming silicate minerals, ore minerals are rare, constituting only a very small proportion of the earth's crust. In general, the ore minerals most commonly exploited for industrial purposes contain a high percentage of various metal elements.

Iron oxide—which is probably most familiar as rust—is one of the most common ore minerals. It imparts a reddish color to many rocks, particularly sandstones formed from desert sands. Hematite and magnetite are among the most abundant forms of naturally-occurring iron oxide. Aluminum and tin are other valuable metals that are often found as oxide minerals, as bauxite and cassiterite respectively.

Some metals are found as compounds of the element sulfur (sulfides). Commercially important sulfide ores include pyrites (iron sulfide), cinnabar (mercury sulfide), and galena (lead sulfide). Occasionally, a metal may occur in its pure form, not chemically combined with other elements; the term "native" is applied to such pure minerals.

Zircon, the mineral zirconium silicate ($ZrSiO_4$), is found in igneous rocks. Several examples of zircon in its various natural forms are shown above, together with cut and polished zircon gems.

The fibrous mass *(left)* **is native silver.** Few metals occur naturally in their native forms, the principal ones (in addition to silver) being copper and gold. Commercially, most metallic silver is extracted from the mineral argentite (silver sulfide—Ag_2S).

Quartz is one of the most common minerals and occurs in numerous varieties. Pure quartz (silicon dioxide—SiO_2) crystals are white and hexagonal with pyramid-shaped ends. Although an essential rock-forming mineral, quartz is also economically important. Sandstone, which consists mainly of quartz, is extensively used as a building stone; and large amounts of quartz sand are used in the manufacture of glass.

Sedimentary rocks

Sedimentary rocks are the most common types on the earth's surface. In general, they were all formed in a similar way—by the deposition, compression, and cementing together of numerous small particles of mineral, animal, or plant origin. The details of these processes are best exemplified by clastic sedimentary rocks, which consist of mineral fragments derived from pre-existing rocks.

As soon as rocks are exposed on the earth's surface they begin to be broken down by the forces of erosion. The rock fragments, and the minerals washed out of them, are carried by the wind, by streams, or by the sea and finally come to rest as a sediment. Eventually, it becomes covered with more sediment, and the underlying layers are compressed and cemented together to form sedimentary rock—a process called lithification. After millions of years, this rock may be uplifted by earth movements—again exposing it to the forces of erosion—and the entire process is repeated. This cycle of erosion, transportation, deposition, lithification, and uplift is known as the sedimentary cycle.

Erosion, transportation, and deposition

By studying the various features of a sedimentary rock, geologists can deduce a great deal about the conditions prevalent at the time of its formation. Sedimentary rocks typically occur as separate horizontal layers called beds, each formed as a result of fairly frequent changes in the sedimentation conditions. When sedimentation stops, the sediments settle; when it resumes, a new layer begins to form on top of the previous one. Unlayered sedimentary rocks—described as massive—therefore reflect long periods of unchanging conditions. Analysis of the grains that make up the rocks may reveal the composition of those from which the fragments originated. In some, the minerals are the same as those in the original rock, but more commonly they have been altered by reactions with water and chemicals in the atmosphere.

The sizes and shapes of the constituent particles reflect the distance they have traveled and the current conditions they encountered. The faster the current of water, the larger are the rock fragments that can be carried by it. Thus, large-grained sedimentary rocks were

A microscopic view of a thin section of sandstone, a typical sedimentary rock, shows its characteristic rubbly appearance. The individual grains are fragments eroded from a pre-existing rock. They have been cemented together by minerals precipitated from percolating ground water.

Millions of years of erosion have exposed the layers of sedimentary rocks in the Grand Canyon, thereby providing a superb record of the area's geological history. The Grand Canyon is about 5,315 feet (1,620 meters) deep at its deepest point, where the rocks are some 2 billion years old. Its walls consist chiefly of limestones, shales, and sandstones.

originally formed from large pebbles and boulders deposited by fast-flowing rivers or by the sea. Such rocks are called conglomerates if their fragments are rounded, or breccias if they are jagged and angular. Sandstones consist of finer sediments that were laid down by weaker currents. Extremely small particles can be carried long distances by even very slow-moving water. The sediments that result are silts and muds, which occur in slow-flowing rivers or on the sea floor far away from a turbulent shoreline. When lithified, these very fine sediments form siltstones, mudstones, or shales.

A mixture of different-sized grains in the same rock may indicate that the current stopped abruptly, thereby suddenly depositing all of the various-sized particles it was carrying; such a sedimentary bed is termed poorly sorted. Well-sorted beds, in which all the particles are of approximately the same size, result from stable current conditions.

The shape of the particles in a sedimentary rock indicates the distance the eroded fragments traveled before being deposited and lithified. The farther the fragments traveled, the rounder they are because of the greater amount of abrasion from rubbing against other particles.

Rocks from sediment

It takes millions of years for a sediment to become rock. After deposition, the sediments are compressed beneath further layers that accumulate on top of them. The weight of the upper layers forces the underlying particles closer together, causing them to interlock and form a solid mass. The mass, however, is not yet rock at this stage; the particles—although tightly packed together—are still separate.

In the next phase—cementation—the particles are bonded together to form rock. Ground water percolating through rock and sediment often has calcite dissolved in it, leached out of lime-rich rocks by the weak carbonic acid formed when carbon dioxide in the air reacts with water in rain. The dissolved calcite then precipitates in the minute spaces between grains, thereby cementing them together; the resulting compressed and cemented mass is the sedimentary rock.

Types of sedimentary rocks

In addition to clastic rocks, there are two other principal types of sedimentary rocks: chemical and organic (or biogenic). Chemical sedimentary rocks are formed when dissolved material precipitates out of water; for example, a bed of salt may be formed when part of the sea becomes cut off from the main body of water and eventually evaporates, leaving a deposit of salt, which may later be overlain and compressed.

Organic sedimentary rocks are formed from the remains of animals or plants. One of the most common is limestone, which usually consists of the remains of small marine shellfish. When these creatures die, they sink to the sea bed, where their shells are broken up and then compressed and cemented together in the same way as clastic rocks.

Coal is probably the most familiar example of an organic sedimentary rock. It consists mainly of carbon, derived from masses of plant matter that accumulated in forested swamps eons ago. Because of the lack of oxygen in the swamp water, the plants did not decompose; instead they became compressed and lithified into coal.

The sedimentary cycle is the process that produces sedimentary rocks. Exposed rocks are broken down by the forces of weathering and erosion. The fragments are carried away by wind, rivers, or sea currents and are then deposited as beds of sediment. Eventually these beds are buried and turned to rock (lithification). At a later time, the beds of sedimentary rock are pushed upward and exposed by mountain-building activity. The exposed rocks are then eroded, and the cycle begins again.

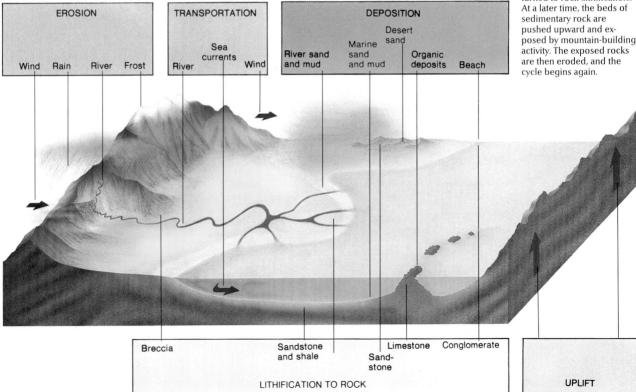

Igneous rocks

A thin slice of a rock placed between polarizing filters and examined through a microscope reveals the rock's individual mineral crystals. In the thin section of granite shown, the well-formed crystals of feldspar, which formed early in the solidification process, show up as rectangular blocks. The colorful crystals of mica and the gray crystals of quartz do not have such well-defined shapes, being the last to form.

Magma that cools quickly, as in a lava flow, forms a very fine-grained rock, such as basalt. Contraction of the cooling rock may cause it to crack and form a series of hexagonal columns that stand perpendicular to the lava surface. The classic example of this phenomenon is the Giant's Causeway on the northeastern coast of Northern Ireland.

Igneous rocks originate in masses of hot fluid that circulate deep within the earth. This molten rock, called magma, may consist of part of the earth's crust that has melted as a result of tectonic or mountain-building activity, or it may arise from the mantle (the layer immediately below the crust).

Rocks from magma

Igneous rocks are formed when molten magma cools and solidifies. Different types of igneous rocks may be produced out of the same mass of magma. As it cools, the components of the magma solidify in a set sequence. The first minerals to crystallize out of the melt are the high-temperature minerals—the oli-

vines and pyroxenes, which are silicates of magnesium and iron. They tend to be denser than the magma and so they sink, leaving the remaining fluid deficient in magnesium and iron. The next group of minerals to solidify are the feldspars (silicate minerals of potassium, sodium, calcium, and aluminum—the lighter metallic elements); the magma thus loses its metallic constituents first. Finally, any remaining silica crystallizes out as quartz. The entire solidification process, or differentiation as it is called, therefore results in dense iron- and magnesium-rich rocks and less dense silica-rich rocks from the same original fluid. This is dramatically exemplified in the rare outcrops in which the different types of rock can be seen as layers in the same rock mass—as occurs in the 1,000-foot (305 meter) thick Palisade Sill in New Jersey, which has an olivine-rich layer at the bottom and rocks with progressively less olivine above. Usually, however, an outcrop consists of only one type of igneous rock.

Geologists classify igneous rocks according to their composition. Those that have a low silica content (and are also usually rich in iron and magnesium) are called basic rocks; those with a high silica content are termed acid rocks. Basic rocks, such as gabbro, tend to be dark in color because their constituent minerals are dark, whereas acid rocks (such as granite) are light in color because they contain white and pink feldspars and glassy quartz. Igneous rocks are also categorized according to their origin: intrusive rocks, formed from magma that solidified beneath the surface, and extrusive rocks, from magma that solidified above the surface.

Igneous textures

When hot magma cools slowly, the minerals in it have sufficient time to grow large crystals and hence form coarse rock. The mineral crystals in rocks that have cooled quickly, on the other hand, are often too small to be seen with the naked eye.

The coarseness of a rock depends on where it was formed. Very coarse-grained rocks, such as the gabbros and granites, solidified deep underground and, therefore, cooled slowly. Volcanic rocks, such as basalts and trachytes, were formed from magma that cooled rapidly on the surface of the earth and are, therefore, fine-grained. The finest-grained igneous rocks originated from volcanoes that erupted underwater or beneath glaciers, as a result of which the lava (magma ejected by a volcano) cooled extremely rapidly.

Occasionally, such igneous rocks are so fine-grained that no crystalline structure is visible, resulting in a natural glass called obsidian.

Sometimes an igneous rock has two textures. It may have large crystals (called phenocrysts) embedded in a matrix of very small ones. This type of two-textured rock forms when magma begins to differentiate slowly then, when some of the crystals have formed, solidifies much more rapidly—probably because it was forced into a cooler location. This texture is known as porphyritic, and the rock is called a porphyry.

The texture and composition of a rock can be studied by cutting a sample into thin transparent slices and examining them with a microscope. The rock's constituents can then be determined by viewing the sections using polarized light, a technique that causes each mineral crystal to appear as a different color. This method reveals that the minerals that formed first have well-defined crystal shapes, whereas those that grew later tend to be distorted.

Igneous structures

It is not possible to observe an igneous rock while it forms (except volcanic rocks, in which the crystallization and solidification can be particularly spectacular) because most igneous rocks form deep under the surface of the earth in structures called intrusions. From these intrusions the magma can push its way through cracks, forcing aside or melting the surrounding rocks; the resultant structures reflect this action.

The largest igneous intrusions are called batholiths, and they form deep below the surface in active mountain chains. They may extend over hundreds of square miles. Underground cracks may fill with magma, forming sheets of igneous rock when the magma solidifies. The sheets are known as sills if they lie parallel to the strata of the surrounding rocks, or dikes if they cut across the strata. Igneous rocks may also form cylindrical structures— called stocks if they are broad, and necks if they are narrow—which may once have led to volcanoes on the surface.

Igneous rocks (and metamorphic rocks) tend to be harder than any surrounding sedimentary formations. As a result, when a mass of rock containing both igneous and sedimentary types is eroded, the softer sedimentary rocks usually wear away first, leaving the igneous masses as hills and other landscape features that reflect their original shapes.

Magma from a batholith pushes its way through the overlying rocks and forms igneous intrusions (stocks, laccoliths, and sills, for example) as it solidifies. Igneous rocks tend to be harder than the rocks surrounding them, and so after the softer rocks have been eroded away, various igneous structures are exposed and form characteristic landscape features, some of which are illustrated below.

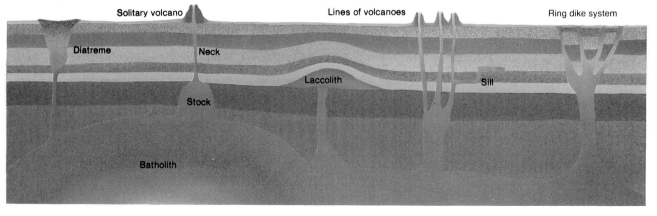

Solitary volcano · Diatreme · Neck · Stock · Laccolith · Lines of volcanoes · Sill · Ring dike system · Batholith

Landscape forms

Diatreme
A diatreme is a funnel-shaped structure formed by the explosive expansion of magma as it rises through areas of lower pressure.

Neck
Erosion of the terrain down to a volcano's neck produces an isolated cylindrical hill, such as Devil's Tower in Wyoming.

Laccolith
When a laccolith is exposed by erosion, it produces a rounded hill surrounded by circular scarps.

Dikes
A longitudinal dike system results from erosion of a line of volcanoes.

Ring dikes
Ring dikes are concentric ridges of igneous rock that are formed when the land around a circular dike system subsides.

Metamorphic rocks

Metamorphic rocks are classified according to their method of formation into two main types: regional (produced predominantly by pressure) and thermal metamorphic rocks (resulting from the effect of heat). Examples of each type are given below.

Regional
Gneiss
Phyllite
Schist
Slate

Thermal
Hornfels
Marble
Quartzite

The new minerals produced by metamorphism can be seen in this microscopic view (using polarized light) of a thin section of mica schist. In the section dark polyhedral crystals of garnet are separated by a contorted mass of mica crystals (which appear multicolored).

Vast slate quarries illustrate the great quantities of rock that can be altered by regional metamorphism. Slate, which is produced by the metamorphism of shale, is used to make roofing tiles and is one of the few metamorphic rocks of significant commercial importance.

When rocks are subjected to different conditions from those under which they originally formed, their mineral composition can change. This alteration can happen when rocks are exposed at the earth's surface, and their minerals react with various chemicals in the atmosphere. Much more marked effects occur when rocks are buried deep in an emerging mountain range and subjected to very high temperatures and pressures. Under these conditions the rocks alter completely, becoming entirely different types of rocks with different mineral compositions. Such transformed rocks are called metamorphic rocks.

The characteristic feature of a metamorphic rock is that its mineral composition changes without the rock itself melting. If the rock does melt and then solidify again, the result is an igneous not a metamorphic rock.

Regional metamorphism

Regional (or dynamic) metamorphic rocks—one of the two main types—are those that have been altered by great pressure but by little heat—as occurs, for example, in the heart of a fold mountain belt while it is being compressed between moving crustal plates. The effects of such a movement are usually extensive, hence regional metamorphic rocks tend to occupy large areas.

At depths in the order of tens of miles, the weight of the overlying rocks produces sufficiently high pressures to alter the mineral structure of the rocks beneath. For example, the minerals in shale (the black, flaky sedimentary rock that is produced by the lithification of mud) recrystallize into the mineral mica as a result of great pressure. The flat, leaflike mica crystals form in parallel bands (known as the rock's foliation). Earth movements associated with metamorphic processes may then deform the mica, forcing it to distort along the lines of foliation and producing, in turn, a schist, a typical regional metamorphic rock. The mineral bands in schist are very pronounced and are often distorted and jagged in appearance—evidence of the great stresses involved in their formation. A schist can usually be easily split along its foliation lines; this tendency to split along certain planes of weakness is called cleavage.

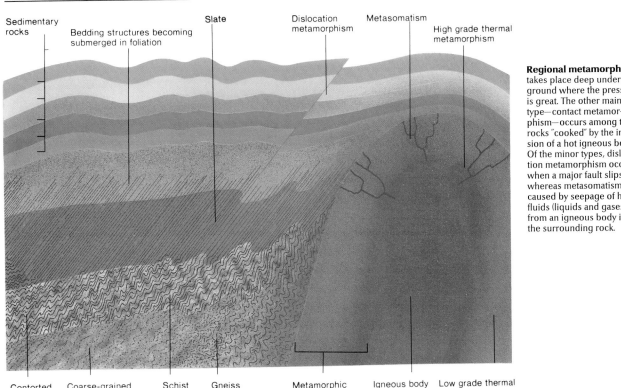

Sedimentary rocks

Bedding structures becoming submerged in foliation

Slate

Dislocation metamorphism

Metasomatism

High grade thermal metamorphism

Contorted foliation

Coarse-grained foliation

Schist

Gneiss

Metamorphic aureole

Igneous body

Low grade thermal metamorphism

Regional metamorphism takes place deep underground where the pressure is great. The other main type—contact metamorphism—occurs among the rocks "cooked" by the intrusion of a hot igneous body. Of the minor types, dislocation metamorphism occurs when a major fault slips, whereas metasomatism is caused by seepage of hot fluids (liquids and gases) from an igneous body into the surrounding rock.

The cleavage of a regional metamorphic rock is exploited commercially in the quarrying and working of slate. Like schist, slate is formed by the metamorphism of shale, but under less extreme pressures. Compared with shale, the minerals in slate are small and are often invisible to the naked eye.

It is sometimes assumed—erroneously—that the cleavage of slate corresponds to the lines of the thin bedding in the shale from which it was originally formed. In fact the cleavage reflects the direction of the pressure to which the shale was subjected during its metamorphism rather than the original structure of the rock.

Contact metamorphism

In the other main type of metamorphism—contact metamorphism—rocks are changed by the effects of great heat but little pressure. Contact metamorphic rocks are formed when a hot igneous mass of magma forces its way through the earth's crust, literally baking the rock surrounding it. In comparison with regional metamorphism, the volume of rock affected by contact metamorphic processes is very small; the newly-formed thermal metamorphic rock may extend for only a few inches around the igneous intrusion (the affected area is called an aureole) or, occasionally, the new rock may be up to about a mile wide around a very large batholith. There is usually a sequence of thermal metamorphic rocks around large intrusions; near such an intrusion there are high-temperature rocks, which gradually give way with increasing distance from the intrusion to low-temperature then unmetamorphosed rocks.

Probably the most familiar contact metamorphic rock is marble, which is produced by the metamorphism of limestone, a sedimentary rock consisting almost entirely of calcite (calcium carbonate). When the calcite is subjected to great heat from a nearby igneous intrusion, it first gives off carbon dioxide then recombines with this gas, thereby re-forming new calcite crystals and transforming the limestone to marble. The newly-formed crystals have a regular form and grain size (as opposed to the random collection of fragments in the original limestone) that gives the marble strength and an even texture.

Usually, however, the elements in the minerals of the original rock recombine during metamorphism to form completely different minerals, as occurs in the formation of hornfels, which often contains cordierite (a silicate mineral found only in thermal metamorphic rocks).

Other types of metamorphism

Dislocation metamorphism is a relatively rare type that occurs when the rocks on each side of a major fault move against each other as the fault slips. In this situation the stresses can be so great that the minerals in the rocks at the fault break down and recrystallize, thereby giving rise to a hard, flinty metamorphic rock called mylonite.

Metasomatism is similar to—and often associated with—contact metamorphism. As an igneous mass cools, it gives off hot liquids and gases, which may percolate through cracks and cavities in the surrounding rock. The hot fluids may then alter the surrounding rock by a combination of heat and deposition of minerals dissolved in the fluids. Many of the most productive deposits of metal ores are from veins that have been emplaced by metasomatic activity.

Volcanoes

Volcanoes are holes or cracks in the earth's crust through which molten rock erupts. They usually occur at structural weaknesses in the crust, often in regions of geological instability, such as the edges of crustal plates. Volcanoes are important to humans because they provide information about the earth's interior, and because volcanically formed soils are highly fertile and good for growing crops. Violent eruptions, however, can devastate huge areas, and accurate techniques for predicting eruptions are essential if major disasters are to be avoided.

Formation of volcanoes

Scientists do not fully understand the process by which volcanoes are formed. It seems that at points where the earth's mantle (the layer immediately beneath the crust) is particularly hot (hot spots) or where part of the crust is being forced down into the mantle (for example, where two crustal plates meet and one is forced down under the other) the heat causes the lower part of the crust or upper part of the mantle to melt. The molten rock—called magma—is under pressure as more magma forms and, being less dense than the surrounding rock, it rises, often along lines of weakness, such as faults or joints in the crust. As the magma rises it melts a channel for itself

in the rock and accumulates, together with gases released from the melting rock, in a magma chamber a few miles below the earth's surface.

Eventually the pressure from the magma and gas builds up to such an extent that an eruption occurs, blasting a vent through the surface rocks. Lava (magma after emission) piles up around the vent to form a volcanic mountain or, if the eruption is from a fissure, a lava plateau. The volcano then undergoes periodic eruptions of gases, lava, and rock fragments. It is termed active, dormant, or extinct, according to the frequency with which it erupts.

Vents associated with declining volcanic activity and the cooling of lava periodically emit steam, or hot water, and are often valuable sources of energy or minerals: solfataras (which are rich in sulfur) and fumaroles give out steam and gas; geysers are hot springs that eject jets of hot water or steam at regular intervals as underground water is heated to boiling point by the magma.

The characteristics of eruptions vary greatly from volcano to volcano, and those typical of any one volcano change over the years. Eruptions are classified according to their explosiveness, which depends on the composition (especially the gas content) and viscosity of the magma involved, which in turn depends largely on the depth at which the rock becomes molten. Relatively viscous magma causes explosive eruptions; sticky magma often forms a plug in the neck of the volcano,

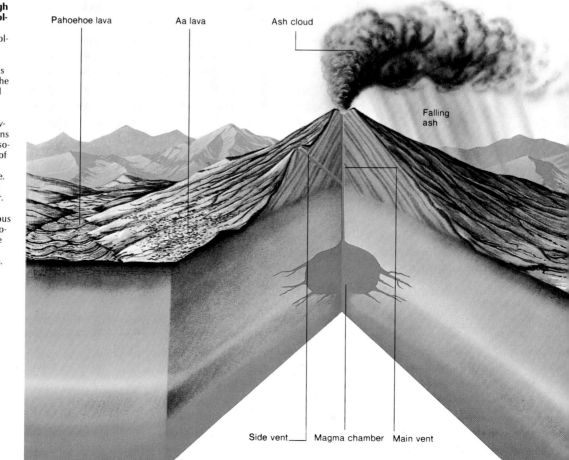

A composite illustration shows a section through a typical continental volcano (not to scale) and many features found in volcanic regions. Pahoehoe and Aa are the two main types of lava; the former is relatively fluid, whereas the latter is more viscous and solidifies to form a rough surface. A tree mold is formed when a tree is covered with lava, which burns away the tree as the lava solidifies, leaving a mound of solid lava with a tree-shaped hole in the middle. Geysers periodically emit powerful jets of hot water. Fumaroles and solfataras give off steam and sulfurous gases. Other volcanic topographical features include crater lakes, hot springs, mud pools, and mud pots.

Pahoehoe lava   Aa lava   Ash cloud

Falling ash

Side vent   Magma chamber   Main vent

blocking further eruptions until enough magma and gas have accumulated for their pressure to blast away the plug and allow the emission of gas, lava, and fragmented magma (tephra). This accumulation may take several decades, or even centuries. Some explosive eruptions are quite small, but others (those in which large amounts of gas are trapped in the magma) are so violent that they blast away a large part of a mountain or a whole island.

Volcanoes formed mainly of rock fragments are generally steep-sided cones (with slopes of between 20° and 40° to the horizontal), because any fragments blasted into the air fall back near the vent. Those formed chiefly of viscous lava are usually highly convex domes typically about 500 feet (152 meters) high and 1,300 feet (396 meters) across, because the lava is too thick to flow far before solidifying. Exceptionally viscous lava may solidify in the vent. The solid mass may then be forced slowly upward, forming a spine that rises several hundred feet above the summit. This movement usually precedes a particularly violent eruption, caused by the sudden release of the accumulated pressure. In 1902, such an event accompanied the destructive eruption of Mont Pelée on the island of Martinique in the West Indies.

At the other extreme, relatively fluid magma is extruded quite freely and quietly, with small eruptions that occur at frequent intervals or even continuously. The lava flows for long distances before it solidifies, and forms a shield volcano (usually with slopes of less than about

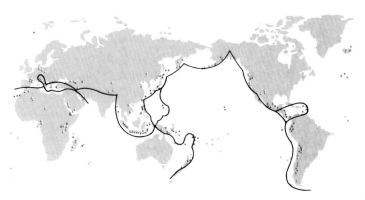

10°), such as Mauna Loa on Hawaii; the island rises about 30,000 feet (9,100 meters) from a seafloor base 60 miles (97 kilometers) in diameter.

Submarine volcanoes

Submarine volcanoes are particularly common near oceanic ridges, where magma is constantly extruded as the continental plates drift apart. Many also form over hot spots. As the crust moves, the volcano also moves away from the hot spot and becomes extinct; a new volcano forms directly over the original hot spot, and a chain of volcanoes gradually forms.

In the map of volcano distribution *(above)* active volcanoes are marked by red dots, extinct ones by blue dots. Most volcanoes are located at the edges of crustal plates (shown as black lines), where earthquakes and mountain building also take place. Some extinct volcanoes mark areas of former crustal instability, such as the Great Rift Valley in East Africa.

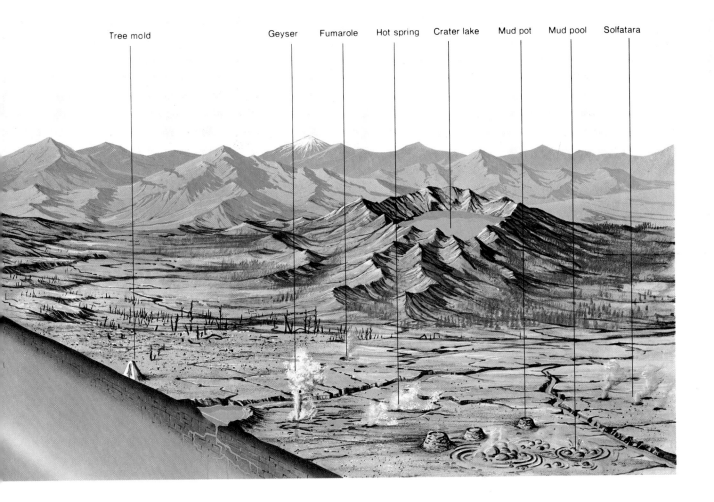

Tree mold   Geyser   Fumarole   Hot spring   Crater lake   Mud pot   Mud pool   Solfatara

Lava fountains (on the skyline) are releasing several lava flows down the eastern slopes of Mount Etna, Italy, during an eruption in 1971.

Pahoehoe lava solidifies into characteristic rope-textured folded sheets. In contrast, Aa lava—the other main type—is rough-textured. The two types often have identical chemical compositions, and it is quite common for a lava flow that leaves a vent as pahoehoe to change to Aa lava as it progresses down a volcano's slopes.

In oceanic ridges and hot spots the lava is formed from mantle material that is forced up by deep convection currents. This lava is dense but fluid, unlike the silica-rich lava produced by melting crustal material, found in continental areas and offshore island chains. Where it appears above the water surface—in Iceland and Hawaii, for example—it forms flat lava plateaus or shield volcanoes.

Marine volcanic activity may lead to the sudden creation of islands, for example, Surtsey, off Iceland, in 1963. Volcanic islands are subject to severe erosion by the sea and may also subside when they move away from a ridge or hot spot and cease to be active. There are more than 2,000 submerged—usually extinct—volcanoes (seamounts) in the world; those that have been eroded nearly to sea level and then subsequently submerged, which are known as guyots, are also common.

Predicting volcanic eruptions

Prediction of eruptions is of great importance because of the extensive damage they can cause to surrounding areas, which are often fertile and densely populated. Volcanic activity used to be assessed in terms of temperature and pressure, measured by means of borings into the sides of the vent. Recently, however, geologists have come to rely instead on seismography, on measurements of changes in emissions of gas and its sulfur dioxide content, and on detecting activity inside the crater (monitored with mirrors). Most of all, they look for changes in the angle of the mountainside (measured with tiltmeters): any expansion in one part of the mountain indicates that an eruption there is likely. Further information is obtained from analyses of the mineral content of the local water, recordings of vertical ground swelling, and readings from geodimeters, which use lasers to measure minute swellings in the ground.

These techniques are, however, by no means perfect. They were in use on Mount St. Helens in the state of Washington, when it erupted in May 1980 but, despite the fact that scientists were aware that an eruption was imminent, they were not able to anticipate the time, force, or exact direction of the blast.

The Mount St. Helens eruption

Mount St. Helens is one of a chain of continental volcanoes in the Cascade Range in the northwestern United States. All the volcanoes in this mountain range are the result of the Pacific oceanic crustal plate being forced down into the mantle by the North American continental plate riding over it. The molten parts of the oceanic plate then rise through the crustal material, forming volcanoes. Normally an eruptive phase involves several of the Cascade Range volcanoes. During the nineteenth century, for example, Mount St. Helens erupted three times, simultaneously with nearby Mount Baker. Because of these coincident eruptions, some scientists believe that the two volcanoes may have a common origin where, at a depth of about 125 miles (200 kilometers) below the surface, the Pacific crustal plate is being overridden by the North American plate.

After 123 years of dormancy, Mount St. Helens erupted in May 1980—one of the most violent (and closely monitored) eruptions in recent times. Volcanic activity was first noticed on March 20, when small tremors began and the mountain top started to bulge; about a week later, fissures in the flank of the volcano emitted steam.

The first violent eruption occurred on May 18, when the slow accumulation of pressure within the volcano was released with explosive force. The north flank of the mountain collapsed, and the contents of the vent were blasted out. The abrupt release of pressure caused the gas dissolved in the magma to come out of solution suddenly, forming bubbles throughout the hot mass—rather like the sudden formation of bubbles in champagne when the bottle is uncorked. A white-hot cloud of gas and pulverized magma (called

a *nuée ardente*) then swept over the surrounding countryside, engulfing everything within a distance of about 5 miles (8 kilometers) from the peak. (This phenomenon also occurred when Mont Pelée erupted in 1902; within a few minutes of the eruption, the cloud had covered Saint-Pierre, then the capital of Martinique, killing its 38,000 inhabitants.) At the same time, a vertical column of dust and ash was blown upward. These two major effects were accompanied by a blast of air caused by the sudden expansion of the freed gases; the blast flattened all trees near the volcano and knocked down some as far as 15 miles (24 kilometers) away.

The *nuée ardente* and the vertical ash column produced cauliflower-shaped clouds 20 miles (32 kilometers) wide that eventually reached a height of 15 miles (24 kilometers). The ash consisted mainly of silica, reflecting the high silica content of continental volca-noes.

The ash falling back to earth and the debris of the collapsed flank, which amounted to about 0.88 cubic miles (3.7 km³), combined with the water of nearby rivers and the melt-water of the mountain snows to form a mud-flow (called a *lahar*). The mudflow plunged along the river valleys at speeds of up to about 50 miles per hour (80 kilometers per hour), destroying bridges and settlements 12 miles (19 kilometers) downstream; in places, the mud deposited by this flow was 425 feet (130 meters) deep.

Although the May eruption is perhaps the best known, Mount St. Helens erupted several times during the later part of the year. Each eruption was preceded by the growth of a dome of volcanic material in the crater left by the initial explosion, and the general pattern of the subsequent eruptions resembled that of the first.

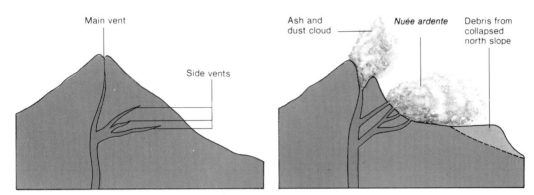

The section, far left, depicts Mount St. Helens before it erupted on May 18, 1980. On the near left is the volcano during the first eruption, when the north slope collapsed and hot volcanic gases, steam, and dust (a *nuée ardente*) were blasted out sideways with explosive force. Simultaneously, a cloud of ash and dust was blown upward.

The most devastating of Mount St. Helens' recent eruptions occurred in May 1980, but volcanic activity continued, and there were several smaller eruptions during the later part of the year. The main explosion was estimated to have had the force of 500 Hiroshima atom bombs and was heard more than 190 miles (306 kilometers) away.

Earthquakes

Earthquakes are among the most devastating natural events that occur on earth and are a reminder that our planet is a dynamic, changing body.

The term "earthquake" has two uses: it may denote the earth tremors (and the resultant damage) at a particular locality, or it may be used to describe the precise source of the tremors caused by a sudden fracture of the ground elsewhere. There are two corresponding measures of the severity of an earthquake. Intensity (usually assessed on the 12-point Modified Mercalli Scale) is a measure of the local effect, which varies according to both the distance from the source of the earthquake and the intrinsic strength of the earthquake. Magnitude is a measure of the strength of the earthquake at its source (focus). It is assessed on the Richter Scale, on which magnitude 7 is severe, magnitude 8 devastating. Since 1904, when seismometers first provided data from which magnitudes could be calculated, there have been very few earthquakes exceeding magnitude 8.4. The highest Richter magnitude ever recorded was 8.9 in Japan in 1933—approximately as powerful as a 100-megaton explosion.

Causes of earthquakes

Most earthquakes occur in narrow belts along the boundaries of crustal plates, particularly where the plates push together (as in the Himalayas, Andes, and Japan) or slide past each other (as happens along the San Andreas Fault in California). Earthquakes may be caused by movement of the plates, itself resulting from convection currents in the hot fluids of the mantle (the layer beneath the earth's crust). Some earthquakes are associated with volcanic activity and are caused by the welling-up or retreat of magma. Collapses of mines or caverns can also produce small earthquakes.

Earthquakes occur when rocks are subjected to stresses that they are not strong enough to withstand; as a result, the rocks break down, thereby releasing the accumulated pressure, which then spreads out in waves from the point of breakdown and produces the earth tremors. The difference between large and small earthquakes is not due chiefly to differences in the strengths of the different types of rocks, but rather to the amount of rock under stress. In the 1964 Alaskan earthquake, for example, the stress was released over a region 500 miles (805 kilometers) long and, with such a large amount of rock involved, the earthquake itself was severe, having a magnitude of 8.6.

Along some parts of the San Andreas Fault, earthquakes are frequent but small because stress accumulates over only a small amount of rock before it is released. A considerable amount of movement occurs along other areas of the fault without producing earthquakes. Yet other parts of the fault—around San Francisco, for example—are "locked" at present, although surveys have shown that stress is accumulating and eventually the rocks will break down, producing a devastating earthquake—probably as severe as that of 1906, which had a magnitude of about 8.3.

Effects of earthquakes

The effects of an earthquake vary enormously, depending on its strength and on the distance from its epicenter. Some are so minor as to be detectable only with sensitive instruments. In contrast, a large earthquake can devastate a huge area, its effects being felt hundreds of miles from the epicenter.

Most direct damage results from shaking of the ground by earthquake (seismic) waves that move through the surface layers—called L waves. (Earthquakes also produce two other main types of waves: horizontally-moving primary, or compressional, waves; and vertically-moving secondary, or shear, waves.)

Various side effects of the shaking include liquefaction of soft, damp ground, landslips, and the appearance of large cracks in the surface. When an earthquake occurs at sea, giant "tidal" waves (called tsunamis) may be pro-

An earthquake occurs when rocks subjected to great stress suddenly break, releasing the accumulated energy, which shakes the ground, the vibrations spreading out from the epicenter like ripples on water. Initially the stress may have little effect (A), but as it accumulates, the rocks distort (B) at faults or other points of weakness and eventually break (C). When this happens, the rock layers "rebound" and the accumulated energy is suddenly released as a seismic shock.

Large cracks in the ground are one of the effects of severe earthquakes. Because of the intrinsic destructiveness of earthquakes, seismologists have devoted much effort to prediction. It has been found that most earthquakes occur along crustal plate boundaries, which are often also areas of volcanic activity; hence the distribution of earthquakes is similar to that of volcanoes.

Severe earthquakes can devastate large areas, causing much loss of life and damage to property. It is therefore important to construct suitable buildings in earthquake-prone areas. Traditional Japanese houses were made largely of wood and paper so that they caused little injury or loss of life when they collapsed. Many modern buildings erected in earthquake risk areas, however, are robustly constructed to withstand even quite large earthquakes.

duced by seismic disturbances of the sea floor. These waves can travel as fast as 470 miles per hour (756 kilometers per hour) and, as they reach the shore, may exceed 50 feet (15 meters) in height. They are so powerful that they can wreck relatively large buildings, sometimes at a considerable distance inland.

Earthquake prediction

It is difficult to predict when earthquakes will happen. One approach to this problem involves studying the historical and geological records of a particular area in an attempt to discover a pattern in the frequency of earthquakes. The records can reveal that they occur at comparatively regular intervals, which enables them to be predicted with reasonable accuracy. Usually, however, there is no easily recognizable pattern.

The other method of prediction involves studying various changes as the stress increases in the rocks of an earthquake-prone region. Many factors (including the shape of the ground, the physical properties of the rocks themselves, and even the behavior of animals) undergo characteristic changes that portend an earthquake, but it is nevertheless extremely difficult to predict exactly when an earthquake will occur.

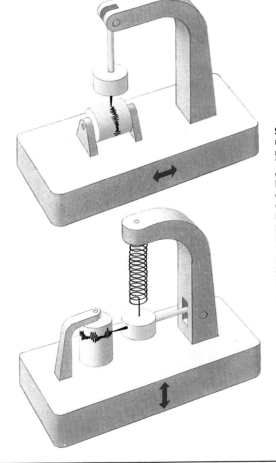

Seismometers are instruments that record the seismic waves of earthquakes. There are two basic types: one *(left, top)* for measuring horizontal movements; the other *(left, bottom)* for vertical motions. Both types of instrument comprise a suspended weight that tends to remain stationary while the rest of the instrument is moved by the earth tremors. Attached to the weight is a pen, which records a tracing on a moving paper strip. In some instruments, tremors are detected and recorded electronically.

Fact Entries

The Mercalli Scale is a measure of earthquake intensity originally formulated in 1902 by the Italian seismologist Giuseppe Mercalli (1850-1914). Subsequently modified, the scale is still used today. There are 12 degrees of intensity on the modern Modified Mercalli Scale ranging from 1 (instrumental), detectable only by seismometer, through 12 (catastrophic), in which there is total destruction of buildings.

The Richter Scale is a measure of earthquake magnitude devised in 1935 by the American geophysicist Charles Richter and later developed by him and another American scientist, Beno Gutenberg. The scale was a measure of the energy released, originally defined as the logarithm of the amplitude of the motion of a standard seismometer 100 km from an earthquake's epicenter. The modern scale (which has no theoretical upper or lower limits) incorporates other factors, such as the strength of the rocks on which the seismometer is resting. Events at the top of the scale may be 100,000,000 times greater than those at the bottom.

Faults and folds

The crust of the earth is subject to movements and stresses that are most clearly visible in the deformations of surface rocks due to the processes of faulting and folding.

Faults

A fault is any displacement of rocks in a plane of weakness in the earth's crust. The earth's surface is crossed with many types of faults, all resulting from stresses caused by earth movements, intrusions, or gravity. Faulting is one of the most important ways that stress is released from rock.

In geological terms, rocks are not solid; they behave like stiff plastic. When stress develops, the rocks absorb it until their rupture point is reached, when they fault. Factors that influence faulting include the nature of the stress, whether it develops gradually or rapidly, and the type, age, temperature, and water content of the rock.

Types and causes of faulting

Because faults are caused by stress, the origin of stress can often help in understanding the types of faulting.

Intrusion of rocks such as basalt or granite may create strong tensional forces that may stretch the overlying rocks beyond their rupture point. At constructive plate margins, such as the Mid-Atlantic Ridge, the intrusion of basalt and pulling away of the sides causes the central area to form a rift valley, or graben, due to the development of two normal faults.

At a destructive plate margin, compressional forces are dominant, and on the margins of the developing fold mountains, huge slices of rock may be pushed over existing rocks, with the formation of thrust faults. These are large-scale features, which can involve several miles of displacement.

Many of the causes of faulting also cause rocks to fold, and when the folding develops, continued stress may lead to faulting in the folding rocks. The most extreme example of this is a thrust nappe. Additionally, many folds have small faults near their axes.

Faults also develop when large areas of the crust move vertically at different rates. One cause of this appears to be the presence of large granite intrusions, which are relatively light and help to stabilize the area into which they intrude. Faults develop when the adjacent areas sink or rise at their own rates.

Faults involving only horizontal movement are called tear faults. These develop when the stresses come from opposing directions but act obliquely to one another. Transform faults are special types of tear faults, which are found in the large rigid plates that make up the Earth's surface.

Faults in the landscape

The displacement of rocks on fault surfaces can produce dramatic effects: the earthquake at Hebgen Lake, Montana, in 1959 was the result of a displacement of over 20 feet (6 meters) and, in addition to the earthquake, a fault scarp of 20 feet appeared instantly. Earthquakes and volcanoes are often associated with faults: Iceland frequently has volcanic eruptions and small earthquakes developing from the rift valley zone. Some large-scale features also develop with faulting, one of the most notable examples being the East African rift valley, which runs for more than 1,800 miles (2,897 kilometers) and appears to be caused by a failed constructive plate margin. The rift valley has become the location of huge lakes, savannahs that support spectacular wildlife, and hot deserts. When land rises between two faults, the feature is called a horst or fault block. The blocks of Western Europe developed in this way—two examples are the Black Forest in Germany and the Alston block in England.

The effects of faults

Faults have affected humankind in many ways. When movement occurs, earthquakes are generated. These can completely destroy artificial

Normal faults involve the downward displacement of the hanging wall block (A), above the inclined fault, relative to the footwall block (B), below the fault.

Reverse faults involve the hanging wall (A) being displaced upward. When the angle (B) between the fault plane and the footwall block (C) is less than 45°, this is called an overthrust fault.

Transcurrent faults involve horizontal displacement (A). When displacement is both horizontal and vertical (B), the fault is called an oblique-slip fault.

Erosion affects all exposed surfaces but is particularly marked where soft rock is exposed or where reverse (A) or overthrust (B) faulting has caused overhanging rock to collapse.

A **normal fault** in an outcrop of sedimentary rock shows clearly the vertical displacement of strata.

A **strike-slip or transcurrent fault** is susceptible to erosion along the fault. This has occurred in the Great Glen Fault in Scotland, where lochs and rivers follow the fault line.

constructions on the surface. But faults may also be important sources of minerals. Because ore-bearing fluids moving through the earth's crust seek out zones of least resistance, fault planes tend to attract such fluids and encourage the deposition of the minerals they contain. Among the valuable metal ores that can be mined as a result of this are galena, a lead ore; sphalerite, an ore of zinc; and gold. Traps for gas or oil are also created by faulting, when impervious rocks are positioned above porous rocks, which can then retain gas or oil. Faulting can affect the water table in a similar way by channeling or collecting subterranean water and either causing springs to form at the surface or creating a water source that can be exploited by an artesian well.

Different types of rocks brought together by faulting can generate important topographical features. For example, when the rocks on one side of a fault are resistant to erosion, and those on the other are not, a prominent scarp in the landscape will be formed.

Folds

Although sedimentary rocks are assumed to form in horizontal layers, according to the Principle of Original Horizontality, when these rocks are exposed at the earth's surface they often appear tilted or folded. There are several possible causes of this folding, the most important being diastrophic, or "earth moving," forces. Intrusions and surface pressures also have significant effects. These processes are very gradual in terms of a human time scale, but geologically they are rapid. Furthermore, the rocks that fold are, normally, geologically young so that they are relatively soft and pliable.

There are two principal fold structures: an arch, or anticline, and a trough, or syncline. The manner of folding varies with the way pressure is applied—for example, it may build up gradually in strength or be short-lived but intense. The temperature, wetness, and type of rock being folded will also influence the effects.

Diastrophic forces

This group of "earth moving" forces is by far the most important cause of the deformation of sedimentary rocks. Folding occurs over a wide range of scale and intensity. Cracking, or faulting, of rocks results from pressures within the crust; as rocks fault, the adjacent blocks of rock move past one another and may fold.

In zones of mountain building, faulting is only one cause of folding, however. Mountains are forced to rise by the convergence of two rigid plates of the earth's surface, which crushes thick piles of young sediments that have accumulated between them. Such crushing results in a shortening of the crust, and folding is one of the principal mechanisms by which shortening is achieved. The intensity of folding increases toward the core of the mountain belt: at the core itself rocks may be folded more than once as the converging plates force and fold into one another. The rocks bend to accommodate the pressures. The most extreme development of this process is the nappe—a structure that has been subjected to such pressure that the folds are themselves folded. This process can be represented by pushing both sides of a tablecloth together: as the sides approach one another, more and more intense folding develops. The moving crustal plates that generate these crushing pressures may develop such nappe folds on their surfaces as sediments pile up and spill over.

Less intense folding in mountain building regions can develop away from the core area, when sediments are forced against a resistant mass. This normally results in a series of asymmetric folds, which are more or less folded according to the pressure exerted on them.

At the margin of mountain belts, young sedimentary rocks may be gently deformed by the mountain-building forces. Western Europe has a series of large but gentle folds, formed as the Alpine mountain system developed 50 million years ago. The rocks affected were principally those formed in the previous 50 to 80 million years—the thick Cretaceous Chalk formation, in this area. The Paris and London Basins are good examples of these fold structures.

Intrusions

Igneous rocks and rock salt (itself a sedimentary rock) are the main types of rock that cause folding of sedimentary rocks by the process of intrusion. Rock salt is deposited as a sediment when salt water evaporates. As other sediments are deposited on top of this, they exert a pressure on the salt layer that causes the salt crystals to flow—a process known as rheid flow. The mobile salt layer has a low specific gravity, which makes it lighter than the enclosing rocks, and encourages it to rise. The salt eventually finds a weak point in the overlying rock and forces its way through, rising vertically. As it rises, it deforms the rocks it passes through and causes overlying rocks to arch into an anticlinal structure. Such formations are known as salt plugs, or domes, and in certain areas form important oil traps, for example, in parts of Texas and in the North Sea.

A similar process occurs with molten rock or magma. When rock melts, dissolved gases tend to make it rise. The pressure they exert, together with the high temperature of the magma, allows it to rise vertically through overlying rocks; this produces folding effects similar to those caused by salt intrusions.

Surface processes

Folding also occurs as a result of surface processes, principally in circumstances that affect sediment before it has lithified, that is, changed into rock. A substantial amount of sediment accumulates on the shallow continental shelf area of the oceans and slides or flows down the slope. This can produce fold structures at a wide range of scales.

Another, though relatively insignificant, cause of folding can occur as a result of vol-

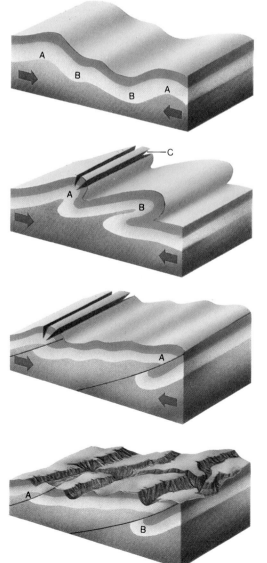

Folding occurs as rocks are compressed. Anticlines (A) and synclines (B) are simple upward or downward folds.

Asymmetrical (tilted) anticlines may be overturned (A) or recumbent (B) folds. When rocks at the apex of an anticline crack without faulting, the fissures are called joints (C).

Overthrust faulting can occur as a result of pressure on a recumbent fold. The low angle thrust sheet is called a nappe (A).

Erosion affects anticlines (A) more than synclines (B), particularly where joints have occurred.

canic activity, particularly if solid material, ejected by a volcano, lands on the layers of fine ash that have been produced by previous eruptions.

The impact of folds

Folding brings rocks of differing characters to the surface. It causes rock to be locally compressed in the syncline cores and stretched on the anticline arch, both of which can affect the rock's response to weathering processes. Anticlines tend to create ridges in the landscapes, but the extension cracks (joints) may concentrate weathering so that the anticlinal structure is deeply eroded.

Most European coalfields lie in broad synclinal troughs. If the coal seams had not been protected from weathering by the folding, the Industrial Revolution might never have occurred. Downfolding is also responsible for many artesian water reserves, of vital importance in areas such as Western Australia. Conversely, upfolding provides an ideal structure to trap oil. After its formation, oil normally collects in suitable reservoir rocks that have been deformed into collecting structures, such as anticlines.

Folding of sedimentary rocks—in this case clays and limestones—is obvious where the sea has eroded the cliff face evenly.

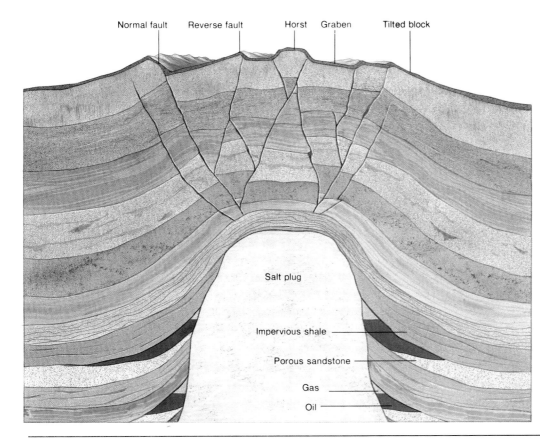

An intrusion, such as a salt plug, compresses and deforms sedimentary layers above it. As the process continues, faulting occurs, typically with the creation of horst and graben formations. A salt plug also creates structural traps in which gas and oil accumulate, seeping through porous strata (typically sandstone) and collecting beneath layers of impervious shale.

Fact Entries

Faults are defined by the angle and direction in which blocks move. Dip is the angle of maximum slope. Strike is the horizontal component of the slope and is at right angles to the dip. In a normal fault, the fault plane is inclined steeply toward the down-thrust block. In a reverse fault, the fault plane is also steep, but movement is in the opposite direction to a normal fault, with the upthrust block rising over the downthrust block. When the dip is less than 45°, a reverse fault is described as an overthrust fault. Lateral movement occurs in a strikeslip, tear, or transcurrent fault, as two blocks slide past each other in a horizontal direction.

Folds are described by the direction of folding: a downward fold is a syncline; an upward fold is an anticline. The line along a trough or crest is the axis of the fold. Asymmetrical anticlines are described as overturned, until the axial plane is nearly horizontal, when they are called recumbent folds. In extreme cases, this is associated with overthrusting and the formation of a thrust sheet, or nappe, in which many folds build up.

Geological time scale

It is now generally believed within the scientific community that the earth is extremely old. However, until the mid-nineteenth century our planet's age was largely ignored by scientists. In 1859, Charles Darwin published his *Origin of Species,* which stated that the earth was several million years old, and this stimulated geologists to begin investigating the earth's age.

Early attempts at estimating the absolute age of the earth varied widely. Most are now known to be grossly inaccurate; nevertheless, considerable progress was made in developing methods of determining the relative ages of rocks and fossils. The discovery in the early twentieth century that certain radioactive isotopes can be used to determine absolute ages led to increasingly accurate estimates of the

earth's age. Scientists today generally accept that our planet is some 4.5 billion years old, although continuing refinements of radioactive dating techniques are likely to produce minor amendments to this figure.

Absolute dating

Radioactive (or radiometric) dating is the most commonly used method of absolute dating (that is, establishing how many years old a rock is, rather than merely whether it is older or younger than another rock). It employs the natural phenomenon whereby radioactive isotopes (which are present in minute amounts in the earth's crust) spontaneously decay into stable, nonradioactive elements at a fairly constant rate.

The central concept in radiometric dating is that of a half-life—the time it takes for half a given quantity of a radioactive isotope of decay. For example, the half-life of uranium-238 is about 4.5 billion years, so after this time has elapsed, only half the original amount of uranium-238 remains, the rest having been transformed into various other isotopes (the final decay product of uranium-238 is lead-206). Thus, by measuring the proportion of parent material to decay products in a rock sample, scientists can calculate the specimen's absolute age.

The other main isotopes used for radiometric dating include potassium-40 and carbon-14. Potassium-40 has a half-life of about 1.3 billion years. It eventually decays into the gas argon-40. Carbon-14 has a half-life of only 5,700 years (eventually decaying to the gas nitrogen-14) and so is used to date recent geological events; it is probably more widely used, however, to date archaeological artifacts.

Although radiometric dating is very useful

Dendrochronology is the use of tree rings to measure absolute ages. A tree grows one ring every year, so the age of the tree can be ascertained simply by counting the rings. This dating method is of limited use because the oldest trees (bristlecone pines in the United States) are less than about 5,000 years old. The dating range can, however, be extended by matching early rings in living trees with distinctive rings in timbers from archaeological sites.

A series of rock strata (comprising mainly igneous rocks and limestone, a sedimentary rock) have been exposed by river erosion in the river canyon *(right).* The rocks at the bottom of the canyon are many millions of years older than those at the top, so by studying the strata scientists can gain much information about the geological history of the area.

for estimating the absolute ages of rocks, the techniques involved require the utmost precision and are capable of yielding ages only within a certain margin of error (which increases with the age of the rocks tested). Furthermore, this dating method cannot tell us about the actual events that occurred in the earth's past. For these reasons geologists still use more traditional methods—such as stratigraphy and paleontology—to study the earth's history.

Stratigraphy

Stratigraphy is the study of the nature and origin of layered (stratified) rocks, their sequence in the earth's crust, and their correlation (that is, identifying rocks of a similar age but from different locations). Analysis of the nature and distribution of stratified rocks enables the geological history of the area from which the rocks were obtained to be reconstructed. In performing such a task, geologists make use of several basic principles, perhaps the most important of which is that of uniformitarianism.

Uniformitarianism

According to the principle of uniformitarianism, present-day geological processes, such as erosion, transportation, and volcanic activity, have operated throughout the earth's history and can, therefore, be used to explain the formation of ancient as well as contemporary geological features. For example, sedimentary rocks containing structures that can be recognized in as yet unlithified sediments can be regarded as having formed under the same conditions as those modern sediments; such structures include ripple marks on beach sands and current bedding in river deposits.

But although the principle of uniformitarianism is fundamental to understanding the stratigraphic record, it does not, by itself, explain all the observed geological phenomena. For example, the African and Canadian banded ironstones (which are more than 2,200 million years old) could have formed only in an oxygen-poor atmosphere, which indicates that the atmosphere during the first half of the earth's history was significantly different from that of the present day. By analyzing rocks, however, it is often possible to discover the conditions under which they formed, and this information can be used to compile paleogeographical maps, which depict the distribution of different environments during the earth's past.

Stratigraphy and dating

Discovering the relative ages of rocks in a stratigraphic sequence and correlating separate outcrops are essential in trying to elucidate the stratigraphic record. Of the principles and techniques developed to help in this work, the simplest is probably the principle of superposition, which states that, in an undisturbed sequence of sedimentary rocks, the older rocks are overlain by younger rocks. There are, however, complications; although all strata are originally deposited sequentially in horizontal layers, subsequent deformation

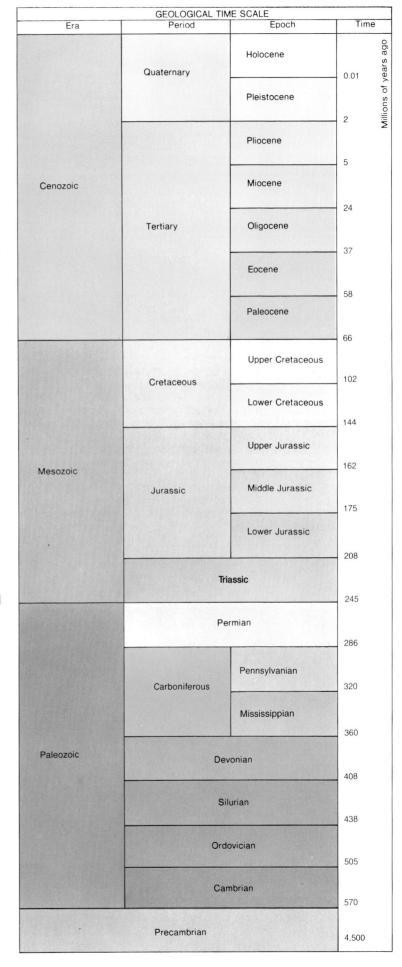

GEOLOGICAL TIME SCALE			
Era	Period	Epoch	Time
Cenozoic	Quaternary	Holocene	
		Pleistocene	0.01
			2
	Tertiary	Pliocene	5
		Miocene	
		Oligocene	24
		Eocene	37
		Paleocene	58
			66
Mesozoic	Cretaceous	Upper Cretaceous	102
		Lower Cretaceous	144
	Jurassic	Upper Jurassic	162
		Middle Jurassic	175
		Lower Jurassic	208
	Triassic		245
Paleozoic	Permian		286
	Carboniferous	Pennsylvanian	320
		Mississippian	360
	Devonian		408
	Silurian		438
	Ordovician		505
	Cambrian		570
	Precambrian		4,500

Millions of years ago

Varves are thin layers of sediments deposited in lakes fed by glacial meltwater. The stratification of the deposits is thought to be a seasonal banding. By counting and correlating these bands geologists have worked out a detailed chronology of the Pleistocene Ice Age in the Northern Hemisphere.

may tilt or even overturn the strata—as happened, for example, when the primordial continents of Africa and Eurasia collided. Hence to establish the correct order of deposition, it may be necessary to use other criteria, such as grading of the rock beds (in the formation of a sedimentary rock mass the coarsest particles are usually laid down first and are subsequently overlain by progressively finer—and therefore younger—sediments).

Rocks folded and deformed during a period of intense tectonic activity may be raised above sea level and severely eroded before further deposition occurs. The younger strata then rest discordantly on the upturned, worn-down edges of the older strata, with eroded fragments of the underlying deformed rocks

marking the unconformity surface—as occurs between the Upper Cambrian (younger) and upturned Precambrian (older) metamorphic rocks in the Grand Canyon in Arizona.

The other main principle used by geologists in determining an area's geological history is the principle of cross-cutting relations: according to which any feature that cuts across rock strata—a fault or an igneous intrusion such as a basalt dike, for example—is younger than the strata themselves. Radiometric dating can be used to ascertain maximum and minimum ages of the strata and, if these strata contain fossils, rocks that occur elsewhere with the same suite of fossils can also then be dated. However, radiometric dating is most useful in assigning ages to rocks containing very few fossils, such as those from the Precambrian Era.

The nature of the stratigraphic record

The stratigraphic record is very incomplete; unconformities are common, and evidence of erosion is widespread. Moreover, although there are many examples of slow, apparently continuous sedimentation—the deep-sea oozes in the Indian Ocean and the estuarine sediments of the Netherlands, for instance—it is probable that catastrophic events, such as landslides and volcanic eruptions, have had the greater effect on the stratigraphic record.

Most near-shore sediments are destroyed almost as soon as they are created, although in some circumstances thick piles of sediment can accumulate rapidly; in the Italian Apennines, single beds of sediment up to about 65 feet (20 meters) deep are thought to have been deposited by a single rush of turbid water. Much better known, however, are the effects of volcanic eruptions, many of which produce vast amounts of ash and other debris; when it settles, the debris tends to form thick, uniformly-graded beds. In the famous eruption of Vesuvius in A.D. 79, for instance, the city of

Zone fossils characterize a particular span of geological time and are used to subdivide and date the various periods and epochs. The Ordovician Period, for example, has been subdivided into five stages *(shown right)* on the basis of the presence of different species of graptolites *(top)* and trilobites *(bottom)*.

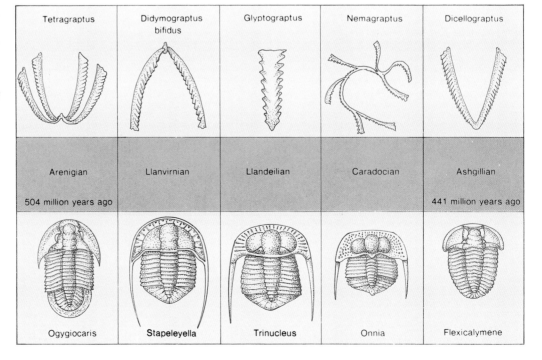

Pompeii was covered with debris to a depth of some 23 feet (7 meters).

The fossil record

Apart from stratigraphic investigations of the rocks themselves, the other major source of information about the earth's past has come from studying fossils (paleontology). Probably only a small fraction of the countless millions of living organisms that once existed have been preserved as fossils; living plants and animals may be attacked by predators, and dead organisms may be eaten by scavengers or their tissues may decay. Even hard skeletal parts such as bones and shells last only a few years when exposed to the elements. For an organism to be preserved it must be rapidly buried in sediment (or another protecting medium) and then not subsequently destroyed by heat, pressure, or weathering.

Most sediment accumulates in the sea, and so the fossil record is heavily biased toward marine organisms. Nevertheless some of the best preserved fossils are of terrestrial lifeforms—insects trapped in the amber resin of trees and woolly mammoths frozen in the Siberian soil, for example.

Fossils and the environment

Most organisms flourish only in certain conditions, and the abundance of different types of fossils is therefore valuable in reconstructing past environments. For example, some present-day species of ghost shrimps live only in the intertidal zone, so the presence of similar fossil ghost shrimps identifies a previous shoreline. Fossils that define the environment in which the rocks were laid down are called facies fossils.

Fossils and evolution

In the early nineteenth century, William Smith (a British canal engineer) and Georges Cuvier (a French zoologist) discovered that rocks of the same age contain the same suite of fossils, which always appear in the same order. This principle of faunal succession was explained by Charles Darwin's theory of evolution (1859): the fossils of any specific past period are unique because that mixture of life forms existed only at that particular time. At some later time the less successful life forms become extinct and new life forms evolve, producing a new, distinctive suite of fossils.

As a result of more than 100 years of collecting and classifying fossils, geologists have determined the times during which the major groups of animals and plants evolved and have compiled a standard stratigraphic column showing this information. By correlating a fossiliferous rock sample with the stratigraphic column, a geologist can date the sample without even needing to know the correct scientific names of the fossils in the rock. For example, if a stratum contains both fossil leaves of a flowering plant and dinosaur bones, then the rock must date from the Cretaceous Period, as flowering plants did not appear until then and dinosaurs were extinct by the end of the period.

On a more precise scale, paleontologists have subdivided the stratigraphic column into a series of zones, each characterized by a particular group of fossils. These zone fossils must fulfil three important criteria: they must have evolved rapidly; they must be easily identifiable; and they must be widely distributed. Ammonites (marine animals with coiled shells) meet all of these requirements and have enabled paleontologists to subdivide the Jurassic Period into 63 zones; the presence of a particular species of ammonite can date a stratum to within one million years. Various other fossils are used as zone fossils, including some corals and shellfish; graptolites (small, marine colonial organisms), which are used to subdivide the Paleozoic Era; and microscopic foraminiferans, which are valuable in Cenozoic biostratigraphy, and also widely used to date rocks in geological surveys for oil deposits.

Ammonites are extinct marine cephalopods (a group of animals that today includes the squid and octopus), characterized by partitioned shells. Widely distributed, the various species of ammonites are important zone fossils in Mesozoic rocks.

Eocene arthropods (the largest is a centipede) have been preserved in amber. In some amber "fossils," the soft body parts have been preserved, whereas in the more common rock fossils usually only the hard parts (shells and skeletons, for example) survive.

Mapping the earth

Cartography, or mapmaking, is the science of representing the features of earth's curved surface on a plane. Its origins date back to prehistoric times, and even today some primitive peoples unable to read and write do, nevertheless, make maps. Cartography was first established on a scientific basis by the ancient Greeks, most notably by Ptolemy. His eight-volume *Geography* (written in the second century A.D.) had a profound influence on mapmaking until the sixteenth century, when the discoveries of the great medieval explorers led to significantly more accurate maps. Cartography continued to improve, and today, with modern techniques such as satellite photography and computer plotting, the discipline is highly sophisticated.

Types of maps

There are many different types of maps, such as those depicting topography, or specific themes, or employing any of various projections (transformations that enable the earth's curved surface to be represented on a plane). All maps are a compromise, however, because of the intrinsic impossibility of accurately representing a three-dimensional object (earth) on a two-dimensional surface (the map). Therefore, in drawing any map a decision must be made as to which element—scale, area, shape, or direction, for example—is the most important for its intended use.

There are an infinite number of possible map projections, each with different character-

istics, but only about 20 types are in common use. Mercator's projection—devised by Gerhardus Mercator in about 1568—is probably the best known and has been more widely used by mariners than any other projection because it gives the true compass direction between any two points. It also shows accurately the shapes of geographical features but distorts areas, having increasing distortion with increased distance from the equator.

Projections that show areas correctly (that is, in the same proportion to that found on earth) are used to show the distribution of features, such as vegetation, geology, or population. But no map can show true scale over the entire earth, and most are correct over only small areas or in certain directions. Only on a globe can shapes and areas be completely accurately represented.

The most fundamental map, on which all others are based, is the topographic map, which shows the earth's surface features—relief, rivers, towns, roads, and railways for instance. Topographic maps are compiled from data collected by field surveys or, more usually, from measurements taken from aerial photographs (photogrammetry). The data may be in the form of a plotted drawing (from which the map itself can be compiled), or it may be encoded and stored in computers, many of which can automatically plot maps.

Maps that do not depict the earth's topographic features are known as thematic maps. They may illustrate something tangible, such as land use, soil type, or annual rainfall, or a

Photogrammetry—aerial surveying of the earth—is now highly developed and is extensively used in cartography. The high-altitude photograph *(below)*, which shows part of San Francisco in the United States, is of such high quality that individual buildings are discernible. Taken on special film, the photograph also yields information about land use and industrial activity: areas that reflect infrared (heat) radiation (such as those covered with crops or natural vegetation) or emit it (heat-producing factories, for example) appear red.

statistical concept, such as the average number of cars per person.

Map design

The design of maps poses two main problems: that of content and degree of detail, and that of symbolization. In compiling any map a decision must be made about what to include and what to leave out. This decision is not necessarily clear-cut, as is apparent when comparing similar maps from different countries, some of which include features that are omitted from others.

Features must be symbolized on a map in such a way that it is easily understandable and positionally accurate. Ultimately the way in which features are represented is determined by the compiler's subjective opinion as to the best method of symbolization. For example, height and slope can be represented in numerous ways, including hachuring (using fine lines following the direction of slope), relief shading (showing the topography by "illuminating" the landscape from one direction), or contour lines, which may sometimes also be separated by different colors.

Map scales

A map's scale refers to the distance on the ground a particular length on the map represents. The scale may be given in terms of a scale bar, so that actual distances can be obtained directly from lengths measured from the map. Alternatively, a representative proportion may be used—that is, 1:100,000 (which may be equivalently expressed as 1/100,000), which means that one unit (say one centimeter) on the map represents 100,000 units (one kilometer) on the ground.

Different scales are used for different maps, depending largely on the amount of detail required. For town planning, scales of 1:1,250 or 1:2,500 are commonly used, whereas for world maps, much smaller scales—typically between 1:50,000,000 and 1:100,000,000—are generally employed.

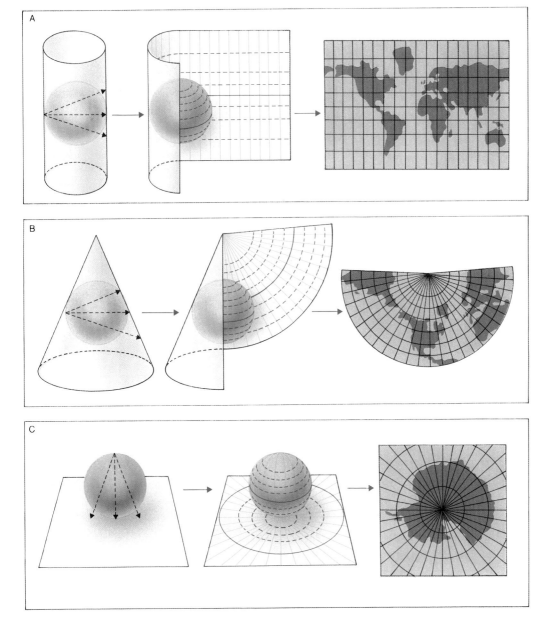

There are three main types of map projection: cylindrical (A), conical (B) and azimuthal, or zenithal, (C). In the first, the earth's surface is projected onto a cylinder; Mercator's projection is probably the best known of this type. In a conical projection, the earth's surface is projected onto a cone, usually drawn with the point above either the North or South Pole and the tangent at a selected latitude. In an azimuthal projection, the earth's surface is projected onto a plane tangential to the earth at one specified point (often the North or South Pole). In addition, any of three viewpoints may be used, giving a total of nine main projections. In stereographic projection (used in the diagrams on the left), the viewpoint is on the earth's surface. In gnomonic projection, the viewpoint is the center of the earth. And in orthographic projection, the viewpoint is at infinity, so that the projection lines are parallel.

Surveying and measuring

The detailed information on maps at basic scales—from which all other maps produced by national survey departments are derived—are now produced almost entirely from aerial or satellite photographs because this method (called photogrammetry) is generally much faster, cheaper, and more accurate than is ground surveying. Nevertheless, it is still necessary to undertake ground surveys to establish accurate coordinates (latitudes and longitudes) of a series of control points against which aerial photographs can be precisely scaled and oriented. In addition, ground surveys are used to produce very large-scale maps of small areas—such as may be needed when erecting a building—and to provide details missing from aerial photographs, perhaps because they were obscured by tall buildings, trees, or even intense shadows.

Ground surveying involves three main tasks: measuring distances, measuring angles, and measuring heights.

Measuring distances

Several methods are used to measure distances on the ground. Direct measurement against a scale or tape of known length is practicable only for comparatively short distances because tape measurements are limited by the landscape and by the cumbersome nature of the technique.

The oldest direct method (dating back some 300 years) involves using Gunter's chain, which has 100 links and is 66 feet (20.12 meters) long; an engineer's steel tape is now used instead of a chain. The tape is aligned by eye between ranging poles set at the points being measured. The distance between the two points is calculated from the number of tape lengths, obtained by physically moving the tape from one point to the other. The tape must be kept taut (at a fixed tension) and horizontal. If the land is not flat, the inclination of slope must be measured and the measured distance must be corrected to obtain the horizontal distance. The tape is held off the ground, free from obstacles, and the end measurements are made against tripods from which plumb lines are suspended.

Problems arise with metal tapes (and chains) because the length of the tape varies with temperature; hence for accurate work, the air temperature must also be recorded at the time of measurement and allowance made for contraction or expansion of the tape. This problem can largely be overcome by using invar (nickel-steel alloy) tapes, the length of which is only minimally affected by temper-

The transit is probably the most commonly used of the various surveying instruments, principally because it can measure both horizontal and vertical angles. The graduated circles against which the angles are read off were originally made of metal but are now usually of glass, which enables much smaller angles (less than one second of arc) to be resolved.

Ground surveying involves establishing the positions of a number of fixed points. This process may present problems in terrain, such as deserts where there are few landmarks. In these circumstances, a surveyor may have to use points that are unmarked by any landscape feature but can be located only from their latitudes and longitudes.

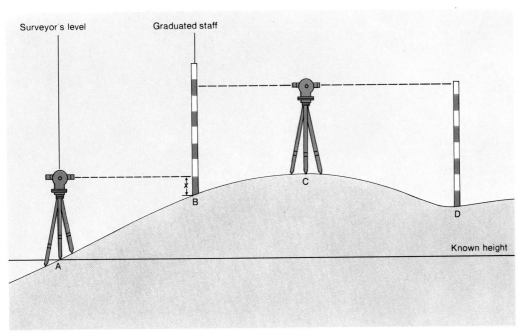

Surveyor's level

Graduated staff

C

B

Known height

A

D

Heights are usually measured by leveling. The level is set up at a point of known height (A) and a graduated staff is held at the point to be determined (B). The height of B equals the height at A plus the height of the level itself, minus the height *x* (read off the graduated staff by sighting through the level). Having determined the height of B, the same technique can be used to ascertain the heights of C and D.

ature. Unfortunately, these tapes are very delicate, and they are used only when extremely accurate surveys are needed.

For surveys requiring a lower degree of accuracy—engineering surveys, for example—distances can also be measured optically (this method is often called tacheometry) using a transit (or theodolite) (a small telescope with scales for measuring horizontal and vertical angles) and a bar (called a subtense bar), the exact length of which is known; a graduated staff may be used instead of the bar. The subtense bar is mounted horizontally on a tripod at one place and the angle subtended by it is measured using the theodolite. Then, knowing the length of the bar and the angle, the distance between the bar and the theodolite can be calculated by simple trigonometry. A similar method is employed when using the graduated staff, except that the staff must be held vertically, and the angle between the graduations is measured. Tacheometry is suitable only for determining short distances.

Until comparatively recently, the only precise methods for measuring long distances were laborious and impracticable over difficult terrain or large expanses of water. As a result, surveys of large areas were compiled from numerous small-area surveys based on only a few accurately-measured base lines. With the introduction of electronic measuring instruments, however, distances could be determined easily and very accurately.

The electronic instruments used to measure distance are of two types: those using light waves and those using high-frequency radio waves. Both systems work in the same basic way as radar: the distance is determined by measuring the time it takes the light or radio beam to travel out to the target and back to a receiver. Using light, a mirror is placed at the target point to reflect the transmitted light beam back to the receiver, which is usually positioned beside the transmitter. This method of distance measurement is more accurate than that using radio waves but is effective over only short distances (typically less than a mile or so) because the light beam is greatly affected by the clarity of the air. Radio waves, on the other hand, can penetrate fog and haze and so can be used to measure relatively large distances—up to about 45 miles (72 kilometers). With radio-wave distance measurement two combined transmitter-receivers are needed; the signals transmitted by one instrument are received and retransmitted by the other. Sophisticated electronic circuitry then measures the time lapse between transmission and reception, and converts it directly into a distance measurement.

Measuring angles

The basic instrument for measuring horizontal and vertical angles is the transit (which is also used in optical distance measurement). Within the transit are cross-hairs, which enable precise sighting of the target and, therefore, accurate measurements of angles, which are read off from the transit's horizontal and vertical scales. Some modern transits are connected to a small computer, which automatically stores the angles measured.

Transits are considerably less accurate in vertical angular measurements than in horizontal ones. As a result, they are seldom used for determining heights, except in surveys requiring only low standards of accuracy. They are, however, commonly used by surveyors when making astronomical observations to determine latitudes.

Measuring heights

In ground surveying, heights are usually determined by a method called leveling. A surveyor's level is similar to a transit in that it is essentially a small telescope, but unlike a transit, a level can move only horizontally. To measure height, the level must first be set up on a tripod so that it is exactly horizontal (which is normally achieved by checking against an ex-

Triangulation, the traditional method of ground surveying, involves establishing the positions of several points by measuring the angles between them (shown in red). The distance between two of the points (the solid blue line) must also be measured so that the other distances can be calculated. Another distance measurement (the broken blue line) may also be made to restrict errors.

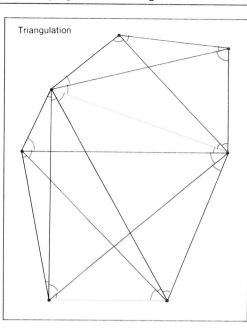

Triangulation

Trilateration, in contrast to triangulation, does not involve any angle measurements. Instead the positions of various points are determined by measuring the distances between them (the blue lines), from which the angles can then be calculated.

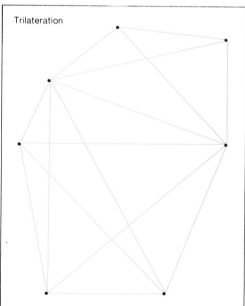

Trilateration

Traversing combines the techniques of triangulation and trilateration: both the angles (in red) and distances (in blue) between the points to be fixed are measured.

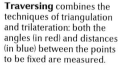

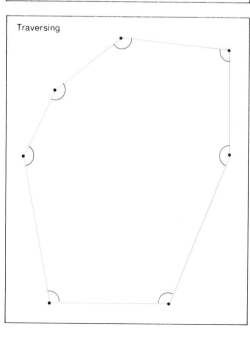

Traversing

tremely sensitive spirit level), after which it is sighted on a graduated rod held vertically on the point whose height is to be determined. The height is calculated from the difference between the measured reading and a point of known height.

Altitude can also be measured approximately by determining atmospheric pressure, which decreases with increasing altitude. The atmospheric pressure may be measured directly with a barometer, or it may be calculated from the boiling point of water, which decreases with decreasing pressure. Although not very accurate (mainly because the atmospheric pressure at any given point varies according to the weather), these methods are useful where leveling is impractical—in determining the heights of mountains, for example.

Triangulation, trilateration, and traversing

All surveys begin with the establishment of a network of accurately located control points. There are three ways in which such a control grid can be established: by triangulation, trilateration, or by traversing. Triangulation was traditionally the fastest surveying technique because it reduced the number of distance measurements (which were slow to make using direct taping) to a minimum. It involves the construction of a triangular system of control points by measuring angles only, apart from the precise measurement of one distance, which serves as the base line on which the entire system is based. In accurate surveys, other base lines a considerable distance from the first are measured to restrict cumulative errors.

Trilateration is similar to triangulation but entails measuring distances instead of angles; the angles can be calculated using trigonometry when the distances are known. This system became practical only with the development of electronic distance measuring equipment in the early 1950's but is now more accurate than is triangulation.

In traversing control points are fixed using a combination of angle and distance measurements. A traverse may be between two points with known coordinates, or it may be between an approximately circular series of points. In the latter, the points are established by measuring the distance and angle from each point to the next until the surveyor returns to the starting place. Thus the first point in the system is also the last, which provides a check on cumulative error.

Triangulation, trilateration, and traversing are used to establish the positions and heights of points within a localized area; this is called plane surveying. But it may be necessary to relate these measurements to a larger region, such as an entire country or continent, in which case it is necessary to take into account the fact that the earth is an oblate spheroid (that is, a slightly flattened sphere). Relating a plane survey to a large area may be done by undertaking an additional geodesic ground survey to determine the position and orientations of the local measurements relative to certain defined points and incorporating highly accurate stellar observations to ascertain latitude, longitude, and true compass

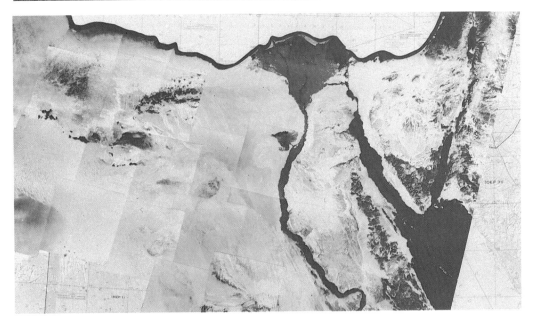

The mosaic of satellite photographs of north-eastern Africa and the Middle East demonstrate the basic technique of photogrammetry: collating overlapping aerial photographs to provide a topographic picture of the earth's surface. Geodesic satellites are also used to monitor a wide range of other factors, such as land use and management, the effects of pollution, and weather patterns.

bearings. Satellite photographs may also be used.

For making detailed, large-scale plans or for supplying details missing from aerial photographs, the traditional method is a plane-table survey. The plane-table is a drawing-board on which fixed points are plotted to scale on a sheet of paper. The surveyor uses an alidade (similar to a theodolite) attached to a graduated straight edge that can be pointed in any direction. The plane-table is set up over a point whose position is known. The features being surveyed are sighted through the alidade; their distances and directions are then marked on the plane-table. Plane-table surveyors often use sighting instruments called clinometers for the calculation of heights so that contours can also be drawn on the plane-table.

Photogrammetry

The topographic detail in the areas between points fixed by ground surveys is usually obtained from aerial photography. Photographs are taken in parallel strips with a 60 per cent overlap between neighbouring photographs and a 10 per cent overlap between adjacent strips. It is necessary to photograph an area from at least two different places in the sky to give complete stereographic coverage.

Each photograph by itself is useless for mapping, being increasingly distorted away from the center. But viewed stereoscopically, photographs can provide a three-dimensional model of the earth's surface. Hence stereographic pairs can be used to obtain contours showing the relief of the land. From this data a conventional orthogonal map (that is, one on which each point is plotted as if viewed perpendicularly from above) can be plotted. The transfer of the information from the aerial photographs is done using a photogrammetric plotting device; positives of the photographs are projected onto a plotting surface and adjusted so that they are in the same position to that from which were taken in the air (to remove distortions caused by tilting of the aircraft). The photogrammetrist then scales and

orients the resulting optical model in relation to fixed points obtained from ground surveys.

Hydrographic surveying

Surveying seas and coastlines—hydrography—to provide charts for mariners involves using both terrestrial surveying techniques and other, specifically marine, methods. In mapping coastlines, for example, normal triangulation is often employed, whereas the ocean floor is mapped using techniques such as echo ranging and echolocation. Mariners are mainly concerned with the positions of reefs, shoals, wrecks, and with the minimum depth of water. For this last reason, hydrographic charts are characterized by having numerous sounding figures, each of which indicates the depth of water at that point.

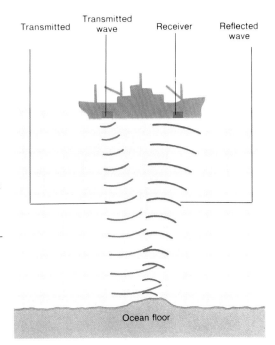

Echo ranging is widely used in hydrography to measure the depth of the ocean floor. A sound wave is transmitted from a ship and the time taken for the reflected wave to return is measured. Knowing the speed of sound through water, the depth of the sea bed can then be calculated.

Terrestrial navigation

Navigation is concerned with determining one's position and direction along a route toward a destination, usually at the best speed consistent with safety, such as avoiding collisions with any obstacles. Navigation on land is comparatively easy if people are equipped with maps; even at night and in adverse weather conditions it is possible to find one's way over open country with a compass. But at sea or in the air, navigation poses more problems.

Position fixing

The first requirement of navigation for a craft is to establish its position and to make sure that it is on the right route. Signposts, buoys and lighthouses, maps and charts, compasses and logs are all objects that serve to determine the route.

At sea, there are few identifiable natural features, so a vessel's position has to be determined by reference to fixed points on the land if the ship is in coastal waters, or in the sky if the ship is far from land. If, for instance, the shore and a lighthouse can be seen and can be identified on a chart, the bearing of the lighthouse from the vessel can be measured. This measurement is usually made in degrees from north, using a compass. In a small vessel, a hand-bearing compass is often used. The bearing line (called a position line) is then drawn on the chart through the position of the lighthouse—the vessel's position must be somewhere along it. If a similar bearing can be made on another identifiable object, such as a church tower, another position line is drawn that will cross the first one. A "fix" is obtained at the intersection of the two or preferably three lines.

Position lines may be drawn by lining up two objects on the shore, such as a church spire and a radio mast on a hill behind it. This bearing is called a transit. It is, of course, essential that the objects are positively identified and are shown in the chart. The angle between objects ashore may also be measured by a sextant to produce a fix using a horizontal angle.

Traditionally, bearings have been obtained by using a compass, but it is now more common for radio methods to be used. Direction finding by radio, or radio detection and ranging (radar), has been made easier since the setting up of beacons for ships and aircraft. Each has a characteristic signal, and the beacons are now listed in nautical and aviation almanacs. Navigators tune in to the appropriate transmission and, by rotating an antenna, can find the bearing of the transmitting station. Some radar equipment is extremely sophisticated. The Decca Navigator, for example, gives a fix anywhere in European waters accurate to within a few meters. Navigation satellites are also used to obtain equally accurate fixes, even for small craft. In addition, "radio lighthouses" now exist whose signals may be picked up on a normal VHF (very high frequency) receiver.

Planning a route

To avoid known natural hazards and obstacles, and to allow for the effects of tides and the wind, a course must be planned. The movement of the tides at any particular time in a given area may be determined by reference to a chart or a tidal atlas. Air streams are also charted. In order to arrive at the course to be taken, the proposed route is drawn on a chart and allowance made for the predicted effect of winds and tides and the estimated duration of the journey. Allowance must also be made in nautical navigation for the fact that the magnetic compass does not point to true north (variation) and may also be affected by its posi-

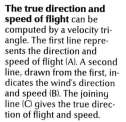

Lightships are usually moored where it is impractical to build lighthouses. They carry powerful lights that are mounted in gimbals to keep the beams horizontal in rough weather. Most modern lightships also carry fog signals and a radio beacon.

The true direction and speed of flight can be computed by a velocity triangle. The first line represents the direction and speed of flight (A). A second line, drawn from the first, indicates the wind's direction and speed (B). The joining line (C) gives the true direction of flight and speed.

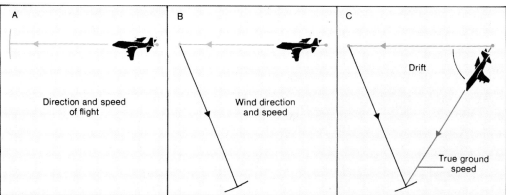

A — Direction and speed of flight

B — Wind direction and speed

C — Drift — True ground speed

tion in the vessel itself (known as deviation).

Along the route, progress is recorded as accurately as possible, and a fix is obtained at least once every hour. Along a coastal route buoys, beacons, and light can be used as signposts from which good fixes can be arrived at when visibility is adequate. But in poor visibility, it is necessary to use dead reckoning—that is, if the speed and distance traveled since the previous fix are known, and allowing for the effects of the tide and wind (leeway), an estimated position can be established.

In aeronavigation, dead reckoning is also used to calculate the true speed of an aircraft. A vector is drawn in the direction of flight, and the length of this line represents the distance the craft moves through still air in an hour. Another vector is drawn from the end of the first toward the direction in which the wind is moving—the length of this line represents wind velocity. A line is then drawn from the beginning of the first to the end of the second vector; this represents the route of the aircraft over the ground, and the distance gives an indication of the craft's true ground speed. The method of dead reckoning therefore enables the position of the craft to be established as well as future positions along the planned course; but these depend on the set speed and wind direction being maintained.

Speed is often measured using Doppler radar. High-frequency radio waves are transmitted by a craft and bounce off a moving object with higher or lower frequency, depending on whether the craft is moving toward the object or away from it. This system is also used in land vehicles. In seagoing vessels, the log is often an electromagnetic detector that calculates the speed of the water flowing past the vessel.

Avoiding obstacles

Ships can be seen some distance away and are obliged to steer to the right if they are approaching each other head-on. But aircraft move too fast for this method to be effective, and so radio detection is used. The principal use of radar is detecting obstacles, especially in poor visibility. Echo rangers used on ships transmit short pulses of ultrasonic sound and calculate the time taken for the echo to return from the sea bed. This method can therefore be used to measure the depth of the ocean floor.

Aircraft use radar altimeters, which employ a similar principle to that of the echo ranger. These instruments emit bursts of radio waves and measure the time taken for their reflection from the ground (thus determining the craft's distance above the ground). In addition, there are radio altimeters that emit continuous waves and measure the extent to which the configuration of reflected waves has deviated from that transmitted by the altimeter. Long-range navigation (Loran) is also employed, which allows craft to establish their positions accurately by timing the frequency of waves from synchronized land-based transmitters.

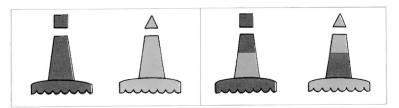

Buoyage System A, used by some nations, has red lateral buoys for port-hand and green for starboard. Striped buoys indicate preferred routes at forks.

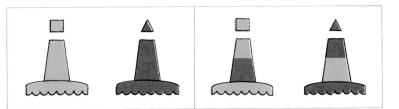

The IALA System, used in the United States, has green lateral buoys for port-hand and red for starboard. Striped buoys again indicate preferred routes.

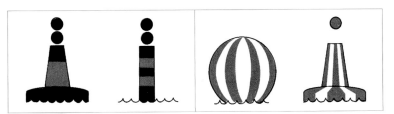

Isolated danger marks (black and red) and safe water marks (red and white) are the same in both buoyage systems and recognized in most countries.

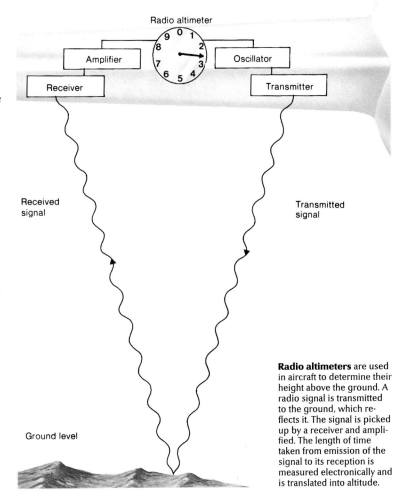

Radio altimeter

Amplifier

Oscillator

Receiver

Transmitter

Received signal

Transmitted signal

Ground level

Radio altimeters are used in aircraft to determine their height above the ground. A radio signal is transmitted to the ground, which reflects it. The signal is picked up by a receiver and amplified. The length of time taken from emission of the signal to its reception is measured electronically and is translated into altitude.

Celestial and inertial navigation

A whole branch of navigation is concerned with the determination of position by reference to celestial bodies, namely the sun, stars, and planets. The positions of these bodies may not be fixed, but their movements can be accurately predicted and are published in almanacs and tables. Celestial navigation, as it is called, relies on the accurate measurement of the angle between the celestial body and the horizon, and after reference to appropriate tables and some simple calculation, the observer's position is expressed in terms of latitude and longitude.

Sun sights

The sun is the most commonly used heavenly body in celestial navigation because normally it can be seen for longer periods during daylight than other bodies. The earth's axis is tilted by about 23.5° from the vertical, and so during the course of a year the sun appears directly overhead at noon within a range of 23.5° north to 23.5° south of the equator—that is, between the tropics of Cancer and Capricorn. The actual angle of elevation at any given time is called the sun's declination. In more northerly latitudes, the sun is directly south of the observer at midday (and directly north to an observer in more southerly latitudes). Measurement of the sun's altitude at noon, with an allowance for declination, enables a navigator to compute the latitude of a position; this method is known as a noon sight. Minor corrections have to be made for meridian passage time (because the sun does not always reach its peak at noon), the height of the observer above sea level (dip) and any sextant inaccuracy (index error).

Longitude is measured by reference to the difference between local time and Greenwich Mean Time, which is recorded on ships by a chronometer. Given that the earth rotates 360° in 24 hours, any point on its surface travels 15° in every hour, or 1° every 4 minutes. A point on longitude 30° W is therefore two hours of sun-time away from Greenwich Hour Angle or GHA. Similarly, hour angles can be measured from any meridian to give a Local Hour Angle, or LHA.

Sun sights can be taken at any time of the day provided that the sun is visible and more than about 10° above the horizon (to avoid refraction). Exact timing is required for these sights. Generally a series of sights is taken, and angles are averaged out. Corrections are then applied to the sextant angle. In order to ascertain the declination of the sun at the time of sight, the tables for the GHA and the LHA (from an assumed meridian) are referred to.

The most common method of establishing a position is to decide on an assumed position, based, for example, on dead reckoning, and by reference to sight reduction tables (which give a vast number of positions for given latitudes, declinations, and hour angles) to compare the results of the assumed position with that actually obtained using a sextant. An intercept line can then be plotted on a chart. The procedure is simplified by the use of a standard sight form, which sets out the steps to be taken.

Moon sights

Moon sights are taken in the same way as for the sun, but there is only a limited time when the moon and the horizon can both be clearly seen. Time must be measured very accurately using a chronometer and a stopwatch because the moon moves faster than the sun. When the moon is waning, it can often be seen in the morning, and if the sun is also visible, both moon and sun sights may be taken and a fix obtained. Plotting a position by the moon is similar to the method using the sun, but be-

The altitude of the sun or a star can be calculated using a sextant. The zero is set (A) by coinciding two images of the horizon—one seen directly through the half-silvered glass, the other reflected by the rotatable index glass to the horizon glass and then to the eyepiece. The pointer fixed to the index glass indicates 0°. The index glass is rotated (B) until light from a star coincides with the image of the horizon. The star's altitude is then double that indicated by the pointer.

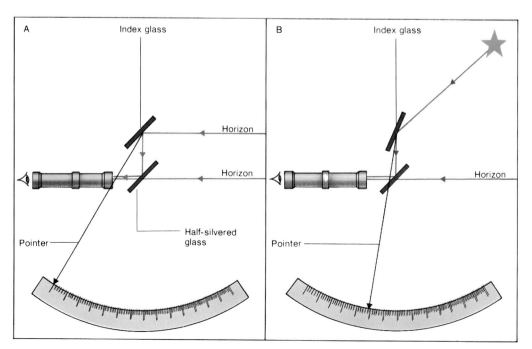

cause the moon is much nearer the earth and its movements are slightly erratic, additional corrections have to be made.

Planets and stars

Four planets are listed in most almanacs: Venus, Mars, Jupiter, and Saturn. The GHA and their declinations are also given, with notes and diagrams to assist identification. In addition, the almanac may list 50 or more stars, and star maps and plans are available to aid their location. A special volume of sight reduction tables is also published, which gives seven stars for each degree of LHA. Three of these stars are marked as being the most likely to provide a fix.

Polaris, the Pole Star, is important to a navigator in the Northern Hemisphere because it is positioned very near to true north; it can be used to determine direction and, with a sight and tables, to establish latitude. The star moves very little and so its altitude above the horizon is nearly the same for the latitude of a position—on the equator (0°), the star is on the horizon at 0°, and at latitude 45° it has an altitude of 45°. There is no comparable star in the skies of the Southern Hemisphere.

Inertial navigation

Inertial navigation is the direction of a craft without the aid of beacons and charts and often requires little human involvement. Direction, for example, can be calculated by the combined use of a gyroscope and an accelerometer. The gyroscope is set at the starting point of a journey to spin in the direction of the force of gravity at that point. The accelerometer measures the direction of the force of gravity at a point on the journey, and the difference between the two directions indicates the direction of passage of the craft and the distance it traveled. This combined system is used both at sea and in the air.

A gyrocompass is a gyroscope set with its axis pointing to true north. As the vessel or air-

The projected map display of an aircraft inertial navigation system enables precise navigation with the aid of gyroscopes and accelerometers. The gyroscope stabilizes the sensitive equipment inside the system and the accelerometer measures acceleration in all directions, including vertical ones. The electronic cluster assembles a detailed image on the screen that makes accurate navigation possible in difficult conditions.

craft changes direction, the instrument tilts and turns so that its axis continues to point to north. A gyromagnetic compass guides a compass indicator and shows accurately the direction of the earth's magnetic field.

Navigation by dead reckoning is the basis of much inertial navigation and is also calculated by computers, which print out information about positioning. Digital computers provide almost instantaneous information. Inertial guidance instruments are particularly useful in submarines because they enable long journeys to be made underwater or under icecaps with reduced possibilities of collision. Auto-helmsmen and automatic-landing pilots control craft with the information given by these guidance and positional instruments.

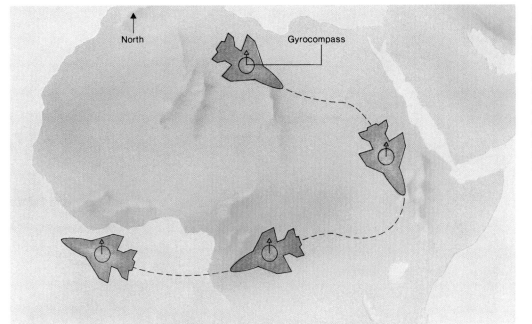

A gyrocompass is often used instead of a magnetic compass as an indicator of north because it is not affected by magnetic fields or gravity. This instrument is a gyroscope or spinning wheel, which is spun with its axis pointing to true north when the carrier starts its journey. As the craft changes direction, the series of pivots holding the axis of the gyroscope swivel so that the axis remains pointing to true north.

Geology and landscape

Most people consider the landscape to be unchanging; in fact, our planet is a dynamic body, and its surface is continually altering—slowly on the human time scale but relatively rapidly when compared to the great age of the earth (about 4.5 billion years). There are two principal influences that shape the terrain: constructive processes, such as uplift, that create new landscape features, and destructive forces, such as erosion, that gradually wear away exposed landforms.

Hills and mountains are often regarded as the epitome of permanence, successfully resisting the destructive forces of nature, but in fact they tend to be relatively short-lived in geological terms. As a general rule, the higher a mountain is, the more recently it was formed; for example, the high mountains of the Himalayas, situated between the Indian subcontinent and the rest of Asia, are only about 50 million years old. Lower mountains tend to be older and are often the eroded relics of much higher mountain chains. About 400 million years ago, when the present-day continents of North America and Europe were joined, the Caledonian mountain chain was the same size as the modern Himalayas. Today, however, the relics of the Caledonian orogeny (mountain-building period) exist as the comparatively low mountains of Greenland, the northern Appalachians, the Scottish Highlands, and the Norwegian coastal plateau.

Some mountains were formed as a result of the earth's crustal plates moving together and forcing up the rock at the plate margins. In this process, sedimentary rocks that originally formed on the sea bed may be folded upward to altitudes of more than 26,000 feet (7,925 meters). Other mountains may be raised by faulting, which produces block mountains, such as the Ruwenzori Mountains on the border of Uganda and Zaire in Africa. A third type of mountain may be formed as a result of volcanic activity; these tend to occur in the regions of active fold mountain belts, such as the Cascade range, which contains Mount St. Helens, Mount Rainier, and Mount Hood. The other principal type of mountain is one that has been pushed up by the emplacement of an intrusion below the surface; the Black Hills in South Dakota were formed in this way.

As soon as land rises above sea level it is subjected to the destructive forces of denudation. The exposed rocks are attacked by the various weather processes and gradually broken down into fragments, which are then carried away and are later deposited as sediments. Thus any landscape represents only a temporary stage in the continuous battle between the forces of uplift (or of subsidence) and those of erosion.

The weather, in any of its various forms, is the main agent of erosion. Rain washes away loose soil and penetrates cracks in the rocks. Carbon dioxide in the air reacts with the rainwater, forming a weak acid (carbonic acid) that may chemically attack the rocks.

The rain seeps underground, and the water may reappear later as springs. These springs are the sources of streams and rivers, which cut down through the rocks and carry away debris from the mountains to the lowlands.

Under very cold conditions, rocks can be shattered by ice and frost. Glaciers may form in permanently cold areas, and these slowly-moving masses of ice scour out valleys, carrying with them huge quantities of eroded rock debris.

In dry areas, the wind is the principal agent of erosion. It carries fine particles of sand, which bombard the exposed rock surfaces, thereby wearing them into yet more sand.

Even living things contribute to the formation of landscapes. Tree roots force their way into cracks in rocks and, in so doing, speed their splitting. In contrast, the roots of grasses and other small plants may help to hold loose soil fragments together, thereby helping to prevent erosion by the wind.

The nature of the rocks themselves determines how quickly they are affected by the various processes of erosion. The minerals in

limestone and granite react with the carbonic acid in rain. These rocks are, therefore, more susceptible to chemical breakdown than are other types of rocks containing minerals that are less easily affected by acidic rainwater. Sandstone tends to be harder than shale, and so where both are exposed in alternating beds, the shale erodes more quickly than the sandstone, giving the outcrop a corrugated or stepped appearance. Waterfalls and rapids occur where rivers pass over beds or intrusions of hard igneous rock that overlie softer rocks.

The erosional forces of the weather, glaciers, rivers, and the waves and currents of the sea are essentially destructive processes. But they also have a constructive effect by carrying the eroded debris to a new area and depositing it as sediment. Particles eroded by rivers may be deposited as beds of mud and sand in deltas and shallow seas; wind-borne particles in arid areas come to rest as desert sands; and the massive boulders and tiny clay particles produced and transported by glaciers give rise to spectacular landforms (terminal moraines, for example) after the glaciers have melted.

In deserts and other arid regions, the wind is the main erosive agent. It carries small particles that wear away any exposed landforms, thereby creating yet more material to bombard the rocks.

The Himalayan range contains some of the world's highest mountains, with more than 30 peaks rising to over 23,000 feet (7,000 meters) above sea level—including Mount Everest, 29,028 feet (8,848 meters). Situated along the northern border of India, the Himalayas were uplifted when a plate bearing the once separate Indian land mass collided with Asia. This occurred comparatively recently in geological terms (about 50 million years ago); there has, thus, been relatively little time for the peaks to be eroded.

Weathering

As soon as any rock is exposed at the surface of the earth it is subjected to various forces of erosion, which reduce the rock to fragments and carry the resulting debris to areas of deposition. The weather is the most significant agent of this erosion and can act in one of two ways. It can produce physical changes in which the rocks are broken down by the force of rain, wind, or frost; or it can produce chemical changes in which the minerals of the rocks are altered and the new substances formed dissolve in water or crumble away from the main rock mass. The different processes involved do not act independently of each other; the resulting erosion is caused by a combination of physical and chemical effects, although in some areas one erosive force tends to predominate.

Effects of rain

The effects of rain erosion of the landscape are best seen in areas of loose topsoil. Rock or soil that is already loose is easily dislodged and washed away in heavy rainstorms. The most spectacular examples of this type of rain erosion occur in volcanic areas, where the soil consists of deep layers of volcanic ash deposited by recent eruptions. Streams of rainwater running down the slopes carry away fragments of the exposed volcanic topsoil, and the force of these moving fragments dislodges other fragments. As a result, the slopes become scarred with converging gullies and small gorges that form where the erosion is greatest. In some places, the lower slopes are worn away so rapidly that the higher ground is undercut, resulting in a landslip. The rain erosion features of volcanic terrain are also found on mining spoil heaps, which, like the surface

layers in volcanic areas, are composed of small particles.

In regions that have a deep topsoil, small areas may be protected from rain erosion by the presence of large rocks on the surface. The soil around these rocks may be worn away, leaving the rocks supported on pedestals of undisturbed material.

Rain falling on grassy slopes may cause soil creep. The soil tends to be washed down the slope, but the interlocking roots of the grass prevent it from moving far, leading to the formation of a series of steps in the hillside where bands of turf have moved slowly downward. (Soil creeps in bands because the force of gravity overcomes the roots' cohesion in the downward direction whereas the root network remains strong in the sideway direction.)

The chemical effect of rain depends on the fact that carbon dioxide in the atmosphere dissolves in the rain, forming weak carbonic acid. The acid reacts with the calcite (a crystalline form of calcium carbonate, the substance responsible for "hardness" in water) in limestone and with certain other minerals, thereby dissolving them. This erosive effect may give rise to any of several geological features, such as grikes, which are widened cracks in the exposed rock, and swallow holes, where streams disappear underground—features that are particularly common in limestone areas, such as northwestern Yugoslavia and the county of Yorkshire in Britain.

Effects of temperature

Temperature changes are an important part of the weathering process, particularly in arid areas where the air is so dry that its insulating effect is negligible (normally, moisture in the air acts as a blanket, reducing heat loss from the ground); the lack of insulation results in a large daily range of temperature.

Repeated heating and cooling of the sur-

Earth pillars *(below left)* are unusual landscape features produced by rain erosion. In wet areas the rain is the principal agent of weathering. The chemical breakdown of the rock, helped by the action of vegetation, produces deep soil. Rain then washes the soil away, especially in areas where the vegetation has been removed. Where the soil has been protected by rocks resting on the surface, earth pillars may form as the surrounding soil is washed away. Weathering in limestone areas *(below right)* can be rapid. The weak carbonic acid of the rain dissolves the calcite component of limestone. This process occurs most rapidly along joints and cracks in the rock, producing enlarged fissures (grikes) that separate prominent blocks (clints). The landscape so formed is called a karst topography, after the area in Yugoslavia where it is well developed.

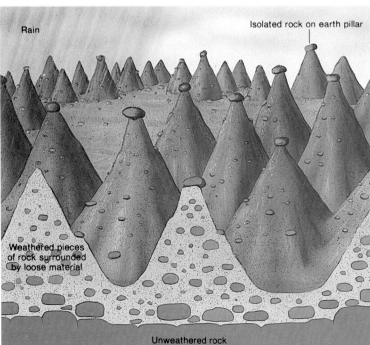

Rain

Isolated rock on earth pillar

Weathered pieces of rock surrounded by loose material

Unweathered rock

face of a rock while the interior remains at a constant temperature weakens the rock's outer layers. When this effect is combined with the chemical action that takes place after the infrequent desert downpours, the outer layers of the rock peel off—a process called exfoliation. Exfoliation may occur on only a small scale, affecting individual rocks, or it may affect whole mountainsides, especially those in which the bedding planes of the rock are parallel to the surface. Exfoliation of entire mountains typically produces prominent, rounded hills called inselbergs, a well-known example of which is Ayers Rock in central Australia.

Effects of wind

As with heat, the weathering effects of the wind are also greatest in arid regions, because the soil particles are not stuck together or weighed down with water and are therefore light and easily dislodged. Coarser soil particles blown by the wind bounce along close to the ground (a mode of travel called saltation), rarely rising more than about 3 feet (0.9 meter) above ground. These particles can be highly abrasive and, where the top of an exposed rock is above the zone of attrition, can erode the rock into a pedestal shape. Stones and small boulders on the ground may be worn smooth on the side facing the prevailing wind, eventually becoming so eroded on one side that they overbalance and present a new face to the wind. This process then repeats itself, resulting in the formation of dreikanters—stones with three or more sides that have been worn smooth.

The effect of the various abrasive processes is cumulative: particles that have been abraded from the surfaces of exposed rocks and stones further abrade the landscape features (thereby increasing the rate of erosion), eventually giving rise to a typical desert landscape.

Human influence and weathering

A natural landscape is a balance between the forces of uplift, which produce new topographical features, and erosion, which gradually wears away exposed surface features. Human activities, especially farming, may alter this balance—sometimes with far-reaching effects. The removal of natural vegetation may weaken the topsoil, and when the soil particles are no longer held together by extensive root systems they can be washed away easily by the rain. This process may result in a "badlands" topography: initially, fields of deep, fertile soil are cut with gullies; then, as erosion continues, the soil is gradually broken down into small particles that are eventually washed away by rain or blown away as dust.

The effects of chemical weathering can be seen in rocks such as dolerite and basalt, which contain magnesium- and iron-rich minerals. The damage takes place at the exposed surface, where the affected rock flakes off layer by layer to produce a characteristic spheroidal weathering pattern.

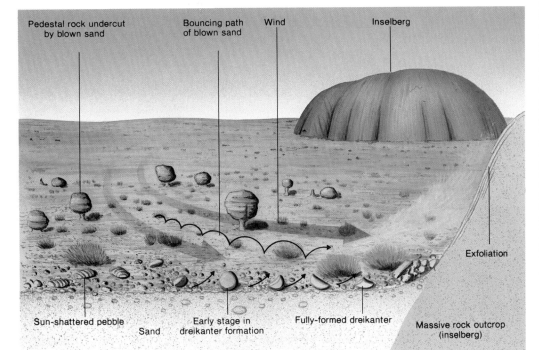

Pedestal rock undercut by blown sand

Bouncing path of blown sand

Wind

Inselberg

Exfoliation

Sun-shattered pebble

Sand

Early stage in dreikanter formation

Fully-formed dreikanter

Massive rock outcrop (inselberg)

In arid regions, temperature changes and the wind are the strongest weathering forces. Chemical action may also affect the surface of exposed rock, although its effect is relatively minor. Temperature changes cause rapid expansion (during the day) and contraction (at night) of the rock surface, as a result of which fragments of rock break off. These fragments are then further eroded into small particles while they are being carried by the wind (a process called attrition). The various weathering processes in dry regions produce characteristic landscape features, such as pedestal rocks, rounded hills (inselbergs), dreikanters and, in hot areas, sun-shattered rocks.

Frost erosion

Of all the forces of weathering that act on a landscape, water—particularly frozen water—produces the most dramatic topographical features. Water expands when it freezes, the expansion being accompanied by great outward pressure. (It is this pressure that bursts pipes when the water in them freezes). This expansive force of frost can affect exposed terrain in two ways: rock may be broken into smaller fragments by freezing water expanding in its joints (a process called frost shattering); or the ground may expand and contract alternatively, known as frost heaving.

The Matterhorn; 14,692 feet (4,478 meters), on the Swiss-Italian border shows the classic features of a frost-eroded mountain. Its peak is sharp, it has straight steeply-sloping walls, and it has been carved into a pyramid shape by the development of cirques on its flanks.

Scree is the product of mechanical weathering and can result from frost action. The material that falls from the flanks of the eroded peaks accumulates at the base of the steep slopes.

In order to be effective, the action of frost erosion must be strong enough to overcome the elasticity of the rock. The breakdown process starts when water seeps into pores or tiny cracks and joints in the rock. Then, when the water freezes, it forces the walls of the pores and joints further apart. On thawing, a slightly greater volume of water is able to enter the enlarged hole, and, thus, a correspondingly stronger force is applied during the next freezing. Successive repetitions of this frost wedging process lead eventually to the shattering of a solid mass of rock into fragments.

Mountain landscapes

Frost erosion is particularly effective in mountainous areas, because temperatures are low and there is a wide daily variation in temperature. In some places, the eroded debris falls and collects in great quantities at the base of steep mountain slopes.

Mountains with needlelike peaks formed by frost action are known as "aiguilles" (meaning needles); they are often further worn away to a pyramidal "horn" by the erosive effect of frost and glaciers on the flanks. Material broken off the side of a mountain gathers toward the foot of the slopes, to form a scree (or talus) slope. Fragments of scree are always angular, and the scree slopes are steep; the larger the fragments, the greater the erosion has been, and the steeper the slope. If the falling debris is guided by natural gullies and channels in the mountain, it comes to rest in a scree slope that resembles the rounded side of a cone as it fans out from its channel. Since they are forming continuously, scree slopes tend to have no soil or vegetation.

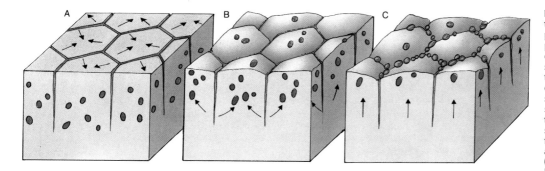

Mountain sculpting

Above the snowline, any hollow in a mountainside is permanently occupied by snow. The steady accumulation and compression of the snow into ice in the bottom of the hollow eventually gives rise to a glacier. The erosive effect of the compressed snow in such a hollow acts in all directions at the same rate and, combined with the downward movement of the glacier, lowers the floor and cuts back the walls so that the hollow becomes a steep-sided, rounded-bottomed feature called a cirque. Neighboring cirques on the flanks of a mountain are divided by a ridge. As the cirque walls are cut back, the ridge becomes steep and sharp-crested and forms an arête, several of which may radiate from all sides of a mountain—by now a pyramidal horn mountain.

Above a glacier, the falling frost-shattered rocks do not form a scree. The blocks that land on the moving ice are carried away and eventually dumped as moraines, which are a significant feature of glacial action.

Layers of snow on the higher areas of mountains may occasionally tumble down steep eroded slopes in avalanches. They usually occur when the lower slopes of snow have melted or been blown away, leaving the top unsupported. The falling snow compacts to ice as soon as it hits anything. The great weights involved can tear away vast quantities of forest and rock from the lower slopes.

Frost effects on flat land

The more complex effects of frost erosion are seen in areas such as the tundra, where temperatures are below freezing point for most of the year and nearly all the visible landscape features have been produced by frost action. The frost heaving that takes place does not break down the rocks, but moves and mixes the soil particles.

As the temperature drops from 32° F. to 4° F. (0° C to −20° C), the already expanded ice begins to contract. When this occurs on the soil surface, the result is a general shrinkage of soil in which the surface cracks up into polygonal sections. These sections may be about 30 feet (9 meters) across and are bounded by deep cracks. During thaws water enters the cracks, and ice wedging takes place when the next freeze occurs. The expansion pressure of the surrounding ice causes the center of the polygon to rise in the shape of a shallow dome.

A stone buried in the soil cools more quickly than the surrounding damp soil because it is a better conductor of heat. The first place in which ice forms during a freeze is therefore directly under any buried stone. The crystals of ice below the stone push it upward slightly as they expand. Over a period of several years, this process brings the stone to the surface. (This frost heaving effect is particularly noted by gardeners in cold weather.) In polygonally cracked ground, the stones are ultimately brought to the surface of the polygons. From there they move down the slopes of the domes and gather in the cracks outlining the polygons.

The force of frost

Most of the effects of frost erosion derive from the peculiar behavior of water at temperatures near its freezing point and from the unique properties of ice. Water contracts as it cools, reaching its maximum density at 39° F. (4° C). On further cooling, it expands slightly, reaching a volume of 1.087cc per gram as it freezes at 32° F. (0° C). As the temperature falls even lower, the ice expands and can exert enormous pressures—in excess of 140 tons per square foot (1,500 tons per square meter). Well below freezing point ice contracts again; for example, at −8° F. (−22° C) it has a volume of only 0.971cc per gram.

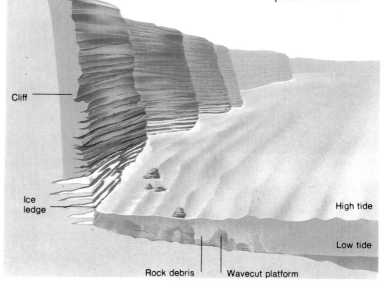

Cliff

Ice ledge

High tide

Low tide

Rock debris   Wavecut platform

Ground water

The rocks immediately below the earth's surface hold over 2 million cubic miles (8 million cubic kilometers) of water—about 40 times as much as in all the rivers, lakes, and marshes in the world. In the ground, water seeps downward through the so-called zone of aeration, in which the pores in the rock are filled with a mixture of water and air. Below this region, ground water accumulates in the zone of saturation, in which the pores are full of water. The boundary between the two zones is the water table; it can be seen as the level at which water stands in wells and boreholes. The height of the water table varies with the season and with the weather. Overall topography is reflected in the conformation of the water table; it rises under hills and slopes down into valleys, where it may reach the surface to form springs.

Porous and permeable rocks

The movement of water underground is controlled mainly by the type of rock through which it passes. Rocks with a large amount of space between their grains are described as porous, and porosity is expressed as the percentage of free space (or voids) in the total volume of rock. Sandstones and limestones, for example, have porosities of up to 15 per cent, but they also allow water to pass through them and are, therefore, termed permeable. Some rocks, such as clays, have high porosity but low permeability because their close-packed grains impede the flow of water. A crystalline rock such as granite, on the other hand, can have low porosity because of its closely interlocking grains but have a high permeability because the joints and fissures in the rock are interconnected and allow the passage of water.

Artesian wells

Any rock that is both porous and permeable contains ground water and is known as an aquifer. Where an aquifer is sandwiched between two impermeable strata, water may be trapped under high hydraulic pressure. If a hole is bored into the aquifer, this pressure forces the water to the surface as an artesian well (so-called after Artois in northeastern France). Such conditions occur in the Paris Basin, where a chalk aquifer is trapped between two layers of clay. Some of the early fountains in Paris made use of natural hydraulic pressure. But today the enormous demands for water by the population have lowered the water table 300 feet (91 meters) or more, and although the aquifer is recharged by rain falling on the exposed rim of the basin, it is insufficient to maintain the original ground water level.

Artesian basins occur on a much larger scale in Australia, where Jurassic sandstones act as an aquifer fed with rainwater from the mountains of the Great Divide. This basin covers an area of 0.8 million square miles (2 million square kilometers) in Queensland and adjoining states. Tube wells, drilled to a depth of 1,000 feet (305 meters), are lined with a metal casing to prevent collapse and contamination of the water. As water is removed, the surrounding water table is lowered and grades down toward the well in a cone of depression, which may extend for 6 miles (9.7 kilometers) or more.

Springs

Where the surface of the ground intersects the water table, water is discharged as a spring. There are various types. Valley springs occur along the lower slopes of valleys where

The strata exposed on hill slopes may give rise to several types of springs. In this example, based on an actual conformation in northern England, a stratum spring at the top of the hill feeds water down to a pothole connected to an underground stream. Water emerges from a Vauclusian spring at the foot of the limestone stratum, below which faulting results in a fault-line spring.

the water table reaches the surface. A line of such springs called the fontanili range along the foot of the Italian Alps, where they emerge from beneath the glacial outwash gravels and feed the rivers that drain the fertile Plain of Lombardy. Stratum springs develop at the junction of an aquifer and an impermeable layer. For example, there is a line of stratum springs at the foot of the Chiltern Hills in southern England where chalk lies on top of a layer of clay. The formation of dry valleys in such chalk country has been accounted for by a lowering of the water table because of the recession of the hills and lowering of the spring line.

Fault-line springs form where water-bearing rocks are brought next to impermeable strata by movement along a fault. Artesian springs occur when the upper surface of an aquifer is breached by faulting or where a synclinal fold traps water in its deep axis. The oases of the Sahara owe their existence to the presence of artesian springs.

Vauclusian springs develop in limestone regions where underground waters emerge from a cave system because of the presence of impermeable rocks beneath the limestone. The classic example of this type of spring occurs in the Fontaine de Vaucluse in Savoy, southeastern France, where the River Sogne flows out from below a sheer limestone cliff. The feature has given its name to this kind of spring.

Many areas of recent volcanic activity have thermal springs. Ground water becomes heated as it passes through hot rocks, as in Iceland and in the Lake Taupo district of New Zealand. In some places, the water boils underground, and jets of steam are forced high in the air as geysers. In other places, the heat supplied by the ordinary geothermal temperature gradient may be sufficient to produce hot springs, such as those in various parts of Europe that were tapped by the Romans and used to provide warm baths.

An oasis south of Adrar in the Saharan part of Algeria derives its water from an artesian spring, which occurs where the top of an aquifer has become eroded away.

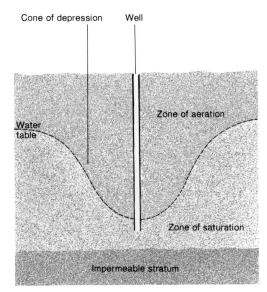

A pump well bored into an aquifer can modify the water table, giving rise to an unsaturated cone of depression in the porous rock surrounding it.

Chemicals in the water from the Mammoth Hot Springs in the Yellowstone National Park have been precipitated out of solution to build up the miniature cliffs of the so-called Minerva Terraces.

Caves and their formation

As rainwater falls, it dissolves carbon dioxide from the air forming carbonic acid. This weak acid corrodes calcite (calcium carbonate), the main mineral component of limestone rocks. The acid dissolves the limestone and sculpts the rock, especially along joints and lines of weakness in the strata. Flowing rainwater makes its way through the dissolved gaps and holes and erodes caverns underground along the level of the water table. Where the water table reaches the surface, as on a slope, a spring forms and drainage is established. The place where the spring emerges is called the resurgence. At the level of the water table, the pattern of linked caves is similar to that of a river, with converging branches and meanders formed by the flow of the water. Below the water table, caves are formed by solution effects, with no current-formed features. These caves are full of water, joined to blind tunnels and hollows.

The cave system

When the water table drops, the current-formed cave system is left dry and empty. Continuing solution effects undermine the rock and the ceilings fall in, producing spacious caverns deep underground. Where a stream of water enters the cave system, sink holes (also called potholes or swallow holes) form as the sides of the original gap are widened by erosion and fall away. A limestone plateau in Kentucky has more than 60,000 sink holes in its surface and there are more than 190 miles (306 kilometers) of interlinked caves and passages underground.

Stalactites and stalagmites

As well as the underground river system, there is a constant seepage of ground water through the rocks. This water carries dissolved

The horizontal network of a cave system forms along joints and weaknesses in the rock. Carbonic acid (formed by carbon dioxide dissolving in rainwater) attacks the calcite in limestone rocks, eventually dissolving the rock. The rainwater then flows underground through dissolved sink holes and corrodes a horizontal cavern system at the level of the water table. Drainage is established when the water breaks through to the surface, forming a resurgence spring. If the water table is later lowered, another cave system develops at the new level. Thus the upper caves become dry whereas the lower, more recent, caves are water-filled.

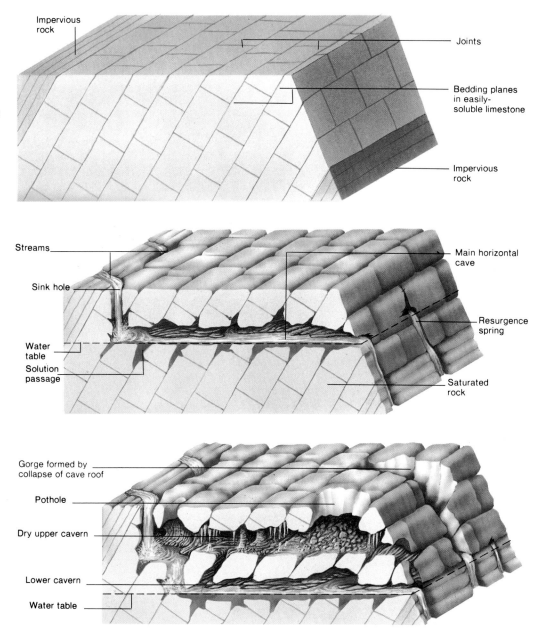

Impervious rock — Joints — Bedding planes in easily-soluble limestone — Impervious rock

Streams — Sink hole — Water table — Solution passage — Main horizontal cave — Resurgence spring — Saturated rock

Gorge formed by collapse of cave roof — Pothole — Dry upper cavern — Lower cavern — Water table

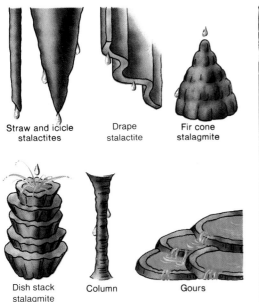

Straw and icicle stalactites

Drape stalactite

Fir cone stalagmite

Dish stack stalagmite

Column

Gours

Stalactites and stalagmites develop in a variety of forms *(far left)*. The most common types are the thin straw stalactites and the broader icicle stalactites. Stalagmites, drapes, columns, and gours (also called rimstone pools) are rarer. In the cave *(near left)* are some fine examples of delicately colored stalactites—and of a column. The red color of many of these is caused by iron impurities in the calcite; manganese impurities—the other main type—stain stalactites and stalagmites various shades of yellow.

calcite, leached out of the rocks. The calcite may be redeposited if the solution evaporates, if its concentration of carbon dioxide is reduced, or if it is agitated. In caves, evaporation is minimal because the atmosphere is saturated, but the other two factors are important. When the solution seeps through to the ceiling of a cave it may hang there as a drip. Mainly through the loss of carbon dioxide, the dissolved calcite is deposited on the ceiling, as a minute mineral particle. This process happens also to the next and subsequent drips and over the years the accumulated particles produce a hanging iciclelike structure. It may take a thousand years to deposit a centimeter of stalactite. The shapes of stalactites vary. Some are long and thin; others form drapelike structures where the seeping water trickles down a sloping ceiling. A constant wind blowing through the cave may cause the stalactite to be crooked or eccentric.

Water from the cave walls, ceiling, and stalactites drips to the floor. There the shock of the impact causes the calcite to separate from the water, which either flows away or evaporates. Constantly repeated, the result is the upward-growing equivalent of a stalactite—a stalagmite. Stalagmites also vary in shape; some resemble stacks of plates, whereas others have ledges and flutes that make them look like gigantic pine cones.

Occasionally, a stalactite and a stalagmite meet and grow into each other, producing a column. At times, the calcite-rich water seeps through the wall into the cave, usually along a bedding plane, and gives rise to a cascadelike structure called a balcony, with stalactites and stalagmites that seem to flow over each other.

In the bed of an underground stream, the calcite-rich water inevitably passes over ridges in the bed. A slight turbulence results, and a particle of calcium carbonate is deposited on the ridge. This action is self-sustaining, because the more calcium carbonate there is deposited on an obstruction, the larger the obstruction becomes and the greater the turbulence. The result is a series of stalagmite ridges with horizontal crests, which act like dams that hold back the water in pools. These little dams are called gours, or rimstone pools.

The calcite that forms these features is a colorless mineral, but impurities (mostly iron and manganese salts) stain the stalactites and stalagmites delicate shades of red, pink, and yellow, as well as white and brown. The staining varies according to the composition of the rocks that the seeping water has passed through and it produces concentric patterns in the iciclelike stalactites, and bands of color on the drape type.

Caves and history

Caves were the traditional homes of early man; his artifacts have been found buried in floor debris, and his paintings have been found on walls. The most important of such sites are in the Spanish Pyrenees and the Dordogne valley in France, which have caves that were inhabited as long as 500,000 years ago.

Fact Entries

Stalactites and stalagmites tend not to be found in Arctic areas, probably because of the low concentration of carbon dioxide in the ground water, which results from the lack of living organisms in the soil.

The largest known cavern is Lobang Nasip Bagus, in Gunung Mulu National Park in Sarawak, Malaysia. The cavern is about 2,300 feet (700 meters) long, 1,000 feet (300 meters) wide and is nowhere less than 230 feet (70 meters) high.

The longest known stalactite, 194 feet (59 meters), is in the Cueva de Nerja, near Malaga, Spain. It is partly supported by a cave wall.

The longest known freehanging stalactite, 38 feet (11.6 meters), is in Poll an Ionain cave in County Clare, Ireland.

The tallest known stalagmite, 95 feet (29 meters), is in the Aven Armand, in Lozère, France.

The tallest known column, 106 feet (32 meters), is in Ogle Cave in the Carlsbad Caverns National Park, New Mexico.

Gouffre de la Pierre St Martin in the Pyrenees is 3,850 feet (1,174 meters) deep.

River action

Most streams are formed in mountains and hills from surface run-off, by the emergence of absorbed rainwater from the ground (as springs), or from melting glaciers. Over many years a stream becomes a river by eroding its bed. The course of a river can be divided into three sections: the upper course, where erosion is predominant mainly because the steep slopes increase the velocity of the water; the middle course, where most of the transportation of the eroded material occurs; and the lower course, where deposition is the major feature because the gentler slopes reduce the speed of the water so that it is not able to carry the debris any farther.

The processes of erosion

The force of flowing water, known as hydrody-namics removes loose material from the surface and forces apart cracks in rocks. Boulders and pebbles carried by the current scour and excavate the bed by corrasion. The rocks carried by the river are themselves worn down by abrasion as they collide with and rub against each other, so that abrasion of the boulders in the upper course provides the fine particles in the lower course. Fine particles are transported in suspension by the water. Rocks that are too large to be suspended are picked up from the bed of the river by the turbulence, only to be dropped again. This bouncing action is called saltation. Boulders are rolled along the river bed by traction.

Solution action is another form of weathering performed by a river. Weak acids in the water, such as carbonic acid, may dissolve the rocks over which the water passes. Most erosion occurs when the river is in spate, when its movement is most turbulent and its speed increases.

Gorges and canyons

In the upper part of its course a river erodes chiefly by vertical corrasion, cutting a steep V-shaped valley that winds between interlocking spurs of high land. The level of a river is changed when there is either an isostatic lift in the land or a eustatic fall in the sea level. In both cases the river is forced to regrade its course to a new base level and in so doing cuts a new valley in the original floodplain. This rejuvenated erosion results in the formation of river terraces.

Incised meanders occur with renewed downcutting so that bends in a river are etched into the bedrock. In some cases, an asymmetrical valley is formed where lateral erosion on the outside of a bend produces river cliffs and a more gentle slipoff slope develops on the inside bend. If erosion is mainly vertical, then symmetrical valleys are formed.

Localized undercutting by lateral erosion on both sides of the narrow neck of an incised meander can produce a natural bridge. When

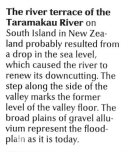

The river terrace of the Taramakau River on South Island in New Zealand probably resulted from a drop in the sea level, which caused the river to renew its downcutting. The step along the side of the valley marks the former level of the valley floor. The broad plains of gravel alluvium represent the floodplain as it is today.

River capture occurs when a major river and its tributaries (A) become so entrenched as they drain an area that they wear through a divide and intercept another river so that its course is diverted (B). The bend at the point of diversion is called the elbow of capture. When the gorge of the captured river beyond the elbow of capture is completely drained, it becomes a wind gap.

A   B

a passage is eventually excavated, the river by-passes the meander, leaving an abandoned meander loop beyond the bridge.

The Grand Canyon, one of the world's scenic wonders, was first cut in Miocene times (about 6 million years ago) as the Colorado Plateau was slowly uplifted by earth movements. The canyon has a maximum depth of about 5,280 feet (1.6 kilometers) from the plateau top to the Colorado River. Differential erosion of the horizontal strata has formed a spectacular terraced valley up to 18 miles (29 kilometers) wide.

River capture, which sometimes occurs in the upper course, results in an elbow-bend in the river and an H-shaped gorge. This happens when a stream erodes the land at its source until it breaks into the valley of another stream, and the adjacent stream is diverted into the new gorge.

Rapids and waterfalls

In the torrent stage of a stream, resistant bands of rock sometimes project transversely across the valley. If the hard band of rock dips gently downstream, then a series of rapids develop, as in the Nile River cataracts, where hard crystalline bands of rock cut across the river as it flows through the Nubian desert north of Khartoum. If the resistant layer is horizontal or dips upstream and covers a softer rock, then a waterfall may eventually result.

In its outlet from Lake Erie the Niagara River plunges 182 feet (55 meters) over a hard dolomitic limestone ledge. The less resistant shales and sandstone beneath have been eroded by eddying in the plunge pool and by water splashing and dripping back under the ledge, leaving the limestone unsupported. Headward erosion has resulted in the formation of a receding gorge 7 miles (11 kilometers) long downstream from the falls.

Waterfalls are also produced by glacial action where, due to the gouging of the main valley by ice, the valleys of tributary streams are left hanging high above the main valley floor. These hanging valleys often produce magnificent falls that plunge down the side of the main glacial trough.

Potholes are also a feature of the upper course of a river. They are formed when eddies whirl around pebbles, causing them to spin and act as grinding tools on the rock below.

River meanders

In the middle course of a river, most outcrops and formations are worn away, and the bed is fairly flat. The current is just strong enough to carry debris from the upper course. But as a river flows onto flatter slopes, it slows down and the coarsest debris is deposited. This debris may form sand and gravel bars around which the river is forced to flow. These deflections in its course develop into bends as the outer edges are eroded and as bars of sediment are deposited on the inner edges. In time, the curves become increasingly exaggerated and the river meanders.

The curves of a meandering river that flows

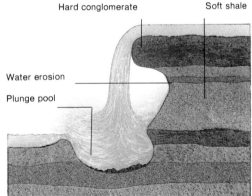

Hard conglomerate — Soft shale

Water erosion

Plunge pool

The Kaieteur Falls in Guyana *(above)* are typical of receding waterfalls. Splashing water from the plunge pool erodes the soft shale *(below)* as does water dripping back under the hard conglomerate and sandstone ledge, which, unsupported, eventually falls away.

The potholes in the Blyde River canyon in South Africa are representative of the cylindrical holes that are found in the bedrock of a stream or river valley. The holes are created by the abrasion of a pebble or boulder that is rotated by eddying water. Uplift of the land can lead to deepening of the vertical erosion.

A levee, a raised bank found on both sides of a meandering river, forms from the accumulation of sediment that the river deposits when it overflows its banks. The river bed is raised by deposited sediment until it is higher than the floodplain.

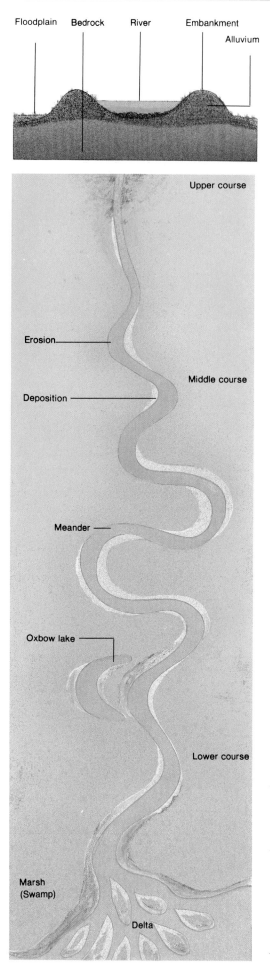

Floodplain   Bedrock   River   Embankment   Alluvium

In its upper course, particularly if the gradient is steep, a river channel is straight and narrow, and the river runs rapidly. But when the slope is reduced, the river slows down and moves around obstacles, such as rocky outcrops, rather than eroding them. In addition, the wave motion of the water moves the river from side to side. Eventually, the river erodes the outer bank of a slight bend and deposits material on the inner bank. The river channel is deepened toward the outer side of the bend and is widened at the same time by lateral erosion. The inner bends are built up with sand and shingle, although they too are eroded during heavy floods. As this process continues over time, the river widens the valley floor and the bends migrate downstream. The meanders increase into ever broadening loops with narrowing necks. Eventually, when a flood carries the water over a neck, the cut off meander becomes an oxbow lake. The lake silts up in subsequent floods and becomes a swamp. Embankments are also built up on the banks during floods. When the river meets the sea or a lake, the immediate reduction in velocity causes it to deposit sediment rapidly and a delta develops.

Upper course

Erosion

Middle course

Deposition

Meander

Oxbow lake

Lower course

Marsh (Swamp)

Delta

across a wide floodplain slowly migrate downstream as erosion occurs on the outer bank of the bends and as sediments are deposited on the inner banks. The changing shape of the bends is due to the current, which usually follows a helical or corkscrew pattern as it goes downstream, flowing faster on the outer bank and sweeping more slowly toward the inner bank where it deposits a series of point bar sediments.

When a river is in flood, silt or alluvium may be spread over the floodplain. The river bed is raised higher than the surrounding land by deposition, while the river itself is contained by embankments, which are formed from the deposition of silt. Embankments may break when the river is swollen and large areas of the floodplain may be inundated. At this time, a river may alter its course, as did the Hwang Ho in China in 1852, when it shifted its mouth 310 miles (499 kilometers) to the north of the Shantung Peninsula. On a smaller scale, individual meanders may be cut off if the river breaks through the narrow neck of land separating a meander loop. The river straightens its course at this point, and the abandoned loop is left as an oxbow lake, which gradually degenerates into a swamp as it is silted up by later floods.

A river is described as braided when it becomes wide and shallow and is split into several streams separated by mid-channel bars of sand and shingle. Braiding often develops where a river emerges from a mountain region onto a bordering plain. The sudden flattening of the slope checks the velocity of the stream and sediment is deposited.

Deltas

Deposition is concentrated where a river is slowed on entering a lake or the sea. A delta forms at this point as long as no strong currents or tides prevent silt from settling. A typical cross section through a delta shows a regular succession of beds in which fine particles of material—which are carried out farthest—create the bottom-set beds, whereas coarser material is deposited in a series of steep, angled wedges known as the fore-set beds. As the delta progrades into the water, the coarsest sediment is laid down on the delta surface to form the top-set beds.

A good example of a lacustrine delta is found where the River Rhône enters Lake Geneva. The river is milky gray in color because it is heavily charged with sediment acquired from its passage through the Swiss Alps. The river plunges into the clear waters of the lake and slows down immediately, leaving the material it has transported to contribute to the outgrowth of the delta. Ultimately, the lake may become completely silted up, although some lakes are initially divided by deltaic outgrowth. Derwentwater and Bassenthwaite in the English Lake District were originally one lake but are now separated by delta flats that were produced by the River Derwent.

Marine deltas are formed when the ocean currents at the river mouth are negligible, as in partially enclosed seas such as the Mediterranean and the Gulf of Mexico. The classic marine delta is exemplified by the arcuate type of the River Nile. Sediment is deposited in a broad arc surrounding the mouth of the river, which is made up of a series of distributary channels crossing the delta. Lagoons, marshes, and coastal sand spits are also characteristic features of most deltas. The Mississippi delta has most of these features including embankments, bayous (distributaries), and etangs (lagoons). The delta progrades seaward by way of several major channels that resemble outstretched fingers.

Alluvial fans and cones

When a mountain torrent flows into a main valley its velocity is greatly reduced and some of its load is deposited as an alluvial fan. This occurs, for example, in the upper Rhône valley in Switzerland, where hanging tributary streams cascade down the mountainside to be abruptly checked on reaching the floor of the main glacial trough. The alluvial fans that have been built up by these streams are now sufficiently high to be the sites of villages.

In semi-arid regions where a river emerges from a canyon or a wadi onto a lowland, often most of the water sinks into the porous alluvium of the fan, and the whole load of sediment is deposited without spreading, creating a steep-sided structure called an alluvial cone.

When closely spaced streams flow down onto a piedmont plain their fan deposits may eventually coalesce to create a bajada, which has a more gently inclined surface than that of the isolated alluvial cone. These features can be seen in the arid intermontane basins of the western United States. They are bordered by fault-line scarps, which overlook rock pediments that are covered by spreads of sand and gravel. Death Valley, in California, is a fault-bounded basin of inland drainage with baja-

das that merge into a piedmont gravel zone around a central salt-encrusted playa lake, which is below sea level. The deposits are formed from material that is washed down from the surrounding mountains by intermittent streams during flash floods. The nature of the sediment varies from coarse fan debris in the piedmont zone to fine sands and salt deposits in the center of the basin.

The delta of the Hsi Chiang River, near Canton in China, is the product of several rivers. The distributaries are many, as in most deltas, because as the accumulation of sediment blocks the path of each distributary, so more channels are created in search for an outlet. The watery terrain represents the built-up sediment.

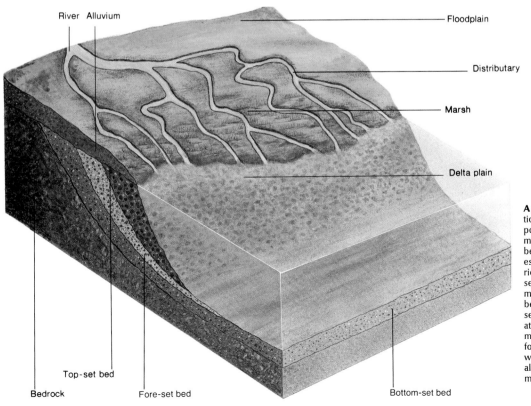

River   Alluvium

Floodplain

Distributary

Marsh

Delta plain

Top-set bed

Bedrock   Fore-set bed   Bottom-set bed

A river delta in cross section can be seen to be composed of several layers of material. The bottom-set beds are made up of the finest particles, which are carried out farthest; the fore-set beds comprise coarser material; and the top-set beds consist of the heaviest sediment that is deposited at an early stage as the river meets the sea. These layers form a sloping fan under water that gradually extends along the sea floor as more material accumulates.

Coral reefs and islands

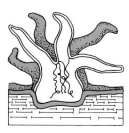

A coral polyp is a very simple animal with fingerlike tentacles, which resemble those of its near relatives the sea anemones.

Not all rocks were formed hundreds of thousands of years ago. Enormous masses of limestone are being formed today in the warmer parts of the Indian and Pacific oceans, built up particle by particle through the activities of corals.

Corals are animals, relatives of the sea anemone, that remain fixed to the same spot throughout life, feeding on organic material that drifts past in the water. They have a hard shell of calcite, formed by the extraction of calcium carbonate from seawater. A coral organism, called a polyp, can reproduce by budding. The result is a branching colony of thousands of individual creatures. Each colony is usually built up on the rocky skeletons of dead polyps, and in this way the coral mass can grow and spread to form a reef.

Corals flourish only in certain conditions. They live in seawater and grow best in clear, silt-free water at a temperature of between 74 and 77° F. (23 and 25° C). Their tissues contain

Turbulent shallow water foams over the reef that fringes a small coral island in the Seychelles. Corals flourish in the warm waters of this part of the Indian Ocean.

single-celled plants that help extract the calcite from water; the plants must have sunlight to survive—in water less than 160 feet (49 meters) deep. For these reasons, coral reefs are found in clear, shallow tropical seas.

Reefs tend to grow in shallow offshore water, especially around islands. They cannot form near river estuaries, where the water carries suspended sand and mud.

Types of reefs

There are three main types of reefs: a fringing reef forms a shelf around an island, just below water level; a barrier reef lies at a distance from the island, forming a rough ring around it and separated from it by a shallow lagoon; the third type of reef is the atoll, which is merely a ring of reef material with no central island at all. The three types can be considered as three stages in a single process.

Usually the island is volcanic, part of an island arc that rises from the sea floor where two crustal plates are converging. Once the island has appeared, corals begin to grow on its flanks, just below sea level. The outer limit of reef growth is defined by the depth below which corals cannot grow. The result is a fringing reef.

As time passes, the island may sink, possibly because, attached to its tectonic plate, it moves from a relatively shallow active area (such as an ocean ridge) towards deeper waters. Alternatively, the "sinking" may be due to a rise in sea level caused by the melting of polar icecaps at the end of an ice age. As this occurs, the exposed part of the island—which is roughly conical in shape—becomes smaller. But the reef continues to build upward from its original position. Sooner or later the island and reef become separated at the surface of the sea, producing a barrier reef. Eventually

New volcanic island   Fringing reef   Barrier reef

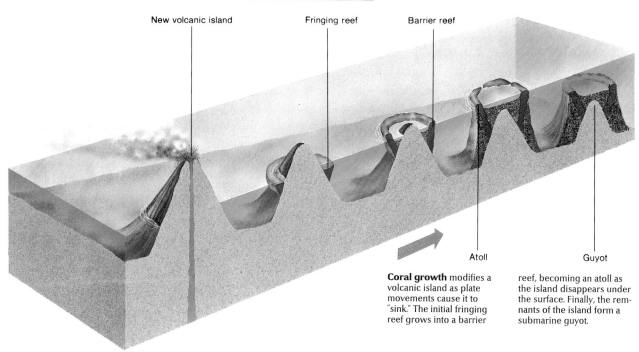

Atoll   Guyot

Coral growth modifies a volcanic island as plate movements cause it to "sink." The initial fringing reef grows into a barrier reef, becoming an atoll as the island disappears under the surface. Finally, the remnants of the island form a submarine guyot.

the island sinks completely, although the reef continues to grow and form the characteristic ring of an atoll.

If the atoll continues to sink and does so at such a rate that the growth of coral cannot keep ahead of it, then the coral dies and the whole reef is carried into deeper water. This may account for the existence of guyots—flat-topped underwater hills whose summits may be 6,500 feet (1,981 meters) below the surface of the sea. Many guyots have been found in the Pacific Ocean. Their distribution suggests that they were originally formed in the same way as the volcanic islands in the area.

The structure of a reef

A living reef forms a narrow plateau just below the surface of the water, producing an area of shallows that can be treacherous for swimmers and small craft. Where the reef crest is above the water it forms a small flat island, often crowned with coconut palms. The island is usually covered with white sand, made from the eroded fragments of coral skeletons. In the lagoon behind the reef there may be boulders of coral material that have been torn off the reef during storms and deposited in the calmer water. In the sheltered water of a lagoon, coral may grow into remarkable mushroom shapes and pinnacles and support a varied community of marine life.

The water in a lagoon is shallow, although not as shallow as over the reef itself. Its floor is covered by sediments of broken coral; this region is known as a reef flat. On the seaward side of the reef its edge may be composed of the skeletons of calcite-secreting algae, because these plants are better than corals at withstanding the rougher conditions. The outer edge forms a scree slope of fragments broken from the reef.

Fossil reefs

Geologically a reef is a mass of biogenic limestone, whose porous nature makes it a good reservoir rock for oil and natural gas. In early times the reef organisms were very different from today's. Modern corals did not evolve until about 200 million years ago (in the Triassic period), yet the first reefs date from the Cambrian of 570 million years ago. Many of the early reefs were built by calcite-producing algae or by shellfish that existed on the heaps of shells left by their ancestors.

Colorful damsel fish seek shelter among the fingerlike growths of coral. The reefs support a wide variety of marine life, from the coral polyps themselves, through numerous species of mollusks and crustaceans, to the predatory fish that feed on them.

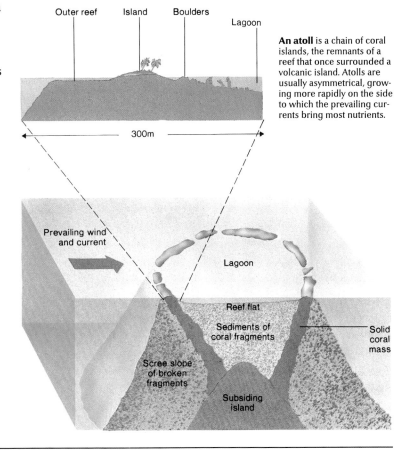

An atoll is a chain of coral islands, the remnants of a reef that once surrounded a volcanic island. Atolls are usually asymmetrical, growing more rapidly on the side to which the prevailing currents bring most nutrients.

Fact Entries

The origin of reefs—from fringing reef, to barrier reef, to atoll—was first deduced by Charles Darwin on the cruises of HMS *Beagle,* and his results were published in 1842, fifteen years before *The Origin of Species.*

An alternative theory was proposed by the American geologist R. A. Daly in 1910. He suggested that the colder conditions in the Ice Age stopped the growth of coral at that time, and the sea level fell because of the water locked up in the ice. The Pacific Islands were then worn flat by wave action, and later corals were built up around the edge when the water level rose again through isostatic readjustment, to form an atoll.

The Great Barrier Reef, of Queensland, Australia, is more than 1,200 miles (1,930 kilometers) long. It is not a continuous structure and is broken at frequent intervals where rivers from the mainland bring mud and silt into the area. Other major reefs near a continental land mass occur in the Red Sea, where the hinterland is sandy desert and there is little contamination by river sediments.

Land emergence
Coast stationary
Land erosion — Advancing coast — Land build-up
Retreating coast
Coast stationary
Land submergence

Valintin's classification defines the stability of a coastline by taking into account whether it is rising or sinking, or being eroded or built up by deposition.

Sea cliffs made of limestone are vulnerable to both weather erosion and the action of waves. Undercutting by the sea creates unstable sections which eventually fall.

Coastal erosion

One of the most impermanent features of any physical map is the coastline. The edge of the sea is in a state of constant modification, however stable the hinterland may be. Sea cliffs erode, deltas build up, sand bars and beaches shift. Around the world's coasts, conditions have not yet stabilized after the changes in sea

level that accompanied the last ice age.

In many places, the land is still subsiding, allowing the sea to reach up the valleys and turn hills into islands. In other places, the land is gradually rising, freed from the weight of overlying ice that melted many thousands of years ago. Former beaches and cliffs are now found inland, well above sea level. It may still take thousands of years more before the coastline becomes fixed and stable.

The type of coastal landscape that develops depends on whether the land is submerging or emerging, and whether the sea is eroding the land or building it up by deposition. When submergence and erosion occur together, the sea works its way inland and creates the most spectacular types of coastal landscape.

Wave power

Waves are the most potent agents of coastal erosion. Their power is threefold and involves hydraulic action, corrasion, and attrition. Hydraulic action is produced by the sheer weight of water flung against the cliffs and rocks, compressing the air in the pores and bursting the rocks apart. Corrasion occurs as the boulders and pebbles suspended in the seawater are hurled against the shore and dragged about on the shallow sea bed. During attrition, the boulders and pebbles themselves are ground down to sand by tumbling.

Much of the power of wave action is concentrated on headlands, which are attacked from both sides. Joints and bedding planes in the rocks are forced open and enlarged into

In an Atlantic type coastline the action of the sea creates bays, eroded out of soft rock, between projecting headlands of harder rock (A). Then the waves attack the headlands from both sides (B), forming caves, arches, and sea stacks. Eventually the headlands are completely eroded away (C), leaving a series of undulating cliffs.

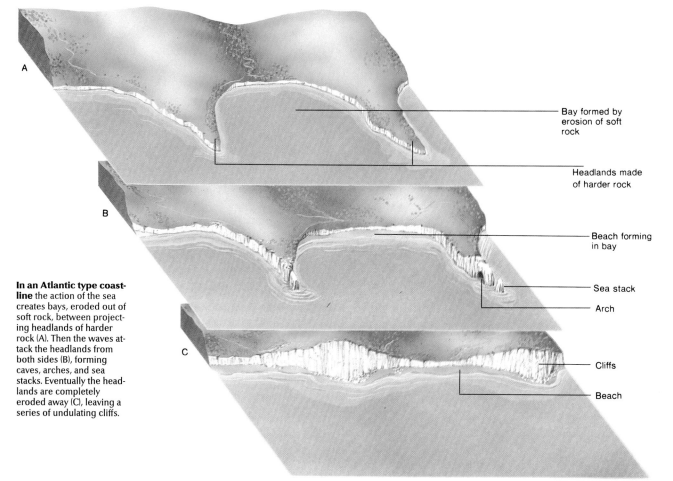

- Bay formed by erosion of soft rock
- Headlands made of harder rock
- Beach forming in bay
- Sea stack
- Arch
- Cliffs
- Beach

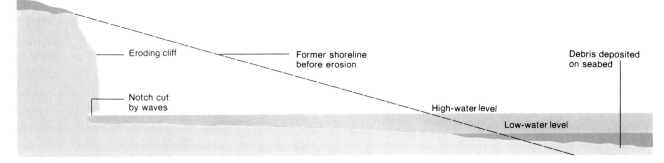

Eroding cliff

Former shoreline
before erosion

Debris deposited
on seabed

Notch cut
by waves

High-water level

Low-water level

caves. Caves on opposite sides of a headland may meet and form a natural arch in the rock. In time the top of the arch (lintel) collapses and leaves the offshore portion of rock standing as a sea stack, which eventually crumbles. This process continues, and the headland is eroded back towards the land. The whole sequence of events may take many thousands of years.

Wave erosion of a cliff usually takes place along a line at the base. The waves cut a horizontal notch in the rock, and the resulting overhang eventually collapses into the sea. Current and wave action clears away the debris, and the undercutting continues, resulting in one of the most unstable types of coastline.

The shape of the cliff that is formed depends largely on its geology. Soft, unconsolidated material like sand forms a sloping, crumbling cliff, whereas harder rock such as chalk, with an even composition and texture, forms a fairly smooth vertical surface. Rocks that are strongly bedded, such as shale, or deeply jointed, such as granite, give irregular cliff profiles because other forms of erosion and weathering accompany wave erosion.

Wave erosion attacks softer rocks and unconsolidated sediments most quickly. As a result, the course of the coastline is determined by the grain of the land. On a large scale, when alternate beds of soft and hard rock run out to sea, the soft rock is eroded into bays while the hard rock forms the headlands, which are thus exposed to wave attack. This is known as an "Atlantic type" coastline. When the grain of the land is parallel to the coast, erosion results in chains of islands and inlets that follow the coast's direction, resulting in what is known as a "Pacific type" coastline.

The sea also erodes some coastlines by dissolving the rocks. This erosive effect is relatively unimportant, however, because most types of rocks are insoluble in seawater. The rocks most vulnerable to the sea's chemical action are those with a high calcareous content, such as limestones.

Human influence

Coastal erosion is often an inconvenience or even a hazard to people, both through the loss of property and the danger to life. But most attempts to prevent it merely introduce another factor into an already complex and little understood process. Groynes erected to prevent sand from being washed along a beach deplete the next beach of its sand. Breakwaters built to provide a sheltered anchorage upset the current pattern and lead to the formation of sandbanks where they are neither expected nor desired. The power of waves is often greatly underestimated when constructing sea walls, and structures that are supposed to withstand the sea for hundreds of years may last only a decade.

A sloping shoreline becomes converted into cliffs by the action of waves. The sea cuts a notch along the base of the cliff; when the unstable part collapses, the tidal current carries the rock debris seaward and deposits it below the low-water line.

The power of the sea is sufficient to smash down the most rugged sea defenses. A single wave can exert a hammer blow of up to 500 tons on each square foot (50 tons/m²) of masonry and hurl stones and boulders for many yards inland.

Fact Entries

Wave power. During winter the pressure exerted by an Atlantic wave is, on average, about 1 ton/ft² (10 tons/m²). In storms this figure can be easily doubled or possibly even tripled. Soft rock forms cliffs that may be eroded by more than 6.5 feet (2 meters) a

year. Cliffs of hard rock tend to be eroded much more slowly by heat, cold, wind, or water but may be relatively quickly eroded if highly jointed or interbedded with softer rock.

Other erosive mechanisms. Although the major agents of marine erosion are the corrasion, attrition, and hydraulic effects of waves, certain minor influences also make their contributions. These include water layer erosion through the repeated wetting and

drying of the rocks, chemical action between the seawater and limestone, the effects of living organisms, such as rock-dissolving bluegreen algae and grazing gastropods, and, according to some authorities, frost weathering, which takes place more slowly on

coastlines than inland because of the salinity of the seawater.

Coastal accretion

While some parts of a coast are being eroded by constant pounding of waves, the material removed is being carried by the sea to other areas where it is deposited, forming any of various characteristic shoreline features, such as beaches and spits.

There are two main mechanisms by which eroded material is transported along coastlines: longshore drift, in which the debris is carried along by currents moving parallel to the shore, and beach drifting, in which the debris is moved by the action of waves on the shoreline itself. Beach drifting usually occurs where waves strike the shore obliquely. The uprush (swash) carries material diagonally up the beach, and the backwash drags the loose fragments back down at right angles to the shoreline. As this process continues, the coastal material (sand and pebbles, for example) is gradually moved along.

Beaches

A beach is an accumulation of (usually) sand and shingle lying in the littoral zone (the region of a shore between the high- and low-water levels). On hilly coasts small bay-head beaches develop where debris is trapped between rocky headlands; many of the coves of southwestern Britain and northwestern France are of this type. In contrast, on low-relief coasts there is often a large expanse of sand with a narrow shingle beach ridge on the landward side. At low tide the sands of gradually sloping beaches may extend seaward for several miles—as occurs in the bay of St Michel on the north coast of France, where the beach extends for about 9 miles (15 kilometers) at low tide.

Beaches are an important economic asset to coastal resorts, many of which have groynes that protect their beaches from removal by drifting. Sand and pebbles accumulate on the side of the groynes facing the direction of drift, whereas on the other side of the groynes material is washed away but is trapped by the next groyne.

Spits and bars

Where both beach drifting and longshore currents occur along an irregular coastline, spits and bars of sand may form. Where the coast turns inward into a bay or estuary, eroded material is usually carried past the inlet and deposited in the deeper water beyond. As this process continues a ridge or embankment is gradually built out from the coast, forming a spit. The spit terminates in open water at a point where cross-currents prevent further forward growth.

Spits—particularly long ones—usually curve toward the shore, an effect caused by the tendency of oblique waves to be refracted (that is, to swing around the end of spits) or by the approach of waves from a different direction. There are many of these hooked (recurved) spits along the eastern seaboard of the United States where southward-flowing currents carry eroded material across river mouths.

If a spit continues to lengthen unimpeded, it may eventually form a bay bar (or barrier beach) linking two headlands. Lagoons and marshes often develop behind such bay bars. Several curved bay bars occur around Danzig (Gdańsk) in Poland; they are composed mainly of sand and are known locally as nehrungen.

A bar that extends from the mainland to an island or from one island to another is called a tombolo. The name originates from the Italian example near Orbetello (about 80 miles (129 kilometers) northwest of Rome), where two bars of shingle (which enclose a lagoon) link the mainland to a rocky island. Another good example is Chesil Beach in Dorset, England, which is a 15-mile (24-kilometer) shingle ridge that begins at Bridport and, after running along the coast, links the Isle of Portland to the mainland.

Where there is a wide zone of shallow

Spits characteristically have a hooked end (caused by wave refraction), which is clearly visible in this example in the Persian Gulf.

Sand and other coastal material is moved along the shoreline—unless impeded by groynes—by beach drifting, caused by the oblique uprush of waves. Eroded matter is also transported by sea currents (longshore drift). Where the material is eventually deposited a spit may form.

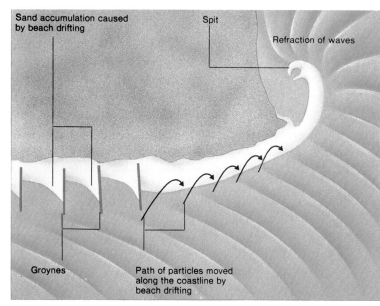

Sand accumulation caused by beach drifting

Spit

Refraction of waves

Groynes

Path of particles moved along the coastline by beach drifting

water, offshore bars may form several miles from the coast. Running parallel to the shoreline, usually discontinuous, these bars are also sometimes known as barrier islands. These are relatively common along the coast of North Carolina, where a series of barrier islands extends more than 90 miles (145 kilometers) north and south of Cape Hatteras.

Cuspate forelands

Triangular outgrowths consisting mainly of shingle ridges are called cuspate forelands, thought to result from either the convergence of two spits or the combined effects of waves from different directions. Cape Canaveral in Florida, for instance, was formed as a result of deposition by opposing longshore currents set up by eddies from the Gulf Stream. Another example is the Darss peninsula in East Germany, where the sediment has advanced about 1,400 feet (427 meters) seaward in the past 200 years and has enclosed several shallow brackish lagoons (known locally as bodden).

Coastal sand dunes

Many beaches are backed by sand dunes, formed as coastal winds blow sand from the beaches farther inland. On the Baltic coast the inland migration of dunes has been measured at the rate of 20 feet (6 meters) per year; some of the dunes rise to more than 200 feet (61 meters) and threaten to encroach on agricultural land. A larger dune belt occurs in the Landes region of western France, where the dunes extend southward along the coast from the Gironde estuary to Biarritz.

To prevent sand dunes from moving inland, pine trees and marram grasses can be planted. Brushwood fences can also control sand drift. In some areas, lagoons and marshes behind the dunes help to prevent the inland migration of sand.

Mobile Bay *(above)* in southern Alabama in the United States is almost completely cut off from the Gulf of Mexico by a spit (at the bottom right of the high-altitude photograph) and an offshore bar *(at the bottom left)*.

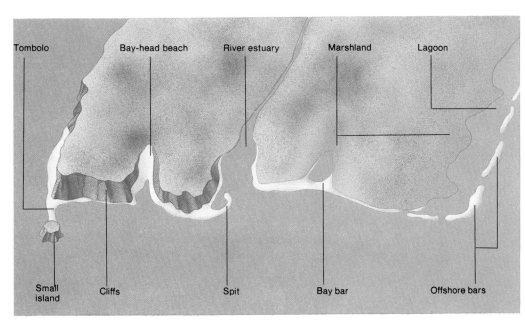

Tombolo — Bay-head beach — River estuary — Marshland — Lagoon — Small island — Cliffs — Spit — Bay bar — Offshore bars

Coastal accretion gives rise to various offshore and shoreline features; the principal ones are shown in the illustration on the left.

The continental shelf

A continental shelf is a submerged, gently-sloping ledge that surrounds the edge of a continent. On the landward side it is bordered by the coastal plain and on the seaward side by the shelf break, where the continental shelf gives way to the steeper continental slope. The coastal plain, continental shelf, and continental slope together comprise what is called the continental terrace. Farther out to sea beyond the continental slope is the continental rise and then the abyssal plain—the sea floor of the deep ocean.

Knowledge of the continental shelf has increased greatly since the 1950's, helped by geophysical techniques originally developed to prospect for offshore oil and gas reserves. Particularly valuable have been the various sonar mapping methods, which use ultrasonic sound to penetrate the seawater. The depth of the sea bed can be measured using echo sounders, and lateral sonar beams can be used to obtain pictorial views of the sea bed that are similar to aerial photographs of the land.

Size and depth of the continental shelf

The continental shelf constitutes 7 to 8 per cent of the total area of the sea floor, forming the bottom of most of the world's shallow seas. The width of the shelf varies from place to place; off the coast of southern California, for example, the shelf is less than 0.6 miles (1 kilometer) wide, whereas off South America, between Argentina and the Falkland Islands, it is more than 300 miles (483 kilometers) wide. It is narrowest on active crustal-plate margins bordering young mountain ranges, such as those around the Pacific Ocean and Mediterranean Sea, and broadest on passive margins such as the Atlantic Ocean.

The shelf slopes gradually (at an average of only 0.1° to the horizontal) down to the shelf break, the mean depth of which is 425 feet (130 meters) below sea level. The continental slope, the other main part of the continental terrace,

begins at the shelf break and extends to a depth of between 4,920 and 11,480 feet (1.5 and 3.5 kilometers). The slope varies from 12 to 60 miles (20 to 100 kilometers) wide and is much steeper than the shelf. In some places it is as steep as 20°.

Influences on the continental shelf

The continental shelf is affected by two main factors: earth movements and sea-level changes. On passive crustal-plate margins the shelf subsides as the earth's crust gradually cools after rifting and becomes thinner through stretching. These processes are often accompanied by infilling with sediments, the weight of which adds to the subsidence of the shelf. And in polar regions the weight of ice depresses the continents by a considerable amount, with the result that the shelf break may be more than 2,000 feet (610 meters) below sea level.

Superimposed on the results of subsidence is the effect of worldwide changes in sea level which, during the earth's history, have repeatedly led to drowning of the continental margins. During the last few million years, sea-level changes were caused mainly by the freezing of the seas in the ice ages. The last major change, the melting of ice at the end of the Pleistocene Ice Age several thousand years ago, released water into the oceans and submerged the shelf. Since then shorelines have remained comparatively unchanged.

Many of the earlier changes in sea level, however, were related to the earth's activity. During quiescent phases, when the earth's surface is being eroded and the resultant debris deposited in the seas, the sea level rises as water is displaced by the accumulating debris. During active mountain-building phases, on the other hand, the sea level falls.

Changes in the rate at which the continents move apart also cause fluctuations in sea level. During times of rapid separation, the rocks near the centers of spreading of the ocean

The narrow margins of the continents slope gradually before descending to the abyssal plain (the floor of the deep ocean). In the profile of the continental margin *(below)*, the vertical scale has been exaggerated to enable the main zones to be clearly distinguishable.

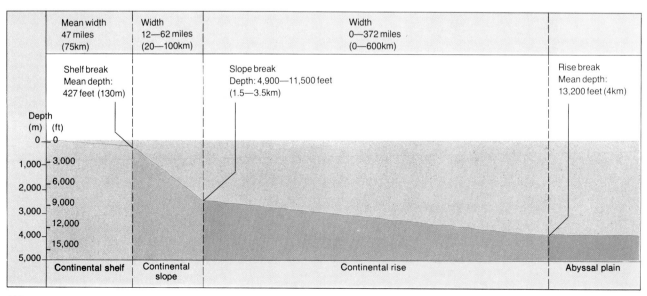

Mean width 47 miles (75km)	Width 12—62 miles (20—100km)	Width 0—372 miles (0—600km)	
Shelf break Mean depth: 427 feet (130m)		Slope break Depth: 4,900—11,500 feet (1.5—3.5km)	Rise break Mean depth: 13,200 feet (4km)
Continental shelf	Continental slope	Continental rise	Abyssal plain

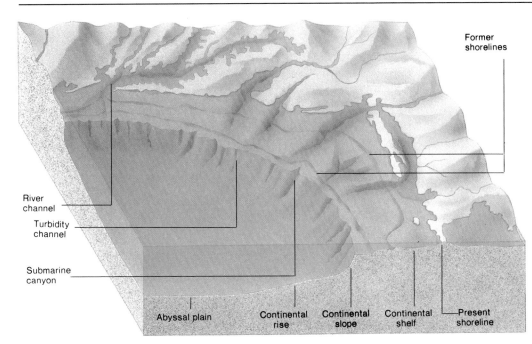

Former shorelines

The continental margin has a varied relief, with such features as submarine canyons and smaller turbidity and river channels. In some areas the former shorelines can also be seen.

River channel

Turbidity channel

Submarine canyon

Abyssal plain

Continental rise

Continental slope

Continental shelf

Present shoreline

floor (from where the continental movements originate) become hot and expand, thereby displacing sea water, which drowns the edges of the continents.

Topography of the continental shelf

The continental shelf has a varied relief. Drowned river valleys, cliffs, and beaches—submerged by the recent (in geological terms) sea-level rise—are common, and in northern latitudes the characteristic features left by retreating ice sheets and glaciers (U-shaped valleys and moraines, for example) are apparent.

Furthermore, the shelf is not unchanging even today. It is being altered by numerous influences that affect the sediments left behind by the sea-level rise at the end of the Pleistocene Ice Age. In strongly tidal areas, such as the Yellow Sea and the North Sea, currents sweep sand deposits into wavelike patterns that resemble the windblown dunes in deserts. If, however, a large amount of mud is flowing onto the shelf from a river mouth, the mud may completely obscure the underlying features. In addition to physical processes, the shelf is also affected by biological activity, i.e., by the growth of coral reefs in tropical areas.

Topography of the continental slope

The continental slope is cut by numerous submarine canyons, many of which are as large as the largest canyons that occur on land. Their gullied sides resemble rugged "badlands." Much of the sediment carried off the continental shelf by wave action passes down the submarine canyons (although some is also distributed along the continental slope). The deeper parts of the canyons show the effects of rapidly flowing turbidity currents—dense mixtures of sediment and water that are often started by a submarine landslide. These turbidity currents may reach speeds of 25 miles per hour (40 kilometers per hour) and travel more than 50 miles (80 kilometers) before coming to rest.

Most offshore drilling for oil and gas is carried out on the continental shelf, partly because the offshore deposits occur mainly in the rocks that form the shelf and partly because it is easier drilling in the relatively shallow waters above the shelf than in the deep ocean.

Earth movements and sea-level changes can affect the continental shelf, as shown by the cliff *(below)*, which was originally an offshore coral reef but was raised by earth movements and became part of the land.

Icecaps

Within the last 1.6 million years the earth has experienced an ice age during which almost one third of the land surface—about 11.5 million square miles (30 million square kilometers)—was covered by ice. Today the area of ice-covered land has dwindled to 6 million square miles (15.5 million square kilometers), and continental ice sheets, such as those that were widespread during the last ice age, cover only Greenland and Antarctica. Smaller ice sheets, known as icecaps, occur in such northern land masses as Iceland, Spitzbergen, and the Canadian Islands. Valley glaciers that flow out over a plain and coalesce with others to form a broad sheet of ice are called piedmont glaciers; the classic examples are along the coast of Alaska.

Ice movement

In very cold latitudes there is no summer thaw, and the snow that falls in winter is covered and compressed by snow in subsequent falls. The compressed snow eventually becomes glacier ice two or three miles thick. The great pressure that builds up underneath the ice makes the ice crystals slide over each other and, because the pressure lowers the melting point of the ice, water is released that lubricates the mass. In addition, glacier ice under pressure can deform elastically like putty. As a result, the ice sheet moves outward away from the build-up of pressure at the center. In Greenland the movement may be as great as 65 feet (20 meters) per day, whereas in Antarctica it may only be 3 feet (1 meter) per year. The bottom layers of the ice move and are deformed, but the top layers remain rigid and are carried along by them, cracking and splitting as they move.

The weight of a continental ice sheet depresses the land beneath it, so that a large percentage of the land surface of Greenland and Antarctica is below sea level. If these ice sheets were to melt, the level of the land below them would rise due to isostasy, as is happening in the areas of the Baltic Sea where the land is still recovering its isostatic balance after having lost the continental ice sheets that covered it during the last ice age. The restoration of balance does not just involve a simple raising of the land level; before this occurs the melting ice increases the volume of water in the oceans and raises the sea level at the same time.

When an ice sheet passes over or through a mountain range and descends to a lower altitude, as they do in Iceland and the Canadian Islands, it squeezes through the passes and cols between the mountains in the form of lobes, which may then become valley glaciers.

The various layers in an ice sheet can be detected by echo sounding, in which pulses of radio waves are sent down into the ice and the resulting echoes analyzed. Reflections from different layers may come from thin layers of dirt, which are probably deposits of volcanic ash that may have periodically drifted into and fallen on the area.

Ice ages

The earth has had a number of ice ages. The

During the Pleistocene Ice Age, about 18,000 years ago (A), two ice sheets covered land in the Northern Hemisphere; one had as its center Scandinavia, and covered the North Sea, most of Britain, the Netherlands, northern Germany, and Russia; the other spread over the North American continent as far down as Illinois. These ice sheets froze enough water to reduce the sea level to about 300 feet (91 meters) lower than it is at present. Today in the Northern Hemisphere (B), only Greenland is covered by an ice sheet, and icecaps lie over Iceland, parts of Scandinavia, and the Canadian Islands.

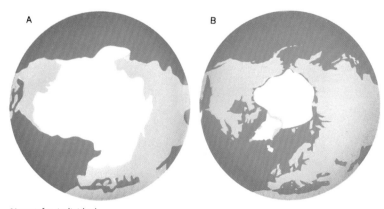

Nunataks, individual mountains that are completely surrounded by ice, occasionally protrude through the surface of an ice sheet. Lower mountains tend to be wholly engulfed. In such cases, ice moving toward the sea can flow uphill as it crosses a mountain range. This phenomenon has been proved by the discovery, on one side of a mountain range in Greenland, of blocks that were plucked from the other side by the moving ice during the Ice Age and transported up and over the range.

area covered by them can be mapped by the distribution of rocks, called tillites, which consist of the same type of material found in glacial deposition. At least three ice ages are known to have occurred in Precambrian times and one in the Upper Ordovician or Lower Silurian period—435 million years ago—evidence of which has been found in South Africa. A particularly important one occurred in Pennsylvanian and Permian times—280 million years ago; the evidence for this has been found in South America, central and southern Africa, India, and Australia. It therefore provides substance for the theory of continental drift and the breakup of Gondwanaland—the great southern continent that may then have existed.

The most recent ice age was during the Pleistocene. It began 1,500,000 years ago and ended within 10,000 years ago. It consisted of 6 to 20 different advances and retreats of the ice sheets, each one separated by a warm interglacial period during which the climate in the temperate latitudes was at times warmer than it is now. It is possible that the glacial advances are not over yet and that we are experiencing another interglacial period before the advance of the next ice sheet.

Causes of ice ages

Many theories have been proposed. It has

been suggested that the distribution of continental masses may be responsible, for example by preventing the warm oceanic water from reaching the poles. Or the albedo of ice sheets reflects a high percentage of solar radiation and so reduces temperatures sufficiently to affect the world climate. Or there may be fluctuations in the proportion of carbon dioxide or dust particles in the atmosphere; a reduction in carbon dioxide or an increase in dust would allow more heat to be lost from the earth and so result in lower temperatures. Others suggest that the reason must be found in space, such as in a fluctuation of the sun's energy output or the presence of a cloud of dust between the earth and the sun.

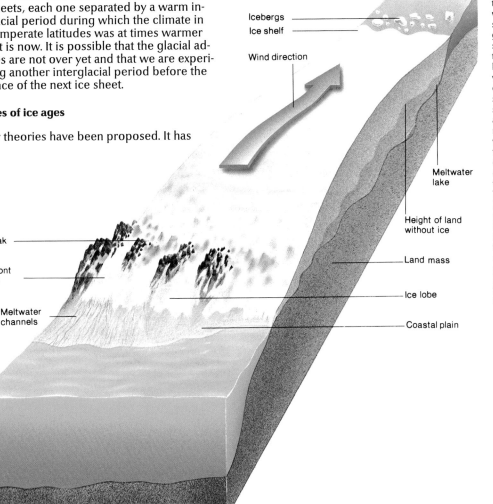

Icebergs
Ice shelf
Wind direction
Meltwater lake
Height of land without ice
Land mass
Ice lobe
Coastal plain
Nunatak
Piedmont glacier
Meltwater channels

Ice sheets have a distinctive surface topography, which includes features such as nunataks, piedmont glaciers, ice lobes, and ice shelves. The land beneath the ice is often depressed to below sea level by the weight of the ice. In this case the icecap covering the subducted areas is dome-shaped from the marginal areas to the interior. The movement of the ice is outward from the raised center, and the rate of flow increases as the ice flows down to the sea and through mountain valleys. The ice moves either as lobes through valleys or as part of the ice shelf into the sea where it melts or calves into icebergs. The friction of the moving ice on the underlying rock or the weight of accumulated ice can lower the freezing point of the bottom layers of ice and cause them to melt.

Fact Entries

Albedo is the surface reflectivity to solar radiation. Dry snow has a very high albedo and reflects a large amount of the sun's radiation back into space. The larger the ice sheet, the less solar radiation would be absorbed by the earth and the lower temperatures would become.

Isostatic rebound is the upward movement of an area of the earth's crust that was formerly depressed by the weight of an icecap.

The Greenland continental ice sheet has a mean thickness of 7,355 feet (2,242 meters), an area of 708,073 square miles (1,833,900 million square kilometers), a volume of 890,000 cubic miles (3.7 million cubic kilometers), and a mass of 3.6×10^{15} tons (3.3×10^{15} metric tons).

The Antarctic continental ice sheet varies in thickness from 1,000 to 6,000 feet (300 to 1,800 meters), has an area of 5.1 million square miles (13 million square kilometers), a volume of 7.2 million cubic miles (30 million cubic kilometers), and a mass of 30×10^{15} tons (27

$\times 10^{15}$ metric tons). This vast quantity of ice makes up 99 per cent of all the ice on earth and locks up, in the frozen state, 75 per cent of the earth's fresh water.

Mountain glaciers

The snowfields on mountain regions are constantly being replenished with fresh falls of snow, the weight of which compresses the underlying material into firn, or nevé. This material is composed of ice crystals separated from each other by small air spaces. With increasing depth and pressure, the firn gradually changes into much denser glacier ice, which moves slowly out from the snowfields down existing valleys. The glacier becomes a river of moving ice, its surface marked by a series of deep cracks or crevasses. The cracks result from the fact that ice under pressure deforms and moves plastically, whereas the upper layers remain rigid and are therefore under tension and they eventually shear. Transverse crevasses often occur where the slope of the glacier increases; these may be intersected by longitudinal crevasses, creating ice pinnacles, or seracs, between them. A large crevasse, known as a bergschrund, may also form near the head of a glacier in the firn zone where the ice pulls away from the mountain wall.

Glacial abrasion and plucking

As a glacier moves it erodes the underlying rocks, mainly by abrasion and by transporting and depositing. Abrasion involves rock debris frozen into the sole of the glacier acting on the rocks underneath like coarse sandpaper. Transporting and depositing happens when the ice freezes onto rock projections, particularly in well-jointed rocks, and tears the blocks out as it moves.

Considerable evidence exists of glacial erosion having taken place during the Pleistocene Ice Age, when glaciers and ice sheets extended over much of northern Europe and North America. At that time ice moved out of the high mountains and spread over the surrounding lowlands. It modified the shape of the land and left various distinctive landforms that can be seen today long after the ice has receded.

In most glaciated valleys it is possible to find rock surfaces that have been grooved and scratched. These striations were caused by angular rock fragments frozen into the sole of a moving glacier. The marks give some indication of the direction of ice movement. Where a more resistant rock projects out of a valley floor, it may have been molded by the passage of ice so that it has a gentle slope on the upstream side (which is planed smooth by the glacier) and a steep ragged slope on the lee side. Seen from a distance, these rocks were thought to resemble the sheepskin wigs fashionable in early nineteenth-century Europe and so were named roches moutonnées.

A melting glacier in the Himalayas, near Sonamarg in Kashmir, lies in the U-shaped valley it has created. The typical rate of flow of a glacier is about 1 foot (30 centimeters) a day, and movement is due to slope and the plastic distortion of ice. Rock fragments that the glacier has plucked from the slopes of the valley can be seen littering the valley floor. They form the lateral moraine of the glacier and, at an earlier stage of glaciation, probably cut in and abraded the valley floor and sides as they were dragged along by the moving ice.

Cirques

An aerial view of a glaciated highland reveals large amphitheater-like hollows arranged around the mountain peaks. These great hollows are called cirques (corries in England and cwms in Wales) and are the point at which glaciers were first formed during an ice age, or where present-day glaciers start in areas such as the Alps or the Rockies. The Aletsch glacier, for example, begins on the southeastern slopes of the Jungfrau in Switzerland and is fed by several tributary glaciers, each emerging from a cirque. Frost shattering of the exposed walls of the cirque results in their gradual enlargement; this process is accelerated by subglacial disintegration of the rock, which occurs when water reaches the rock floor through the bergschrund crevasse (esker) at the head of the glacier.

During an ice age most cirques were probably filled to overflowing with glacier ice, and their walls and floors were subject to vigorous abrasion. When the ice melted, a cirque often became the site of a mountain lake, or tarn, with morainic material forming a dam at the outflow lip.

Cirques are bordered by several precipitous knife-edged ridges known as arêtes. These develop when the walls of two adjoining cirques meet after glacial erosion has taken place from both sides. When the arêtes themselves are worn back, the central mass may remain as an isolated peak where the heads of several cirques meet. The Matterhorn in the Swiss Alps is a peak that was produced in this way.

Glacial valleys

When a glacier passes through a pre-existing river valley it actively erodes the valley to a characteristic U-shaped profile. The original interlocking spurs through which the former river wound are worn back and truncated. In this way, the valley is straightened, widened, and deepened, and its tributary streams are left high above the main trough as hanging valleys. The streams in them often plunge down the valley side as spectacular waterfalls, as in the Lauterbrunnen valley between Interlaken and the Jungfrau.

Where several tributary glaciers join the head of a major valley, the increased gouging by the extra ice flow results in the formation of a trough end, or steep step in the U-shaped trough. The floor of a glaciated valley is often eroded very unevenly, and elongated depressions may become the sites of long, narrow ribbon lakes. Some of the deeper ribbon lakes are dammed by morainic material at their outlets, as in lakes Como and Maggiore in northern Italy.

In mountainous regions glacial troughs may extend down to the coast where they form long steep-sided inlets, or fjords. The classic fjords of Norway, Scotland, and British Columbia all result from intense glaciation followed by a eustatic rise in sea level at the end of the Ice Age, and the lower ends of the U-shaped valleys were converted into deep, flooded fjord inlets.

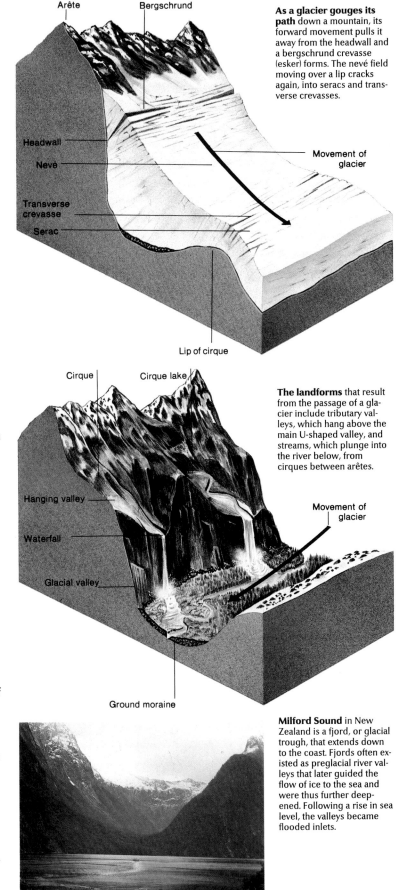

As a glacier gouges its path down a mountain, its forward movement pulls it away from the headwall and a bergschrund crevasse (esker) forms. The nevé field moving over a lip cracks again, into seracs and transverse crevasses.

Arête   Bergschrund
Headwall
Nevé
Transverse crevasse
Serac
Movement of glacier
Lip of cirque

Cirque   Cirque lake
Hanging valley
Waterfall
Glacial valley
Movement of glacier
Ground moraine

The landforms that result from the passage of a glacier include tributary valleys, which hang above the main U-shaped valley, and streams, which plunge into the river below, from cirques between arêtes.

Milford Sound in New Zealand is a fjord, or glacial trough, that extends down to the coast. Fjords often existed as preglacial river valleys that later guided the flow of ice to the sea and were thus further deepened. Following a rise in sea level, the valleys became flooded inlets.

Past glaciation

When a glacier emerges from its U-shaped valley, it spreads out over the surrounding lowlands as an ice sheet. Much of the surface material eroded by the glacier and carried by it to the plains is deposited when the ice starts to melt. The pre-glacial lowland landscape is, therefore, often markedly modified by various deposits left behind by the ice.

Surface deposits

When the great northern continental ice sheets reached their most southerly extent, they deposited a ridgelike terminal moraine that was contained at the ice front. Similar ridges, known as recessional moraines, have resulted from pauses during the retreat of the ice sheet. The North German Plain is traversed by a series of parallel crescent-shaped (arcuate) moraines, which were formed as the Scandinavian ice sheet advanced across the Baltic. The main line of low morainic hills can be traced southward through the Jutland peninsula, and then eastward through northern Germany and Poland. The Baltic Heights represent the most clearly defined moraine, reaching more than 1,200 feet (366 meters) in height near Gdańsk. Similarly, a series of moraines cross the plains to the south of the Great Lakes, marking the various halts in the recession of the North American ice sheet.

Behind each terminal moraine, groups of low, hummocky hills known as drumlins often occur. These hills were formed as the ice sheet retreated, and most are elliptical mounds of sand and clay, sometimes up to 200 feet (60 meters) high, and elongated in the direction of the ice movement. How they were formed is not known, but it is thought that they were formed by the overriding of previous ground moraines. Drumlins are arranged in an echelon, or belt, and form a distinctive drumlin topography. A drumlin field may contain as many as 10,000 drumlins—one of the largest known is on the northwestern plains of Canada. In Strangford Lough in County Down, Ireland, drumlins form islands.

Winding across glaciated lowlands, there are often long sinuous gravel ridges called es-kers. They are thought to be deposits formed by subglacial streams at the mouths of the tunnels through which they flowed beneath the ice. Eskers are common in Finland and Sweden, where they run across the country between lakes and marshes.

When a delta is formed by meltwater seeping out from beneath the ice front, it develops into a mound of bedded sand and gravel known as a kame. In some areas, kames are separated by water-filled depressions called kettle holes, formed originally as sediment piled up around patches of stranded ice that melted after the recession of the ice sheet.

The chief product of glacial deposition is boulder clay, which is the ground moraine of an ice sheet. It comprises an unstratified mixture of sand and clay particles of various sizes and origins. For example, deposits in southeastern England contain both chalk boulders of local derivation and igneous rock from Scandinavia. Blocks of rock that are transported far from their parent outcrop are known as erratics. The largest blocks are commonly seen resting on the boulder clay surface or even perched on exposed rock platforms.

The unsorted ground moraine behind the ice front contrasts strongly with the stratified drift of the outwash plain beyond. Meltwater streams deposit sand and gravel on the outwash plains to form the undulating topography so typical of the Luneburg Heath of West Germany or the Geest of the Netherlands.

Proglacial lakes

At the end of the Ice Age, many rivers were dammed by ice, and their waters formed proglacial lakes. During the retreat of the North American ice sheet, for example, a large lake—Lake Agassiz—was dammed up between the ice to the north and the continental watershed to the south. The remnants of this damming can be seen in Lake Winnipeg, which is now surrounded by lacustrine silts that were deposited on the floor of the ancient Lake Agassiz.

Beach strand lines are sometimes visible, which indicate the water levels at various stages in the draining of a lake. This probably occurred when the proglacial lake overflowed through spillways at successively lower levels

During the last Ice Age the northern polar icecap covered Greenland and Scandinavia, extending as far south as Britain, Denmark, and the northern United States.

During the Ice Age, encroaching ice sometimes diverted the course of a river. In northeastern England, originally (A) the land was drained by rivers flowing eastward to the North Sea. The advancing Scandinavian icecap dammed a river (B), creating a lake, which overspilled southward. Further ice movement created yet another lake (C), forcing the river southward once more. Today (D) the River Derwent still follows the diverted course.

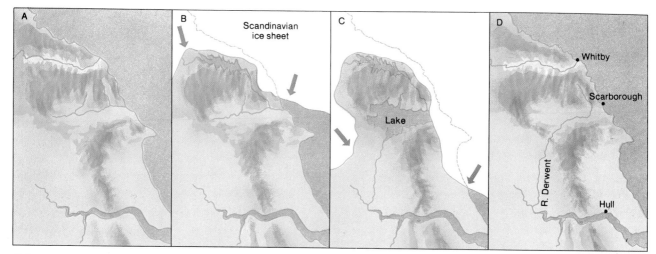

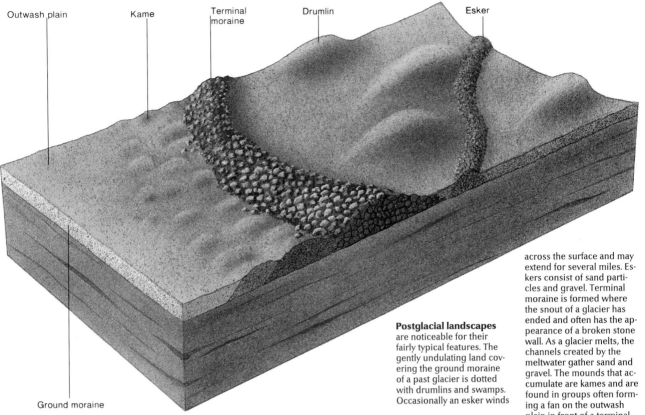

Outwash plain   Kame   Terminal moraine   Drumlin   Esker

Ground moraine

Postglacial landscapes are noticeable for their fairly typical features. The gently undulating land covering the ground moraine of a past glacier is dotted with drumlins and swamps. Occasionally an esker winds across the surface and may extend for several miles. Eskers consist of sand particles and gravel. Terminal moraine is formed where the snout of a glacier has ended and often has the appearance of a broken stone wall. As a glacier melts, the channels created by the meltwater gather sand and gravel. The mounds that accumulate are kames and are found in groups often forming a fan on the outwash plain in front of a terminal moraine.

as the ice began to recede. In northeastern England there is striking evidence of the diversion of drainage by ice. Pre-glacial rivers flowed eastward into the North Sea, but were blocked by the Scandinavian ice front as it approached the base of the North York Moors. The Eskdale valley in the moors was turned into a lake, which overflowed southward via a spillway into Lake Pickering, about 15 miles (24 kilometers) distant. This lake in turn drained through the Kirkham Abbey Gorge about 6 miles (10 kilometers) away. Today the River Derwent still follows the southward route to the River Humber, having been diverted by ice from its eastward course.

Erratics, blocks of till or bedrock, have been known to be carried for more than 500 miles (800 kilometers) by a glacier. They are prominent on glacial landscapes, and their positions often suggest the direction of the ice movement.

Pre-glacial features

Beyond the ice sheet margin lies the periglacial zone of permafrost, in which repeated freeze and thaw cycles result in the breaking of the soil surface and the differential sorting of loose fragments of rock so that a pattern is produced. On flat surfaces, polygonal arrangements of stones occur, whereas on sloping surfaces, parallel lines are formed. Another periglacial landform is the pingo, or ice mound, created when a body of water freezes below ground and produces an ice core that raises the surface into a low hillock.

Evidence of solifluction is also found in periglacial areas—a special type of soil flow in sloping ground in which a highly saturated soil layer overlies the permafrost. Solifluction debris, of frost-shattered fragments in a clay matrix, is referred to as head or coombe rock and often occurs at the foot of scarp slopes or in chalk valleys.

Drumlins, shown here protruding out of a lake in Ireland, usually occur in groups, each one parallel with the direction of the glacier's movement. They comprise morainic till or bedrock and sometimes both.

Biological and gravity erosion

The principal erosive forces are weathering, glacial action, and water erosion, but plants and animals also have a considerable effect on the breakup of the rocks of the earth's crust. The force of gravity, too, causes broken rock or loose soil to move from its original site.

Biological erosion

Small pockets of soil in exposed rocks may be large enough to allow a tree seed that lands there to germinate. As the seed grows, the roots of the young tree force their way down through the pocket and enlarge it by pushing its sides apart. The material broken down by plant roots in this way forms the basic inorganic component of new soil.

Once the rock is broken down into soil the presence of vegetation tends to keep it stable. Decaying vegetable matter produces the humus content of soil, and the interlocking network of roots and stems holds the individual particles together. This inderdependence is dramatically demonstrated when natural vegetation is removed to make room for cultivated crops; the soil breaks down and is eroded by wind and water so that in a few years a dustbowl results. To prevent the removal of coastal sand dunes by the wind, marram grass *(Ammophila arenaria)* or pine trees are often planted on them, the roots of which bind the sand particles together.

Animals, too, have an influence on the landscape, although the breakdown of rocks by animal activity is not as extensive as that by plants. Certain marine mollusks, such as the piddock (family Pholadidae), burrow into solid coastal rocks and so accelerate the rate at which they are eroded. The destruction of shrubs and overgrazing of grasslands by increased populations of herbivorous animals can also lead to rapid erosion of the soil. Constant grazing by the herds of the Bedouin nomads, for example, has caused the destruction of large areas of grassland on the margins of the Sahara and the Arabian deserts, enabling the deserts to extend their boundaries.

Slow earth movements

Loose rock material that results from weathering and erosion always moves downhill due to gravity, and it may do so slowly or rapidly. The slower process is called soil creep.

During soil creep, the soil surface tends to hold together, and the movement—often less than an inch per year—is perceptible only from its effects on the things growing in or placed upon it. Fences and telephone poles that were originally erected upright may lean downhill, for example. Tree trunks curve outward and upward as the progressive lean caused by the creep is overcome by the natural upright growth of the tree. Any steeply dipping rock structure under the creeping soil can be seen, in cross section, to curve over near the surface as the downslope movement pulls it away.

Soil creep may be caused by expansion and contraction in the soil produced by moisture or frost. During expansion, soil particles rise perpendicular to the surface, whereas when the soil contracts, the particles settle vertically downward. As a result, every time the soil expands and contracts on a slope the particles move a little farther downhill.

The soil creep process is particularly marked in the periglacial areas of arctic and subarctic regions, where the spring thaws may cause many square yards of topsoil to move downhill in the form of a lobe or a tongue. This process is known as solifluction and occurs only in the spring, producing a movement of about 4 inches (10 centimeters) per year down slopes as gentle as only 2 degrees.

Rapid movements

Slumps and landslides are similar phenomena and are more rapid downslope movements than solifluction and soil creep. A slump is characterized by the splitting up of the slope into concave slices that rotate over each other

Pholas dactylus is a species of piddock that, like the other members of its family, bores into rock with the serrated cutting edges at the end of its shell.

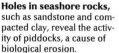

Holes in seashore rocks, such as sandstone and compacted clay, reveal the activity of piddocks, a cause of biological erosion.

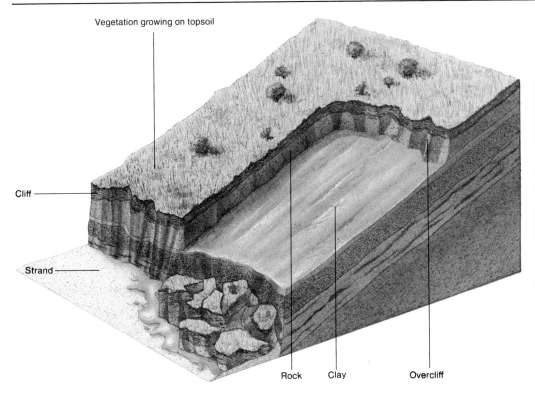

Vegetation growing on topsoil

Cliff

Strand

Rock   Clay   Overcliff

Landslides occur principally when the bedding planes on a slope dip at a steep angle and when there is no support at the end of the slope. Various types of landslides occur depending on the slope and the composition of the rock. This example shows heavy, massive rock overlying a layer of clay that has become saturated with water so that it lubricates the movement of the rock above it. In a typical landslide, the mass of rock moves rapidly downslope in a unit that disintegrates into rock fragments before it comes to rest.

with a downward movement. Slumping can begin slowly, the first stage being the appearance of a series of concentric cracks at the edge of the slope or cliff, outlining the area that is about to slump. As the slump continues, the slices break up and become a jumbled earthflow that takes the form of a tongue reaching out from the area of slip.

A landslide usually occurs with a mass or rock that is lubricated by a bed of slippery material, such as shale or clay, which may break down under wet conditions. If the support at the lower end of the bed is removed, a rapid landslide may take place. Other landslides occur because of the undercutting of a rock surface by the sea or river currents. The undercutting eventually becomes so great that the weight of the rocks above causes a collapse. Natural joints or bedding planes, or other lines of weakness in the rock, determine the shape of the fracture.

Another form of downslope movement is mudflow. This usually occurs where dry, loose material in an arid area is suddenly saturated by a seasonal downpour and flows down a dry canyon and across flatter areas beyond. Mudflows sometimes take place in volcanic regions during eruptions. Loose volcanic dust that has been ejected over the landscape soaks up the water from the torrential rains that usually accompany eruptions and causes destructive flows called lahars.

Slopes and landscapes

The effect of such soil flows is to reduce the slopes of the ground. Steep faces, for example, are carved away, and the eroded material is spread out over hollows. In addition, hills are flattened, and plains are built up. Incipient slopes can be divided into several parts consisting of a free slope, which is the outcrop of bare rock, surmounted by a gentle, upper

wash slope, which is formed by the material above the outcrop. Below the free slope is the debris slope, which is the pile of material that has been worn from above. This slope lies at a constant angle of repose, which tends to be the same however eroded the rest of the slope is on which the spread of material washed away from the area collects.

Over a long period of time, slopes tend to retreat under constant weathering until they are softened and worn down to a series of gentle convex and concave curves. A mature landscape has, theoretically, all its surface features worn away to sea level and is known as a peneplain.

Soil creep is a slow, downslope movement and is the result of a number of factors including climate. Rock is shattered by contraction and expansion during winter and is moved to the surface by the heaving effect of frost. When spring thaws the loosened rock, it moves down the slope, dragging along anything that is planted in it.

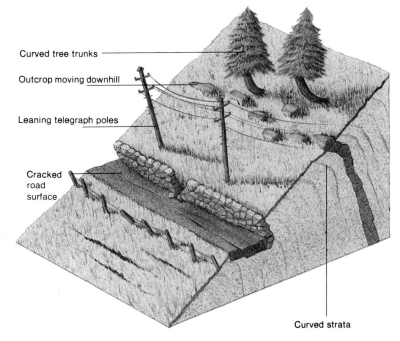

Curved tree trunks

Outcrop moving downhill

Leaning telegraph poles

Cracked road surface

Curved strata

Soil formation and distribution

Soil is made up of weathered rock with a small, but crucial, organic content that distinguishes it from other weathered material, which has no organic component. Weathering of the parent rock, climate, vegetation, and surface slope are the main influences on the processes that determine the actual type of soil.

The parent material

All soils form a blanket over underlying rock. In most situations this rock has been broken down by physical and chemical weathering processes to produce the mineral component of the soil. The mineral fraction can range in size from coarse gravel to minute particles of clay and is largely responsible for the texture of the soil. The products of the chemical decomposition of the parent rock's minerals also determine the way in which a soil develops—and its fertility. Clay minerals, which result from the chemical breakdown of silicates, such as feldspar, are especially important, because they can retain vital nutrients until they are required by growing plants.

Igneous rocks tend to form rich soil, whereas the soil produced from sedimentary rocks varies; sandstones weather to form thin, acid soils; limestones form thin, alkaline soils; and shales have little influence.

The formation of a mature soil from a bare rock surface takes approximately 10,000 years. In this time other controlling influences also exert their effects, reducing the importance of the parent rock as the soil develops.

Climate

Climate is an important element in soil formation and is often the basis for soil classification. It influences the soil by dictating the dominant weathering processes that affect the parent rock. As the mineral fraction of the soil accumulates, temperature influences the degree of biological activity that occurs and also the amount of water in the soil. Soil water, particularly rainfall, also plays an important role. Excess water seeps through the soil and may remove soluble minerals and fine solids, whereas too little water can slow the breakdown of minerals that are the source of vital nutrient chemicals.

Vegetation and slope

Young soils have small amounts of nutrients and can, therefore, support few plants, except for the hardy pioneering species, such as moss and lichen. These plants assist the liberation of nutrients from weathering minerals; and they ultimately decay in the soil. Decayed vegetable matter becomes humus, which is the richest source of nutrients because it retains nutrients, losing little to water moving through the soil.

Humus is concentrated at the soil surface, giving the surface layers a distinctive dark brown or black color. As soil matures, it becomes richer and can support more demanding vegetation that in turn, improves the soil still further until the soil and the plants it supports reach an equilibrium. The natural recycling of nutrients is vital to the maintenance of the fertility of soil. Arable farming removes vegetation (and with it the nutrients in the plants), and therefore, fertilizers have to be added to the soil to maintain its fertility.

Soils developing on slopes have to adjust to a constant movement of material through them. On the steeper areas, because the downslope movement is fairly rapid, the soil is thin and immature. The parent rock is often predominant in the soil in such situations. On

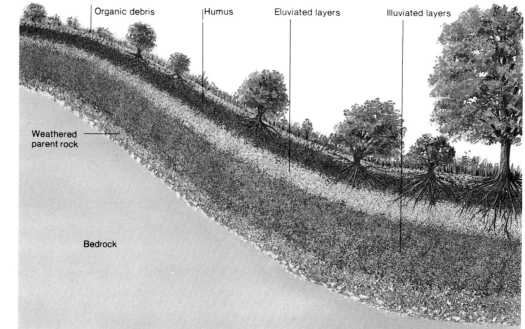

A profile of the different layers of which a soil is composed is usually divided into the A, B, and C horizons. The top layers, or the A horizon, consist of loose organic debris, humus, and leached, or eluviated soil. The dissolved substances collect in the lower layers, the B horizon, which comprise illuviated soil. The A and B horizons form the topsoil. Beneath them is the C horizon, the layer of weathered parent rock that has contributed to the makeup of the upper layers. The bedrock under it all is sometimes called the D horizon.

Organic debris   Humus   Eluviated layers   Illuviated layers

Weathered parent rock

Bedrock

lower parts of the slope the soils thicken as material accumulates and as minerals are carried downslope by water, which improves their fertility. Under such conditions a sequence of soils forms determined by their positions on the slope. This sequence is called a catena when the parent rock is the same throughout the slope.

Soil-forming processes

Other processes also affect the development of soils. Leaching, for example, is the movement of soluble material from the upper layers of a soil. It is often combined with eluviation, which involves the washing through of fine solid material. This second process encourages distinctive horizons to form in a soil, the upper ones losing material by eluviation while lower horizons may accumulate it and are then said to be illuviated.

Podsolization describes the removal of all soluble material and thus includes eluviation, but it also encompasses the chemical breakdown of clay minerals and the removal of many of the resulting products. It is therefore an extreme type of leaching. The soils produced are Podsols, the upper layers light gray and rich in mineral silica, the lower layers tending to be dark brown.

Laterization occurs in regions that have high temperatures and rainfall, such as the tropical rain forest areas of Africa and South America. Chemical decomposition in Laterite soil is rapid, and soluble material is quickly carried away, leaving an inorganic horizon containing iron or aluminum oxides with a distinctive yellow-orange color.

Calcification of soils results from a shortage of rainfall. When the soil water evaporates, it carries soluble minerals, especially calcium bicarbonate, to the surface. A rich Chernozem soil forms when the calcification is moderate, but excessive calcification leads to infertile, impermeable soils such as Caliche, or calcrete.

Podsols, Laterites, and Chernozems are common soil types. Brown Earth is another, which develops with mild leaching and is typical of areas with temperate climates, such as western Europe. In areas with extreme climate, such as hot and cold deserts, thin poor soils occur. Mountainous areas develop a wide range of soil types that are grouped together as mountain soils.

The Soil Survey Staff of the United States Department of Agriculture uses a different system of soil classification than the international system described above. The U.S. classification consists of 10 orders of soil: Alifisols, gray to brown leached topsoils; Aridisols, desert and other dry soils; Entisols, shallow soil of little development; Histosols, organic soils, such as peats; Inceptisols, very young soils, only slightly developed; Mollisols, thick, dark, rich topsoils; Oxisols, highly weathered, reddish soil; Spodosols, very acid, light colored, naturally infertile soils; Ultisols, well developed, acid soils; and Vertisols, subhumid and arid warm climate soils that develop wide, deep cracks during the dry seasons.

Podsols (*left*) occur mainly in regions of low temperatures. The gray iron pan results from the eluviation of iron hydroxides and humus, which collect in lower layers. This leaves the upper soil bleached and ash gray in color.

The world's climate and soil types are correlated. Glacial and tundra soil occur in polar regions, and Podsols are found in temperate latitudes with cold winters and mild, humid summers. In those grass-covered areas, which are humid to semi-arid and temperate to tropical, with discrete wet and dry seasons, Vertisols predominate. Chernozems are found in arid and semi-arid regions, with desert soils in the extremely dry areas. Laterites occur in tropical savanna and monsoon regions, and the soils in mountainous areas are grouped simply as mountain soils.

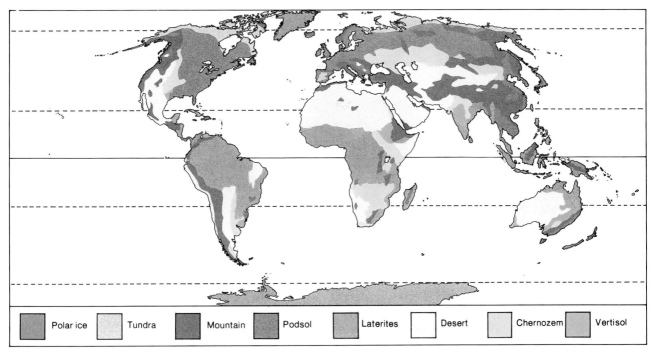

| | Polar ice | | Tundra | | Mountain | | Podsol | | Laterites | | Desert | | Chernozem | | Vertisol |

Man and the landscape

The landscape is the visible result of various natural geological processes—the formation of rocks, their uplift into mountains, subsequent erosion of the mountains, distribution and deposition of eroded sediments, movements of the continents, and the modification of coastlines by the action of the sea. But most natural processes (with the exception of brief, powerful phenomena, such as earthquakes) tend to take a long time to produce noticeable alterations. During the past few thousand years, by far the most significant landscape modifications have been produced by man.

Human beings are unique because of their intelligence and technological ability. Thus humans are less restricted by the constraints of ecology and evolution than are the other species that inhabit the earth. Instead of adapting to their surroundings, humans can modify the environment to provide for many of their needs.

Because of the relatively rapid development of technology and medicine, the human population has increased exponentially during the last 5,000 years; in geological terms, this period is extremely short—less than one-millionth part of the time the earth has existed—but during that time, the world's population has increased to about 5 billion. This population will probably double in the next 40 years. In the process of providing food and dwellings, civilization has substantially altered the

natural world. Today, very little of the earth's land surface remains in a virgin state.

Early human influences

The earliest known fossils of modern man *(Homo sapiens)* date from about 375,000 years ago. At that time most human communities obtained their food by hunting animals and by gathering edible wild plants from the surrounding countryside. Because of their simple lifestyle and sparse population, these early hunter-gatherers had a negligible effect on the environment. With the development of primitive technology—the use of fire and the production of clothing—they were able to migrate from the warm areas of Africa, southern Europe, and southern Asia to colder regions farther north; they managed to penetrate the American continent by crossing the land bridge across what is now the Bering Strait.

The next stage in the development of human civilization was the adoption of a nomadic way of life. In areas with large seasonal climatic variations, the animals on which the hunting tribes relied for food migrated to avoid the worst extremes of climate. And the tribes followed the animals to ensure a continuing food supply. Like the hunter-gatherers, nomadic hunters had a minimal effect on the environment.

The first change that had a major and last-

Much of the rural landscape, although natural-looking to many people, has been extensively modified. In densely-populated areas especially, almost all of the suitable land has been given over to agriculture to provide food.

ing environmental effect was the development of agriculture some 10,000 to 12,000 years ago. Initially, this involved collecting wild plants from the surrounding countryside and replanting them close to the human settlements. As agriculture became established, crops were grown from seeds obtained from the previous season's yield. Although still relatively small-scale (because the total human population was sparse), early agriculture had a noticeable effect on the landscape because it required the clearing of natural vegetation to provide land for cultivation. Animal husbandry followed, necessitating the clearing of more natural vegetation to provide grazing land. Furthermore, the development of farming as the main source of food was accompanied by the establishment of the first permanent settlements.

The earliest agriculture took place in river valleys where frequent flooding ensured that the soil remained fertile—the Nile, Tigris, Euphrates, and Indus valleys, for example. Elsewhere, "slash and burn" (or shifting) agriculture was employed. This method (which is still used in some parts of the world) involved clearing an area of its natural vegetation and burning it, then cultivating that land for a few years until the soil lost its fertility, after which the community moved on and cleared a previously untouched area.

The overall result of the development of agriculture was to ensure a relatively reliable source of food that was easy and safe to gather (unlike the much more hazardous hunting lifestyle), which, in turn, led to an increase in the human population. But the advent of settled agriculture also marked the beginning of extensive alterations to the environment.

Industrialization

The most dramatic changes to the landscape have been caused by industrialization, which, although its origins can be traced back to the Stone Age, has had by far the greatest effect in Western Europe since the Industrial Revolution of the mid-nineteenth century.

Primitive industry began in areas where there was a natural resource suitable for exploitation. Such a resource—a deposit of flint from which Stone-Age people could make arrowheads, for example—was worked by the local community, which could then trade its surplus for commodities it lacked.

Later, with the development of efficient transport and communications, trade was eventually possible between places anywhere in the world. Good communications affected the environment not only directly (by the building of roads and railways, for example) but also indirectly by stimulating industrialization throughout the world—a process that is continuing today, most notably in underdeveloped countries.

Hence our agricultural and industrial civilization has altered almost all of the natural landscape: forests have been cut down, and the land used for crops; mountains have been quarried for valuable minerals; animal and plant communities have been changed irrevocably; and the communications networks extend across the globe. Even if civilization suddenly disappeared from the face of the earth, the results of its environmental modifications would be long-lasting, and it would probably take thousands of years for a truly natural landscape to re-establish itself.

Man's effect on the landscape is most obvious in large cities, such as Los Angeles in the United States, part of which is shown left. In addition to their immediately apparent impact on the environment, urban areas also have a more subtle effect—by discharging large amounts of effluent into the air and waterways, for example.

Land for agriculture

About 70 per cent of the earth's surface is covered by ocean. Of the remaining 30 per cent, most is too cold, too dry, or too steep for agriculture. Only about 11 per cent of the land area is sufficiently warm, moist, and level to be used for arable farming, and about twice as much is under permanent pasture or meadow. The actual proportions vary from continent to continent and from country to country, with Europe being the best endowed with agricultural land. But even though such countries as Denmark till more than 75 per cent of the land, other parts of Europe suffer from aridity or permanently frozen ground, and only about one-third of the continent is arable. South America and Australasia suffer from much more severe limitations, and only about 15 per cent of their land area is suitable for growing crops.

Colonization and increase

Large new areas of farmland in the North American prairies and the Argentinian pampas were brought under agriculture during the late 1800's and early 1900's. These regions were used mainly for growing wheat and for raising livestock. European settlement there and in other parts of the world such as Australia and New Zealand, where a large dairy and sheep industry was established, led to a rapid expansion of the total farmed area and in food production. Sugar cane, cocoa, rubber, tea, and coffee were among the products exported from the new colonial plantations in the tropics.

In countries with large populations and small surface areas, such as the Netherlands, reclaimed land has also been farmed. The arable area of the world doubled during the 100 years before 1970. The rate of expansion has, however, now slowed. It is expected that there will be a further increase of only 4 per cent by the end of this century. At that time, the population per arable acre is likely to be 1.6.

Climatic and physical factors

The climate and physical environment impose limitations on agriculture. Huge areas of Africa, Asia, Australia, and America, for example, are desert or semidesert. Irrigation can overcome the difficulties that arise from aridity in some regions, but the extent of irrigation is restricted in turn by the availability and distribution of fresh water. Therefore, most large perennial irrigation schemes are found in riverine plains such as the Indus valley in Pakistan.

As crop breeders produce new fast-maturing strains of plants, the growing of crops may be extended into higher latitudes and altitudes, and into drier regions. In Alberta, Canada, for example, strains of wheat have been grown successfully in the short three-month summer season. Some of the extensions of

Farming in Portugal is carried out increasingly on smallholdings or fragmented farms. Most farms are less than 12 acres (5 hectares) in area, and most holdings are only about 5 acres (2 hectares). A little more than 33 per cent of the working population is occupied with the land, frequently using traditional, unmechanized methods. The total area under wheat is about 780,000 acres (316,000 hectares). But this crop is often farmed with others, such as rye, olives, and grapes.

The demand for land, both for settlement and agriculture, is great in Hong Kong, so much so that reclamation and multiple use of the land are high priorities. Land has been reclaimed from the sea by using a filling of stone and earth from nearby hills. The construction of paddy fields involves minimal earth-moving because they need only a bank surrounding a basin. Rice is the largest crop in the colony, and often the flooded fields are also used as breeding ponds for fish.

growth areas have been substantial at the local level, but dramatic expansion on a global scale is less likely because many of the climatic limitations on agriculture are unyielding and beyond human control.

Deficiencies in the soil may sometimes be rectified by, for example, the use of artificial fertilizers and the application of trace elements. Rapid loss of soil from steep mountain slopes can also be overcome—at great expense and in small areas—by terracing. This solution is not practicable for large areas, however, and is worthwhile only if enough water is available.

Increasing areas of arable land are suffering from soil erosion, or from the accumulation of salt or insoluble minerals, as a side effect of irrigation. Soil is eroded from most cropland faster than it forms and is therefore a wasting asset. The rate of soil loss varies from area to area and, in some places, poses a real threat to continued cropping. The amount of land lost to salinization or alkalinization is usually small but significant, because such irrigated regions often produce high yields. In Pakistan, 150,000 acres (60,000 hectares) of irrigated land have been affected by salinization.

The outlook

Arable land is being lost mainly as a result of the growth of towns and cities. About 2 per cent of the present arable area will probably be built over by the year 2000, and this area, assuming average yields, is capable of feeding nearly 85 million people. In addition the land lost in the vicinity of urban areas increasingly has to be replaced, if it can be replaced at all, by the recovery of marginal land in remote areas where until recently there was insufficient demand to bring the land under cultivation.

Because the area of land used to grow crops can be increased only slightly and slowly, increased yields will be necessary if the growing world population is to be fed.

Vestiges of the rural past of Clydebank in Scotland can be seen in the few outlying fields that have managed to ward off the encroaching city. With a rapidly growing world population the arable area per head is decreasing, during the first half of the 1970's, each arable acre worldwide supported an average of 1 person, whereas the figure is projected to rise to 1.6 people by the year 2000.

Higher yields may be achieved by advances in plant breeding (to produce crops that mature sooner and yield more), by the increased and improved use of fertilizers, and by the greater use of pesticides to safeguard crops. But fertilizers are expensive, and their widespread use is sometimes detrimental to wildlife. In developed countries, yields have doubled since World War II. Agricultural systems, however, require a great deal of capital and fossil fuel, and in the poorer developing countries, these resources are not always assured. The outlook for the world food supply is therefore uncertain. The arable area is probably incapable of great expansion because of environmental limitations and other demands for land.

Only about one-tenth of the land on earth is suitable for growing crops and just more than 20 per cent serves as grazing land. Deserts, mountainous and ice-bound regions, as well as forests, account for the rest of the land surface. With irrigation and hardier strains of plants, some of these areas, too, may gradually come under cultivation.

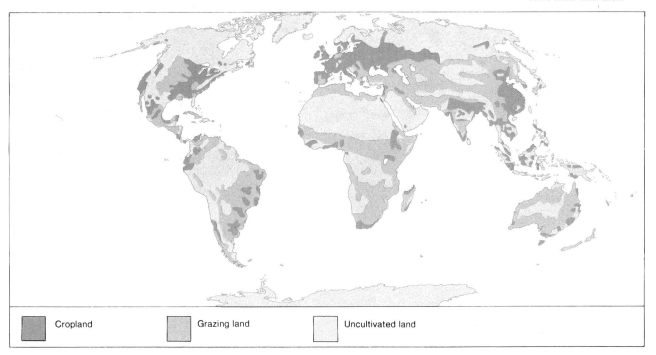

| Cropland | Grazing land | Uncultivated land |

Modifying farming land

Agriculture unavoidably involves changes to the land. The soil itself, machinery used on it, crops grown on it, and animals fed off it are all continually being improved to raise the level of productivity. Until the 1930's most of the increase in crop production resulted from an increase in the area under cultivation. With the development of chemicals for fertilizers, herbicides, and pesticides, less of an increase was needed in land and labor. During the next 30 years, the total area of cropland rose by only 46 per cent whereas agricultural output went up by 94 per cent.

Land improvement

Agricultural methods include the modification of the natural soil, which has to be prepared to create the ideal conditions for plants to grow. The simplest techniques are tillage and plowing, which change the soil structure but also kill weeds, aerate the soil, improve drainage, and distribute nutrients.

If soils are too sandy or clayey, as they often are in Denmark, for example, the problem is overcome by marling, which involves transporting clay to sandy areas and mixing the two materials to produce a more balanced, loamy soil.

Soil water can be another problem, either in excess or deficit. Excess water can be removed by mole drains, which allow richer soils to develop through aeration. But the land surface may be lowered following drainage, as in the Fenlands of England, which makes it vulnerable to flooding.

Leaving the soil exposed after tillage often promotes soil erosion, so that minimum tillage is sometimes practiced, which involves cutting slits into the sod in which the seeds are planted. Alternatively, some farmers use the no-tillage method, one of the more dramatic changes that has affected farming. The system involves planting seeds into a shallow furrow cut into the stubble of the previous crop, which is pressed down immediately. Savings in time and fuel can be great because conventional tillage, which involves up to 10 operations per field, is replaced by only 3 or 4. No-tillage agriculture allows steeper slopes to be cultivated because the soil is not exposed to surface runoff. Contour tillage and terracing on sloped farmland also help to prevent excess runoff.

Cultivation depletes the soil's fertility over the years, necessitating the use of fertilizers. Farming is dependent on natural and artificial fertilizers to maintain the high yields that are now common in areas of intensive farming, such as Western Europe. Fertilizers today include combinations of the three vital nutrients: nitrogen, phosphorus, and potassium.

Irrigation

The distribution and regulation of water is essential to agriculture. Irrigation has extended farming areas and increased their level of production. One of the simplest methods, which has been used for centuries, is water conduction by means of canals and ditches. Saudi Arabia has many flourishing farming enterprises based on oases from which water is pumped. In the Sudan, a huge, formerly uncultivable region called the Gezira (situated between the Blue and White Nile rivers) has been developed by irrigation from the Sennar Dam.

Irrigation can involve even more extensive systems. In Australia, for example, an irrigation project was carried out in the arid but fertile region of the Snowy Mountains. The drainage system included steel and stone drains, contoured terraces, and grassed canals. The steeper slopes were supported with matting and woven fences, sprayed with bitumen, and then covered with vegetation.

The topography of Peru—a narrow coastal plain, high mountains, mountain plateaus, and a forest basin—leaves little room for sufficient agriculture to support the country's population. This means that land must be modified as much as possible to be able to support crops. By terracing mountain slopes, the poor mountain soils can be retained and stabilized so that rice and other cereals can be grown on them.

Crop control

Other means of minimizing soil erosion include strip cropping, in which rows of different crops are alternated, one of closely spaced plants, the other with widely spaced plants. Crop rotation also performs this function when row crops are cultivated alternately with grass. Potatoes, cotton, and sugar beets are alternated with grass-legume mixtures that control soil loss and increase the availability of nutrients and water.

In addition, crop rotation and strip cropping help to control insects and other pests, as do irrigation, pesticides, and the use of fertilizers. Weeds are suppressed by flooding, burning, and herbicides. Unfortunately, irrigation can spread weed seeds, and some pesticides leave inorganic deposits that are harmful to crops. Intensive small-scale agriculture carried out close to urban centers where there is a ready market for salad crops makes great use of PVC in cloches and greenhouse-type structures, to protect and accelerate plant growth. The greenhouses vary from small sheds to large commercial structures that cover hundreds of square yards. The more traditional glasshouses also produce early crops and extend the growth limits of plants. Iceland, for example, has thousands of acres of heated greenhouses in which even pineapples can be grown.

The tremendous improvement in crops has also expanded areas under cultivation. Research into crop development has created early maturing varieties and higher yielding and disease-resistant strains.

Much of Australia's land supports only livestock because of the lack of water. Irrigation has enabled some of these dry areas to support crops.

The use of greenhouses for vegetables, particularly in cooler regions, has meant that crops such as green peppers can now be grown all the year round.

Polyethylene is increasing in popularity as a means of retaining the moisture in the earth around the roots of a plant. These tomato plants, growing on reclaimed swampland in Florida, require less frequent watering by being cultivated through polyethylene because the amount of water they lose through evaporation is reduced.

Transportation

The movement of goods and people has always been essential to economic, social, and political development. To enable this movement to take place, modern societies have created various kinds of transportation systems, such as canals, railroads, roads, pipelines, airports, and seaports. The form of any system and its relationship with the physical landscape in which it is built result from the interaction—and interdependence—of many factors. They include the system's function—particularly the characteristics of the traffic it has to carry; the technological knowledge at the time it is built; and the level of finance and organization available.

Inland waterways

Rivers can be modified for commercial navigation by dredging and straightening, or a canal can be dug to by-pass part of a river's course. On the River Rhône, for example, canal by-passes not only improve navigation along the river but are also the sites of hydroelectric power stations. For a canal to cross a major watershed between rivers, it must be made to ascend and descend, and water must be supplied to the summit level. The usual method of negotiating gradients is by locks, such as those in the Panama Canal or in the Soo canals between Lakes Superior and Huron. Alternatively, a vertical lift can be used, which has the advantage of saving the water consumed by a boat's passage through locks. Cheaper surface crossings (but at the expense of more locks) can be made at higher levels; in this case water may have to be pumped up to the summit. Canals are efficient as a means of moving freight; the Panama Canal, a vital link between the Atlantic and Pacific seaboards of the Americas, can, for example, take 80,000-ton ocean-going vessels. On the Great Lakes, ore and grain from ports such as Chicago are carried to the St. Lawrence Seaway by canals, which have become an international trade route.

Railroads and roads

Pioneering railroad engineers in early nineteenth-century Britain planned routes for railroads with profiles that included gently graded sections and short, steeper sections. Cable haulage was used on the steeper grades and steam locomotives on the gentler slopes, until it was found that heavier, more powerful locomotives could haul trains up more severe grades than was first thought—1 in 70 or steeper in normal use, and up to 1 in 14 in extreme cases. Cables and racks are still used on mountain railroads, with grades of up to 1 in 3. But conventional railroads are demanding in their route requirements because their motive power and braking rely on friction between steel and steel; track curvature is also determined by the traffic's speed requirements. In anything but the gentlest terrain, therefore, railroads need large scale earthworks, often including tunnels, bridges, and viaducts. Long, steep climbs may be achieved by spirals or switchbacks. New routes for high speed trains have been built in Japan, France, and West Germany. The present trend in developed countries is to reduce the track mileage, cut out uneconomic rural routes, and concentrate on fast, efficient intercity and commuter routes.

The variety of roads through time has closely reflected the demands of their traffic. Purpose-built motor roads, which first appeared in the United States and Western Europe in the 1920's, are potentially the most demanding of all. The German Autobahnen and the French Autoroutes, for example, are designed to carry large volumes of traffic at speeds of 75 miles per hour (120 kilometers per hour) or more and require gentle curves—an average radius is about 1.8 miles (3 kilometers)—and grades—1 in 3 is typical for the steepest—to maximize traffic flow and safety.

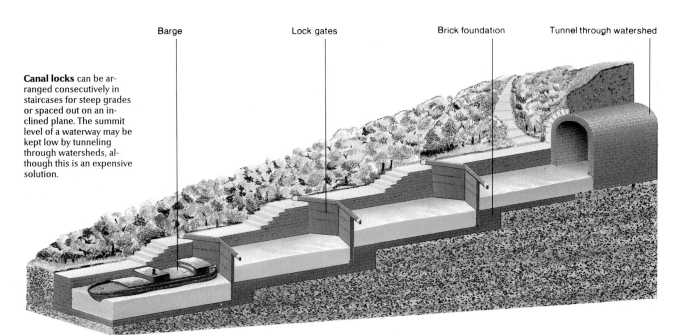

Barge   Lock gates   Brick foundation   Tunnel through watershed

Canal locks can be arranged consecutively in staircases for steep grades or spaced out on an inclined plane. The summit level of a waterway may be kept low by tunneling through watersheds, although this is an expensive solution.

Pipelines

Large quantities of liquids or liquidized solids can be moved continuously along pipelines, with the benefit to the environment that, once the pipeline is buried underground, the landscape can be restored. In some areas, however, the nature of the ground makes surface laying necessary, such as the oil pipeline from the Alaskan fields (which would be affected by the permafrost if it were laid underground).

Pipelines can also be laid under water, such as those used in the development of North Sea oilfields. Very steep, even vertical, ascents and drops can be incorporated in a route, although the cost of pumping then increases. Liquids, such as some crude oils, may have to be heated to reduce their viscosity, especially in cold climates. In inhabited areas, corridors of open land have to be designated to allow safety margins between pipelines and buildings.

Airports and seaports

Unlike most land transportation systems, air and sea transportation does not need extensive, constructed routes (apart from ship canals), although the radar, radio, and light beacons that control the airways and seaways are necessary land-based facets of aviation and shipping.

A modern airport may cover 25,000 acres (10,000 hectares) or more and requires that there should be no high ground or tall buildings nearby—at least in line with landing and take-off paths.

Modern seaports also require large areas of level land, which must be adjacent to deep water. Increases in ship size since the 1950's, particularly of oil tankers and bulk ore and grain carriers, have made older ports obsolete. New facilities have to be built, or a completely new terminal may be required. Containerization of freight has increased the demand for new land-based facilities, notably large open areas for container stacking, with road and rail access.

Complex road junctions abound in California and testify to the fact that the state has the most extensive system of freeways in the world. In the early 1980's it had about 3,700 miles (5,933 kilometers) of freeway.

An airport, such as Heathrow, London, needs at least one runway of 1.8 miles (3 kilometers) or more, as well as large terminal buildings, car parks, road, and sometimes rail access, all of which can cover more than 25,000 acres (10,000 hectares).

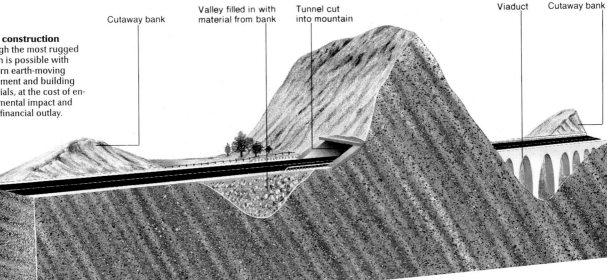

Cutaway bank

Valley filled in with material from bank

Tunnel cut into mountain

Viaduct   Cutaway bank

Road construction through the most rugged terrain is possible with modern earth-moving equipment and building materials, at the cost of environmental impact and large financial outlay.

Land for settlement

The pattern of settlement at a particular time and place results from the choices people make from those offered by the natural environment. These choices are based on three variable factors: population, the materials and technology available, and cultural requirements. The accelerating increase in numbers of people in modern times has led to vastly greater pressure on land. Technological progress, however, enables people to overcome the constraints and to exploit the opportunities presented by nature. Ultimately, many societies may emulate the United States legislation that now requires studies of environmental impact to be made before construction is carried out using government funds. The conservation-exploitation debate about land and what to do with it acknowledges that land, which covers about 30 per cent of the earth's surface, may be limited whereas human's numbers, capabilities, and demands are not.

The growth of settlements

The term settlement includes the establishment of villages and towns as well as the pattern of human concentration at a given time and place. For fewer than 10,000 years mankind has lived in places where specialized activity was possible. Towns and cities have come to dominate large hinterlands from which they draw food and other resources, although they occupy small areas of land. With the rise of the European colonial systems during the last 500 years, certain cities such as London or Paris were able to expand the hinterlands from which resources could be drawn because the means were found to move people, commodities, and goods over long distances.

Today urbanization continues apace with some groups of cities merging into a super-city or megalopolis, as has happened in the north-eastern United States along the Atlantic seaboard from Philadelphia to Boston. Individual cities expand as migrants move into them from smaller settlements and from rural areas, and birth rates remain high in most countries.

In the 1920's, there were about 24 cities with more than 1 million inhabitants. Today there are 225 such cities. There has been a gradual trend in recent decades for "million cities" to develop in the tropical latitudes. The fastest growth in the late twentieth century has occurred in some Third World cities. Mexico City, for example, is forecast to have more than 31 million citizens by the year 2000, considerably larger than the Tokyo-Yokohama (26 million) or the New York conurbation (22 million). By that year, long-established large cities, such as London and Paris, with a population of little more than 12 million each, may seem modest in comparison.

Modern cities and land use

Growing major cities in modern times consume land for industry, commerce, housing, administration, and such public services as health and education, as well as open space for recreation. Linking such urban subdivisions and connecting the city to other parts of a system of settlement is "transport space." This space carries transportation networks, such as road, rail, and other routes, to terminal sites, such as stations, airports, and ports. It also includes ancillary transportation storage and supply land, such as gas stations and parking lots.

Another major feature of modern urban settlement is the multiple use of land. Buildings in the center of a metropolis may have several stories; street levels may be used for retail or transportation, and upper floors may be used for residential, commercial, or manufacturing functions. The greatest concentrations come in downtown or central business districts. Such settlements depend on land far beyond their own limits, for food and other supplies and for markets. At the other end of the settlement scale, modern villages may be small but are increasingly "urban" and no longer expect to subsist on production from local land. Many villages today are dormitory settlements for commuters working in nearby urban centers.

The settlement of Mexico City began in the 1300's when the Aztecs founded their capital, Tenochtitlàn, on an island in the middle of Lake Texcoco (A). They partially drained the lake, thereby forming one large oval island, which was connected to the mainland by three causeways (B). By 1519, when the Spanish arrived, Tenochtitlàn contained over 100,000 people. The Spanish drained the lake completely and replanned the city. A cathedral was built near the site of the Aztec temple, roads were constructed, and ranches and mines were established. In 1824 the boundaries of the Distrito Federal were created—an area of 580 square miles (1,500 square kilometers)—and in 1865 the city limits were extended with the expansion of outlying residential areas (C). By 1970 Mexico City contained 18 per cent of the total national population. The metropolitan area spilled over the limits of the Distrito Federal. Today the Mexico City metropolitan area covers about 883 square miles (2,287 square kilometers) (D). Mexico City's population is now 14,445,000 people. At present the population density exceeds 15,000 per square mile. The projected growth rate is 113 per cent for the year 2000.

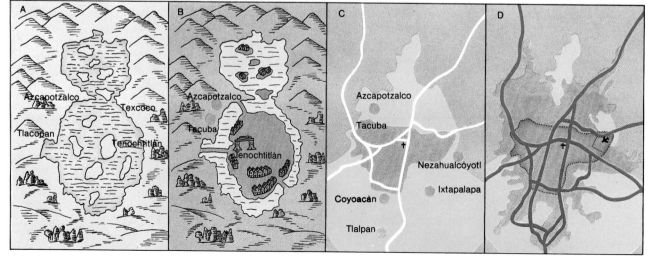

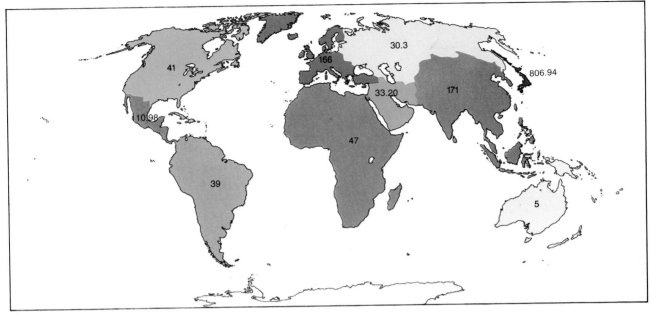

Nomads have long used inhospitable land that was not able to support fixed communities but where water and other resources were adequate for temporary use. Such specialized people-land relationships have expanded the usable land area (ecumene) in a transient and thinly spread way. Modern people can also live in such marginal areas. Supplies and equipment for a comfortable lifestyle can be transported to outlying areas, and radio communications can keep them in touch with the metropolis. Prudhoe Bay on the north Alaskan oilfield, for example, is an isolated community maintained by inland contact.

Effects on the land

Land consists of subsurface and surface features that constitute, along with climate, the natural environment. It may be thought of as a constant until we realize the extent of the impact of settlement on the land; ground water tables are lowered by pumping; and forests are replaced by farmland and settlements. In the cities, vast areas are relentlessly buried under concrete and asphalt. Such losses can to some extent be countered by the extension of the usable land area with irrigation and reclamation projects or reafforestation—perhaps eventually by schemes to change the climate of large areas.

The population densities of the world, given here in persons per square mile, reflect a variety of influences, including religious attitudes toward procreation, suitability of environment for settlement, and the amount of exploitable resources available, as well as the size of the area analyzed.

Tokyo-Yokohama, the capital of Japan, is typical of a modern, built-up city. Neon lights, skyscrapers that indicate a need to expand upward rather than outward, and crowds milling on the sidewalks can be found in most of the world's capital cities.

A village in the Amazon forest contrasts strongly with urban settlements in westernized nations. The villagers are hunter-gatherers and the search for food is a continual problem in the forest interior, so the communities in these areas tend to be small, supporting about only 50 people. Their isolation has protected these villages from outside influences, and their pattern of settlement remains largely unchanged.

Land reclamation

The term reclamation applies both to the reworking of land that has been damaged—as a result of mining, for example—and also to land won from the sea. The principles and techniques of land reclamation vary according to the setting, but the common reason is that land is a scarce and valuable resource that should be made available for productive or beneficial use wherever possible. Reclaimed land can be used for agriculture—for arable or pastoral farming; as sites for new towns and villages; for transport systems such as new airports, harbor facilities, or road networks; and for industry. Usually the most pressing need is for more living space. Many of the world's most ambitious reclamation schemes have been carried out in countries (such as the Netherlands and Japan) that have high population densities.

Land reclamation from the sea

The most spectacular schemes to reclaim land are those that have been carried out in coastal zones. In the Netherlands, land has been reclaimed from the sea since the seventh and eighth centuries when the first dikes were built in Zeeland and Flanders. About a quarter of the present land area of the country has been created in this way. At first, earth embankments or dikes were constructed to enclose shallow, sheltered areas of water, and wind-driven pumps were installed to transfer the water from the enclosed lagoons into drainage channels. On a much larger scale, the Zuider Zee project was begun in the 1920's. A barrier dam was built to enclose the Ijssel

Meer so that it could be turned into a freshwater lake, and several areas behind the dam were drained and eventually brought into agricultural use. These reclaimed areas, called polders, lie below sea level and require continual pumping and protection from encroachment by the sea.

Other, less ambitious, forms of land reclamation have been carried out on the other side of the North Sea, in eastern England. Some areas of coastal marsh (which lie just above mean sea level, but are at least occasionally inundated at high tide) have been protected by earthen sea walls. In this way, the marsh is cut off from salt water and, as happens in the Dutch polders, any remaining salt in the soil is gradually washed out by the rain. Grass is eventually planted, and after some years of cattle or sheep grazing, the soil may be suitable for crops. Heavy yields can then be obtained from the fertile, silty soil. Land reclamation from the sea has been on only a small scale in England, but has been carried out to such a large extent in the Netherlands that new farms, villages, and road networks have been established on land that was once permanently under salt water.

Reclamation of land from the sea has also been carried out elsewhere in Europe: in Belgium, northern Germany, Denmark, northwestern France, and in areas of the Mediterranean. In Italy, the scale of the operation has been larger than in the Netherlands; reclamation has been concentrated in the deltaic areas of the Adige, Po, and Reno rivers, where the Plain of Lombardy meets the Adriatic Sea. A large reclamation project was also completed in Japan in 1966, using Dutch technical aid. The new polder is now densely settled and used for rice growing and fish farming.

The rising sea level in the first century A.D. altered the coastline of the Netherlands (A). To protect the land from inundation, dikes were built; and from the fifteenth century (B) to the present (C), the areas that were drained and empoldered increased.

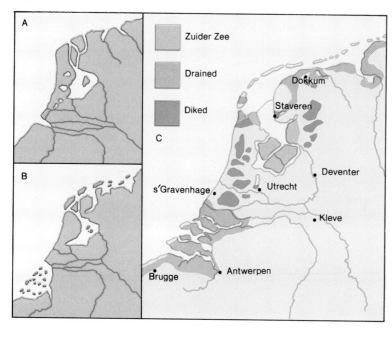

The Alblasserwaard is a drained and diked polder in south Holland that is protected by the Kinderdijk.

Reclamation of waste land

The reclamation of land that is laid waste by mining or industry poses quite different problems. Such waste materials are often rocky and infertile in nature, and in the absence of a proper mantle of soil, it is difficult to establish a vegetation cover. Rock waste usually holds little water, and plant nutrients are often either unbalanced or totally absent. Wastes from mining or the processing of such metals as copper, zinc, and lead may be toxic. In the lower Swansea valley in Wales, for example, waste tips are still toxic as a result of nonferrous smelting activities in the past 200 years.

The reclamation of land damaged by poisonous waste is usually a slow and costly process. Generally, the most effective treatment is to spread a layer of good soil on top of the rocky waste. If topsoil is available from a neighboring development site, then in one operation a fully developed soil of adequate structure, texture, and nutrient status can be quickly established. But to be really effective, a blanket of at least 4 inches (10 centimeters) of topsoil is required on the waste; if trees and shrubs are to be grown on the reclaimed area, a far greater thickness is needed.

Because of the cost and lack of availability of topsoil, this treatment is not always possible, and other less effective solutions may have to be employed. Sewage sludge, hog slurry, or peat may be used to improve the fertility of the soil, and in some cases one waste material is used to counteract the damaging effects of another. Hydraulic seeding—the application of grass seed mixed in water with fertilizers and soil stabilizers such as latex—may, for example, also be used in the treatment of sloping banks of waste material or on exposed land that is suffering from soil erosion.

Desert reclamation

Many arid and semi-arid regions have fertile soil potentially able to support crops if water were available. In the Middle East, for example, traditional methods of irrigation, such as pumping up water from wells sunk into wadi beds, have been used to cultivate land. In addition, many desert areas, such as the Negev desert in Israel, have a heavy dewfall that is sufficient to be collected and used to water plants. More sophisticated methods of irrigation include water-carrying pipelines.

New plantations are being established in the Amazon basin to counterbalance the clearing of the forest for timber and farmland. The soil in this region needs a thick vegetation cover to provide nutrients and stability. Once exposed, the soil becomes infertile and is washed away by heavy rainfall. To regain the soil's fertility the land has to be reafforested.

Wadi Hadramawt, in the People's Democratic Republic of Yemen, is a seasonal watercourse in a desert region. Cultivation is carried out on its bed and along its banks. With a complex system of irrigation and water conservation, using subterranean water and the little rain that falls, the farmers have been able to plant an area of about 15,000 acres (6,000 hectares) with date palms. Other crops include cereals, vegetables, and fruit trees.

Landscape destruction

Land is easily damaged and degraded. In some industrial areas, severe air pollution has damaged soils and vegetation to the extent that agriculture is no longer possible there. The dumping of industrial waste has also contaminated land and made it unproductive; sizable areas have been rendered useless by the effects of mining. The side effects of industry on the land may be severe, but they are usually confined to relatively small areas. Conversely, agriculture, grazing, and forestry may have extensive destructive effects on land although they seem less dramatic and are less rapid than those of industry.

The effects of industry

The pollution of the air from industrial plants (such as metal smelters) can cause considerable damage to plant life and soil. Some gases, such as sulfur dioxide, released by factories dissolve in rain to form a weak acid, which is extremely harmful to the environment and to human health.

Quarrying and mining, particularly strip mining, leave soil unprotected and accelerate erosion. Attempts are being made in some places to refill strip-mined areas with topsoil and to plant vegetation on it to reduce the damage. But this is not always done and erosion follows. In addition, rain leaches salts out of the exposed soil, which increase its acidity, and the acid run-off sterilizes the soil downslope.

Mining also leads to subsidence of the land—which damages buildings and roads—and heaps of waste material mar the landscape. The Potteries near Stoke on Trent in England illustrate early industrial dereliction with disused pits, slagheaps, and coaltips.

Deforestation

To create new land for agriculture and settlement and to satisfy the need for timber, the world's tropical rainforest is being felled and burned at a rate of about 13.5 to 55 million acres a year; at this rate, it will have disappeared completely in 80 years. Forest removal has been practiced for centuries, but the onslaught on the tropical forest is especially drastic because its complex of soils and vegetation is so fragile. The chief source of plant nutrients is in the vegetation rather than in the soil; if the vegetation is removed, much of the land's fertility is lost.

Once a forest is cleared, a greater degree of rainfall runs off the soil surface directly, and soil erosion is increased. The erosion of topsoil makes the land less productive and also causes land and waterways downstream to silt up. In the Himalayas, for example, farmers and peasants gathering fuel have denuded hills, thus increasing erosion and flooding in the lower plains.

In the 1930's, the United States suffered badly from soil erosion. The North American plains had been deforested, and the exposed topsoil was blown away, leaving a barren, extensive dustbowl.

Soil usually develops very slowly, even when undisturbed under natural vegetation. It may take from 100 to 400 or more years to generate half an inch of topsoil. On cultivated land the soil is usually unprotected by crops or vegetation for part of the year, and the rate of soil loss is almost always higher than the rate of soil formation. It is estimated, for example, that the amount of soil lost in one year from corn-growing land in Iowa is equivalent to the amount that forms naturally in eleven years. Soil erosion may result in a loss of both nutrients and soil-rooting depth. Whereas it may be possible, at a price, to replace nutrients by the application of fertilizers, the loss of rooting depth is irreplaceable.

Overgrazing

Soil erosion is not confined to cropland, but also takes place on grazing land. If pastures are overstocked, or if grazing is uncontrolled, then the vegetation is adversely affected. Such reduction of plant cover occurs especially in the semi-arid areas where many of the world's pasture lands are located. If the vegetation cover is reduced, then the soil surface is less protected and erosion is accelerated.

As population pressure increases, there is a tendency for agriculturists to move into more marginal areas, and pastoralists are in turn displaced into more arid areas. In the Sahel of Africa, for example, which extends from Senegal in the west to Ethiopia in the east, overstocking has severely degraded huge areas of land and contributed to the spread of the Sahara. In addition, the slash-and-burn agriculture practiced on the margins has reduced the vegetation cover, and a severe drought in that area has further aggravated the problem.

Failed projects

In a few parts of the world, the desert has been made to bloom by the use of irrigation.

The effects of strip mining can be devastating to the landscape. In addition to the remolding of the land on the site of the mines, roads for access to the sites have to be built that often carve up the natural contours. The heavy earth-moving equipment and other machinery needed in such an operation also break down and compress the soil irreparably.

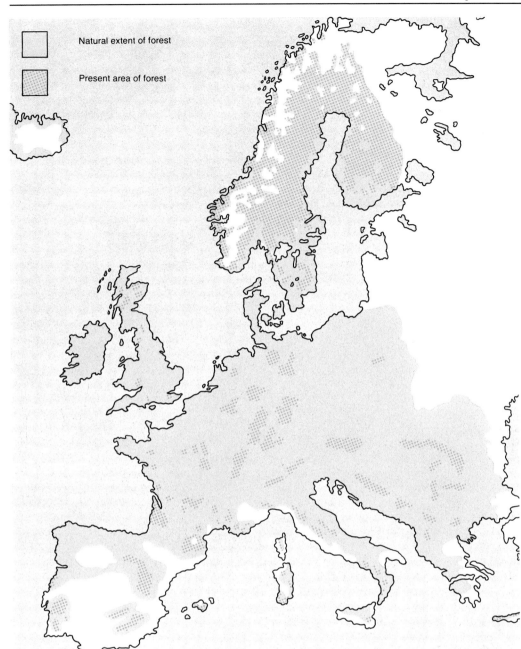

Natural extent of forest

Present area of forest

Almost 60 per cent of the earth's surface was once covered with forest. Now, less than a third of that area is forested. The removal of natural forests is a continuing trend in land use at present. As populations increase, there are great pressures to clear forests to use the land for agriculture and settlement. In addition, there is a growing demand for timber for fuel and other purposes.

Mismanagement of grazing lands occurs in developing and developed countries. In the semi-arid regions of Ethiopia, for example, the livestock of nomadic pastoralists has severely depleted the vegetation by overgrazing.

Such programs transform the productivity of the land, but sometimes they suffer from technical problems: waterlogging of the soil, or growth of crusts of salt or other chemicals that render the land unproductive. In Pakistan, for example, an irrigation project backfired when the amount of salt in the soil rose so high that it became unusable for agriculture.

In addition, dams constructed to bring water to dry areas have caused massive damage to the landscape with the loss of plant and animal life as well as of agricultural land. With modern population pressures, many agricultural problems are more acute than ever before. Unless more appropriate forms of land management can be practiced in many parts of the world, the prospects for adequate resources in the future are gloomy.

Land management

If food production is to keep up with population growth, then sensible land management is essential. The basic resource on which food is produced is soil; the maintenance of the nutrient level of soil and the control of erosion are, therefore, objectives of the utmost importance.

Streamflow erosion in semi-arid areas is responsible for the formation of dustbowls and badlands riven with gulleys. Much less obvious is sheet erosion, in which a broad sheet of surface run-off washes soil particles downhill. On plowed land, such erosion may be imperceptible at first, and it often passes unnoticed until crop yields start to decline because of the reduced level of nutrients in the soil. Losses in production can be considerable, as shown by a 16-year study in Tennessee, where corn yields were found to be 32 per cent lower on eroded than on uneroded land.

Contour plowing and terracing

One requirement of land management is that the land should be used only for purposes for which it is suitable. Because soil loss is greatest on sloping land, the natural vegetation is best left undisturbed on particularly steep slopes. On gentler slopes, contour plowing can reduce erosion by half, because the furrows retain rainwater and so reduce the velocity of the run-off. Contour plowing becomes even more effective if there is strip cropping along the contours, because the plant roots also check the downhill flow of water.

In parts of Asia and South America, the population density is so great that steep slopes have to be cultivated as well as flat areas, in which case the slopes are terraced. Terracing is expensive, but by breaking a slope into a series of level steps, the run-off never attains much erosive power. Bench-type terraces are bordered by rock walls or by earth banks covered with vegetation. On gentler slopes, low mounds of earth are thrown up along the contours to form terraces.

Soil protection

Fertilizers and crop rotation are essential parts of any conservationist land management program. When fallow, the soil should be protected by grass crops, such as clover. Clover is especially useful when it is eventually plowed back into the ground because it also helps to fertilize soils that are deficient in nitrogen. In fields of corn, tobacco, cotton, and other crops that are grown in rows, the intervening strips should be covered either by the planting of some other crop or—a costlier method—by covering the soil with a protective mulch, which decomposes to become humus. Humus not only enriches the soil, but also increases its water-holding capacity.

Oil-rich Middle Eastern governments have halted the advance of desert sands by financing the spraying of petroleum on the dunes. The oil dries to a gray crust which stabilizes the loose sand and retains moisture beneath the surface. In such improved conditions, grasses and such trees as acacias, eucalyptus, and pines, whose roots bind the soil particles, can take root. The plants return humus to the soil, which helps to retain more moisture. In this way, once desolate regions are reclaimed.

Consequences of mismanagement

Any regional land management program should be appropriate to the natural factors that determine the local environment. Erosion has often been the result of the introduction of inappropriate farming methods. For example, the enormous damage done to the soils in much of eastern North America came about because the pioneering farmers from western Europe had brought with them agricultural techniques that proved unsuitable in North American conditions.

In the nineteenth century, European colonizers introduced into tropical regions plantation agriculture and intensive ranching, which were forms of land management that often proved more damaging to the soil than the traditional shifting agriculture. In recent years, a commercial adaptation of shifting agriculture has been successfully applied in Zaire. It in-

The Philippines are a mountainous group of islands with several volcanoes and few plains flat enough for cultivation. Much of the agriculture, therefore, is practiced on steep slopes into which terraces have been built to prevent soil erosion. Rice is the principal crop grown on these terraces—more than 7.5 million acres (3 million hectares) is given over to rice cultivation. The banks on the edges of the terraces retain water long enough to allow the rice seedlings to develop.

volves clearing strips of land in the forest, practicing crop rotation until the soil fertility starts to decline, and then reafforesting the land and moving on to new strips. Often, traditional farming methods have to be stopped, such as livestock grazing in semi-arid regions. In this case, government aid is needed to find other employment for the herdsmen.

The Appalachian mountains were largely deforested in the nineteenth and early twentieth centuries. The effects of the consequent soil erosion in the upper courses of the Tennessee River included rural poverty. In addition, the Tennessee River carried massive quantities of silt. The bed of the river silted up, and the water level rose so that disastrous floods were common on the plain. The establishment of the Tennessee Valley Authority (TVA) in 1933 provided for the control of the Tennessee River and its tributaries through a series of large dams. The TVA also launched a reafforestation and soil conservation program, including the instruction of farmers. Similarly, the problems of the overgrazed, drought-stricken Sahel zone in sub-Saharan Africa apply to several countries. In these cases land management programs are most effective when there is multinational cooperation.

All such programs should take account of ecological factors. For example, the creation of some large reservoirs in tropical Africa, which provide irrigation water and energy to generate hydroelectricity, has led to epidemics of bilharzia. Another project that has had some dire consequences is the building of Egypt's Aswan High Dam. It stopped flooding in the Nile valley, but it also deprived the valley of fertile silt, which now accumulates on the floor of Lake Nasser. In addition, before the dam was built, the supply of silt reaching the Nile delta roughly balanced the erosive power of the sea. But by the early 1980's, the rate of erosion at Rosetta headland (Masabb Rashid) near Alexandria was 75 feet (23 meters) a year and salt water was advancing inland.

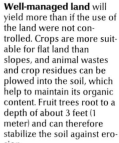

Well-managed land will yield more than if the use of the land were not controlled. Crops are more suitable for flat land than slopes, and animal wastes and crop residues can be plowed into the soil, which help to maintain its organic content. Fruit trees root to a depth of about 3 feet (1 meter) and can therefore stabilize the soil against erosion.

Gower peninsula in south Wales has an area of sand dunes that is being stabilized by marram grass (Ammophila sp.). This plant has extensive underground stems that can spread up to 43 feet (13 meters) from the parent plant and from which new shoots are sent up. To protect the seedlings from the wind, pine barricades have been constructed.

Controlled irrigation and drainage of desert areas can make them suitable for supporting cash crops, which in turn, bind the soil. By building a bank around the foot of each plant, water can be prevented from running off the soil and eroding its nutrients away. In the United Arab Emirates, the Arid Lands Research Centre has used water from desalinization plants to irrigate crops in the desert.

World Facts and Figures

Earth—Planetary Data

Weight	6.6 sextillion short tons	6.0 sextillion metric tons
Equatorial circumference	24,901 miles	40,075 km
Polar circumference	24,859 miles	40,008 km
Total surface area	196,951,000 sq. miles	510,100,000 km²
Land area	57,259,000 sq. miles	148,300,000 km²
Water area	139,692,000 sq. miles	361,800,000 km²
Total area	196,951,000 sq. miles	510,100,000 km²
Mean atmospheric pressure at sea level	14.7 lbs. per sq. inch	1.03 kg per cm²

Earth—Major Components

	(tons)	(kilograms)
Atmosphere	5,600 trillion	5,100,000 trillion
Hydrosphere (surface water)	1,540,000 trillion	1,400,000,000 trillion
Biomass	1.1 trillion	1,000 trillion
Oceanic crust	700,000 trillion	7,000,000,000 trillion
Continental crust	17,600,000 trillion	16,000,000,000 trillion
Mantle	4,490,000,000 trillion	4,080,000,000,000 trillion
Core	2,080,000,000 trillion	1,890,000,000,000 trillion
Total	6,600,000,000 trillion	5,980,000,000,000 trillion

Atmosphere—Main Layers

	Altitude range	Mass	Volume
Troposphere	0–6 miles (0–10 km)	442 billion tons (400,000 billion kg)	1.34 billion miles³ (5.6 billion km³)
Stratosphere	6–30 miles (10–50 km)	105 billion tons (950,000,000 billion kg)	4.82 billion miles³ (20.1 billion km³)
Ionosphere	30–300 miles (50–500 km)	5.5 billion tons (5 million kg)	81.6 billion miles³ (340 billion km³)

Atmosphere—Main Constituents

	Percentage (by volume)	Approximate mass (tons)	Approximate mass (kilograms)
Nitrogen (N_2)	78.09	4,240,000 billion	3,840,000,000 billion
Oxygen (O_2)	20.95	1,300,000 billion	11,800,000 billion
Argon (Ar)	0.93	72,000 billion	65,000,000 billion
Carbon dioxide (CO_2)	0.033	2,870,000 billion	2,600,000 billion
Neon (Ne)	0.0018	70.5 billion	64,000 billion
Helium (He)	0.00052	4.08 billion	3,700 billion
Methane (CH_4)	0.00015	4.74 billion	4,300 billion
Krypton (Kr)	0.0001	16.6 billion	15,000 billion
Nitrous oxide (N_2O)	0.00005	4.42 billion	4,000 billion
Hydrogen (H_2)	0.00005	.198 billion	180 billion
Ozone (O_3)	0.00004	3.41 billion	3,100 billion
Xenon (Xe)	0.000008	.198 billion	180 billion

Sea Water—Major Dissolved Constituents

	Concentration (parts per million)
Chloride (Cl^-)	19,000
Sodium (Na^+)	10,550
Sulfate (SO_4^{2-})	2,460
Magnesium (Mg^{2+})	1,290
Calcium (Ca^{2+})	400
Potassium (K^+)	380
Bicarbonate (HCO_3^-)	140
Bromide (Br^-)	65
Boric acid (H_3BO_3)	25

Oceans

	Area (sq. miles)	Area (km²)
Pacific Ocean	63,800,000	165,200,000
Atlantic Ocean	31,530,000	81,662,000
Indian Ocean	28,356,300	73,441,700
Arctic Ocean	3,662,000	9,485,100
Total	127,348,300	329,788,800

River Water—Major Dissolved Constituents

	Concentration (parts per million)
Bicarbonate (HCO_3^-)	58.4
Calcium (Ca^{2+})	15.0
Silicon dioxide (SiO_2)	13.1
Sulfate (SO_4^{2-})	11.2
Chloride (Cl^-)	7.8
Sodium (Na^+)	6.3
Magnesium (Mg^{2+})	4.1
Potassium (K^+)	2.3
Iron (Fe^{2+})	0.67

Crust—Major Constituents

	Percentage composition (by weight)
Oxygen	46.6
Silicon	27.7
Aluminum	8.1
Iron	5.0
Calcium	3.6
Potassium	2.6
Sodium	2.8
Magnesium	2.0
Other	1.6

Famous Rivers of the World

Name	Length In Miles*	In Kilometers	Location	Interesting Facts
Amazon	4,000	6,437	South America	Carries more water than any other river; world's second largest river; only the Nile is longer.
Arkansas	1,459	2,348	United States	Rapid currents have worn many rocky canyons into the land.
Colorado	1,450	2,334	United States	River's current, combined with other agents of erosion, created the Grand Canyon.
Congo	2,900	4,667	Africa	Fifth largest river in the world and second in the amount of water carried.
Danube	1,777	2,860	Europe	Its beauty inspired Austrian composer Johann Strauss, Jr., to write the famous waltz "On the Beautiful Blue Danube."
Ganges	1,540	2,478	India-Bangladesh	Considered sacred by members of the Hindu faith.
Huang He	2,903	4,672	China	Name means *yellow river;* large amounts of yellow silt are deposited along its course.
Hudson	306	492	United States	Harbor of New York City lies at its mouth.
Indus	1,800	2,897	Tibet-Pakistan	Source of one of the largest irrigation systems in the world.
Jordan	100	160	Israel-Jordan	River mentioned most often in the Bible.
Mackenzie	1,071	1,724	Canada	Canada's longest river.
Mekong	2,600	4,180	Asia	Largest river on the Indochinese Peninsula.
Mississippi	2,348	3,779	United States	Longest river in the United States.
Missouri	2,315	3,726	United States	Second longest river in the United States.
Niagara	35	56	United States-Canada	Famous for its spectacular Niagara Falls; connects Lake Erie and Lake Ontario.
Niger	2,600	4,180	Africa	Third longest river in Africa; its delta is the largest in Africa.
Nile	4,145	6,671	Northeast Africa	World's longest river.
Potomac	287	462	United States	Historic river; forms boundary between the states of Maryland, West Virginia, and Virginia.
Rhine	820	1,320	Europe	Most important inland waterway in Europe; a German symbol of national history and strength.
Rio Grande	1,885	3,034	United States-Mexico	Spanish name for *large river;* forms part of international boundary between United States and Mexico.
St. Lawrence	800	1,287	Canada-United States	Canada's second longest river; links the Great Lakes and the Atlantic Ocean.
Seine	475	764	France	Flows through the heart of Paris, where more than 30 bridges span it.
Thames	215	346	Great Britain	Longest and most important waterway entirely within England; flows through the center of London.
Volga	2,193	3,530	Soviet Union	Longest river in Europe.
Yangtze	3,915	6,300	China	China's longest river; third longest river in the world; only the Nile and the Amazon are longer.
Zambezi	1,700	2,736	Africa	Separates the African countries of Zambia and Zimbabwe.

*Refers only to the length of the river itself and not the length of the river system.

Principal Mountain Ranges

	Location	Highest peak	Length (miles)	(kilometers)
Himalayas	Asia	Mount Everest 29,028ft (8,848m)	1,500	2,400
Andes	South America	Aconcagua 22,831ft (6,959m)	4,500	7,200
Alps	Europe	Mont Blanc 15,771ft (4,807m)	750	1,200
Rocky Mountains	North America	Mount Elbert 14,433ft (4,399m)	3,300	5,300
Atlas Mountains	Africa	Jbel Toubkal 13,665ft (4,165m)	1,500	2,400
Scottish-Norwegian Highlands	Europe	Glittertind 8,104ft (2,470m)	1,550	2,500
Great Dividing Range	Australia	Mount Kosciusko 7,310ft (2,228m)	2,300	3,700
Appalachian Mountains	North America	Mount Mitchell 6,684ft (2,037m)	1,900	3,100
Ural Mountains	Soviet Union	Mount Narodnaya 6,214ft (1,894m)	1,500	2,400

Continents

	Land area (square miles)	(km²)
Asia	19,968,000	43,947,000
Africa	11,694,000	30,330,000
North America	9,363,000	24,249,000
South America	6,886,000	17,835,000
Antarctica	5,100,000	13,209,000
Europe	4,066,000	10,532,000
Australia	2,966,150	7,682,300

Population

Major Area	Population (1988 estimate)
World	4,792,000,000
Africa	600,000,000
Asia	3,000,000,000
Australia	16,000,000
Europe	678,000,000
North America	418,000,000
Pacific Islands (including New Zealand)	12,000,000
South America	287,000,000

Glossary

In the following glossary small capital letters (for example, IGNEOUS ROCK) indicate terms that have their own entries in the glossary.

A

abrasion An erosion process in which particles carried by wind or water currents are worn away against each other.

absolute zero The zero point on the absolute temperature scale, theoretically the lowest temperature possible and equal to about $-460°$ F. $(-273°$ C).

acid igneous rock An IGNEOUS ROCK containing more than 65% silica, often in the form of quartz.

aeration The process by which the pores of the SOIL are filled, partly by water and partly by air, enabling the soil to mature by physical, chemical, and biological processes.

albedo The ratio of the amount of light reflected from an object in various directions to the amount of incident light. Thus an albedo of 1.0 corresponds to a perfect reflector.

alkalinization The degradation of farmland that results in making the SOIL more alkaline.

alluvium Loose material carried in suspension by a river and deposited on a FLOODPLAIN or DELTA. Sands and silts are typical alluvial deposits.

almanac Calendar of days, weeks, and months with added astronomical and other data, used extensively in NAVIGATION.

amber Fossilized RESIN from CONIFEROUS TREES. It has a yellowish color, is transparent or translucent, and is often regarded as a semiprecious stone.

ammonite Extinct cephalopod MOLLUSK with a coiled and chambered shell. The form and ornamentation of the shell evolved so rapidly during the MESOZOIC that ammonites are widely used for CORRELATING TRIASSIC, JURASSIC and CRETACEOUS rocks.

andesite A fine-grained INTERMEDIATE IGNEOUS ROCK; the extrusive equivalent of DIORITE and often produced by VOLCANOES in fold-mountain areas.

angle of repose The maximum slope of the ground at which loose material remains stable. At a greater angle, the material slips or falls until that slope is again reached.

anticline A FOLD in SEDIMENTARY ROCKS in which the STRATA are arched upward. Where the folding is complex, an anticline lies between two SYNCLINES.

apogee The point in the Earth-centered ORBIT of a satellite or the moon at which it is at its farthest from the earth. See also PERIGEE.

aquifer A rock formation that holds water.

asthenosphere The region of the earth's MANTLE, extending from about 60 to 435 miles (100 to 700 kilometers) below the surface, in which plastic movements can take place. PLATE tectonics and isostatic adjustments occur by means of the movement in the asthenosphere. It can be detected seismically by a zone in which earthquake waves slow down. See also ISOSTASY; LITHOSPHERE.

aurora A display of lights in the night sky usually near the North Pole (aurora borealis) or the South Pole (aurora australis), caused by the interaction of SOLAR WIND particles with the earth's magnetic field.

axis The theoretical line around which a body rotates. The earth's axis runs between the geographic North and South poles and is tilted at an angle of 23.5° to the plane of the earth's ORBIT.

B

bacteria Single-celled microscopic organisms that belong to the class Schizomycetes and are responsible for wide-ranging biochemical effects in the earth's ECOLOGY, including decay of dead matter and increasing fertility of SOIL.

bajada An alluvial plain formed by the confluence of fans of sediment washed on to a depositional BASIN from surrounding mountains.

basalt A fine-grained BASIC IGNEOUS ROCK, the extrusive equivalent of GABBRO and DOLERITE, usually produced by the eruption of LAVA from a VOLCANO at a constructive PLATE margin or over a HOT SPOT.

basic igneous rock An IGNEOUS ROCK containing between 45% and 55% silica. Basic rocks tend to be dark in color because of their large constituent proportion of dark MINERALS such as pyroxine.

basin, depositional An area into which rivers flow and sediments accumulate, such as an inland sea.

basin, structural A geological structure similar to a SYNCLINE in which the BEDS curve upward all around.

beach drifting The movement of sand and shingle along a beach by continuous and repetitive wave action. Waves strike a beach obliquely and pebbles are carried obliquely up the slope. They then roll down at right angles to the shoreline, ending up a little further along than before.

bed A distinctive layer in stratified rock, easily distinguishable from those above and below it and separated from them by a bedding plane. Beds form originally from horizontal layers of sediment but may later be tilted or contorted.

biostratigraphy The dating of rocks and the determination of past events using FOSSILS.

block mountain An upland area bounded by FAULTS. It has either been thrust upward, or the surrounding land has been downfaulted.

breccia A CLASTIC SEDIMENTARY ROCK consisting of large angular fragments, like a lithified scree.

C

calcite The mineral calcium carbonate ($CaCO_3$). It forms the main constituent of LIMESTONE.

Cambrian The PERIOD of geological time from 570 to 504 million years ago at the beginning of the PALEOZOIC Era. It is characterized by the first widespread FOSSILS of animals with hard shells.

Cenozoic The last ERA of geological time, dating from 66 million years ago and comprising the TERTIARY and QUATERNARY PERIODS.

centrifugal force The force acting on a body moving on a circular path that tends to push the body away from the center of the circle.

chemical sedimentary rock A SEDIMENTARY ROCK produced by the precipitation of the MINERALS dissolved in seawater or ground water, usually as the water evaporates, e.g. rock salt, TRAVERTINE.

clastic sedimentary rock A SEDIMENTARY ROCK formed by the accumulation of fragments broken away from preexisting rocks, e.g., CONGLOMERATE, SANDSTONE.

climate The atmospheric conditions of a particular place—temperature, humidity, PRECIPITATION, etc. —averaged over a long period of time.

col A saddle or a gap between two peaks.

conglomerate A CLASTIC SEDIMENTARY ROCK consisting of large rounded fragments, like a lithified shingle beach.

coniferous tree A cone-bearing tree, usually evergreen, and characteristic of the vegetation of high LATITUDES and altitudes.

Conrad discontinuity The boundary between the upper and lower parts of the continental CRUST, separating rocks with a predominantly granitic or dioritic composition above from those with a predominantly basaltic composition below.

containerization The packing of goods into containers of a standard size so that they can be conveniently handled and transported.

continental drift The slow movement of the continents from one part of the globe to another through long periods of geological time. The phenomenon can nowadays be explained by PLATE TECTONICS.

conurbation A large built-up area formed by the merging of growing towns.

convection current A current formed by the rising of a warmed fluid and the movement of denser, cool fluid to take its place. Such currents are found in the atmosphere, in the sea, and even in the earth's MANTLE.

core The central portion of the earth below the GUTENBERG DISCONTINUITY that separates it from the MANTLE. It forms a sphere 2,160 miles (3,470 kilometers) in diameter and comprises an inner, solid part and outer, liquid part.

Coriolis effect The effect whereby a north- or southward moving object is deflected to the east or west because of the earth's rotation.

corrasion An erosion process in which a surface is worn away by the passage over it of particles driven by the wind or water currents.

correlation The technique of determining that two rocky OUTCROPS are of the same age despite their being separated by some distance. This is usually done by comparing their FOSSILS.

craton A particularly solid and ancient part of the continental CRUST that has been unaffected for a long time by mountain-building activity.

Cretaceous The PERIOD of geological time from 144 to 66 million years ago, characterized by widespread deposits of chalk. It was the last period of the MESOZOIC

ERA and saw the extinction of the spectacular dinosaurs of that era.

cross-cutting relations The determination of the relative ages of geological formations by examining which cuts through another. For example, if a dike cuts across a sequence of BEDS, then the beds must have been emplaced before the dike.

crust The outermost layer of the earth's structure. The crustal material of the continents (SIAL) is lighter than that underlying the oceans (SIMA). The continental crust is about 25 miles (40 kilometers) thick whereas the oceanic crust is about $4\frac{1}{2}$ miles (7 kilometers) thick. The crust and the solid uppermost portion of the MANTLE constitute the earth's PLATES.

crystal The natural three-dimensional shape produced by certain solid substances when they form. A crystal usually has flat faces, straight edges, and angles that are constant for every crystal of that substance. The crystal shape reflects the arrangement of the atoms in the MOLECULE of that substance.

cyclonic rain Rain associated with a low atmospheric pressure area (cyclone).

D

deciduous tree A tree that loses its leaves seasonally.

declination In NAVIGATION, the angle between the sun and the horizon.

Deep Sea Drilling Project The project organized by the Joint Oceanographic Institutions Deep Earth Sampling organization (JOIDES) to sample the earth's oceanic CRUST. The drilling ship *Glomar Challenger* began operations in 1968 and obtained valuable material from the floors of the deepest oceans.

delta An area of sandbanks formed at the mouth of a river where the sea currents cannot remove the material brought down by the river current. As the river weaves through the sandbanks, it splits up and reaches the sea in a number of mouths.

desalination The removal of salt from seawater to make it suitable for drinking or for irrigation. The process usually involves distillation of the seawater.

Devonian The PERIOD of geological time from 408 to 360 million years ago, characterized by extensive river and desert deposits and the first forests on land.

dew point The temperature at which a cooling atmosphere is unable to hold all its moisture as vapor. At this temperature water droplets form and clouds appear.

diastrophic force A force acting on the earth's crust that produces such deformities as FOLDS and FAULTS.

dinosaur A member of the reptilian orders Saurischia and Ornithischia, abundant during the MESOZOIC ERA and often attaining a large size, e.g., *Tyrannosaurus, Triceratops.*

diorite Coarse-grained INTERMEDIATE IGNEOUS ROCK consisting largely of feldspars.

dip The direction on a dipping BED that is at right angles to the STRIKE. Water runs down the bedding plane in the direction of the dip.

doldrums Region of calm weather near the EQUATOR at the convergence of the Trade Winds.

dolerite Medium-grained BASIC IGNEOUS ROCK, similar in composition to GABBRO and BASALT.

Doppler effect The apparent change in frequency (and wavelength) of a wave (sound wave, radio wave, etc.) caused by the relative approach or separation of the wave source and the receiver. An everyday example is the change in pitch of a train horn as the train passes the observer.

dune A mound of windblown sand that slowly moves as the wind blows particles up the slope from one side and deposits them on the other.

dustbowl An effect of overfarming in which the binding

components of the SOIL are used up too quickly, reducing the soil to dust that is soon blown away.

E

ecology The study of the interrelationships of organisms with each other and with their ENVIRONMENT.

Ekman spiral The change in direction of an ocean current with increase in depth. The CORIOLIS EFFECT deflects a wind-generated current to one side of the wind track, and the water layers below are, in turn, deflected still further, thereby producing the spiral effect.

element The simplest form of a substance, which cannot be broken down by chemical means. The atoms of each element consist of an inner nucleus of protons and neutrons, and an outer cloud of electrons. An element's atomic number indicates the number of protons present (equal to the number of electrons in a neutral atom).

eluviation The removal of a component of the SOIL by water percolating through it.

environment The sum total of the conditions in a (usually specified) region. The environment includes the terrain, climate, amount of water present, and types and numbers of living organisms.

Eocene The EPOCH of geological time from 58 to 46 million years ago.

epicenter The point on the earth's surface directly above the focus of an earthquake. It is the place where most damage occurs.

epoch A geological time unit, subdividing a PERIOD.

equator The imaginary line around the earth midway between the poles; latitude 0°.

equinox One of the two points in the calendar, one in spring and the other in autumn, at which day and night are of equal length. This occurs when the Sun is overhead at the EQUATOR.

era The largest unit of geological time, incorporating several PERIODS.

erratic A boulder that has been transported many miles from its original outcrop by means of GLACIERS.

estuary A broad river mouth that is tidal and can obtain both salt and fresh water.

eustasy A worldwide change in sea level.

evolution The process by which organisms change from generation to generation, producing forms that are adapted to changes in the ENVIRONMENT and eventually give rise to new species.

exosphere The outermost layer of the atmosphere above about 250 miles (400 kilometers).

F

facies The total description of a body of rock—including its mode of formation, its age, the FOSSILS it contains, its texture, and its color.

fault A region of weakness in a rock mass at which the rock cracks and the rock masses at each side of the crack move in relation to each other.

faunal succession, principle of The principle that states that particular FOSSILS are found only in rocks of a particular age and that different sets of fossils always appear in the same order.

firn Compacted snow, in the form of granular ice, representing an early stage in the formation of GLACIER ice. Sometimes regarded as synonymous with NÉVÉ.

floodplain Part of a river valley covered by river sediment that has been deposited during times of flood.

fold A geological structure in which BEDS of rock are bent.

foraminifera Members of the order Foraminiferidae; single-celled marine animals that secrete a CALCITE shell.

fossil The remains of an early animal or plant preserved in a SEDIMENTARY ROCK.

fossil fuel Hydrocarbon fuel derived from the remains of ancient life, e.g., coal, oil, natural gas.

front In meteorology, the boundary between two air masses.

fumarole A fissure in the ground of volcanic areas through which gases are given off.

fusion, nuclear The nuclear process in which two atoms, under the influence of great heat and pressure, unite to form an atom of a different substance, with the release of energy. This is the process by which energy is generated in the sun.

G

gabbro A coarse-grained BASIC IGNEOUS ROCK containing a large proportion of pyroxene and often olivine.

geothermal activity The action of heat within the earth's crust, usually referring to the heating of ground water.

geyser A hot spring in which underground water is heated by GEOTHERMAL ACTIVITY and periodically boils, the sudden pressure produced blasting a fountain from a surface vent.

glacier A mass of ice, produced by the accumulation and compression of snow, which moves slowly downhill or seaward under its own weight.

glass A solid substance, mineral or artificial, which has solidified from a melt so quickly that it has not had sufficient time to form CRYSTALS.

gneiss A high-grade REGIONAL METAMORPHIC ROCK with a very coarse grain.

Gondwanaland The SUPERCONTINENT present during the Upper PALEOZOIC and the MESOZOIC ERAS, consisting of the present-day continents of South America, Africa, India, Australia, and Antarctica.

grading In SEDIMENTARY ROCKS, the change from coarse to fine material that may be found between the bottom and the top of a particular sedimentary BED, caused by the larger fragments coming out of suspension before the fine material during the formation of the original sediment.

granite A coarse-grained ACID IGNEOUS ROCK consisting of quartz, feldspars, and mica, and usually having a light color.

granodiorite A coarse-grained ACID IGNEOUS ROCK similar to granite but with a different composition of feldspar.

graptolite An extinct colonial organism consisting of several individuals encased in a chain of chitinous cups. They were widespread in Lower PALEOZOIC seas and are useful in BIOSTRATIGRAPHY.

gravimeter A device for measuring minute differences in the effect of GRAVITY at different places on the earth's surface.

gravity The force by which objects are attracted to one another because of their mass. On the earth's surface it is responsible for the sensations of weight and of falling.

greenhouse effect The trapping of heat radiated from a planet's surface. This happens when an atmosphere is rich in particular gases, e.g., carbon dioxide, and causes the planet's surface temperature to continue to rise.

groyne A barrier built on a beach, at right angles to the shoreline, to prevent BEACH DRIFTING.

Gutenberg discontinuity The boundary between the earth's CORE and MANTLE. It can be detected by the change in the path of seismic waves that pass across it and is named for the American seismologist Beno Gutenberg (1889-1960). *See* SEISMOLOGY.

gyre A large-scale circulation of ocean currents. Gyres often occupy half an ocean.

gyroscope A spinning instrument which, by virtue of its own inertia, always points to the same direction irrespective of how its carrier moves.

H

Holocene The most recent EPOCH of geological time, beginning 10,000 years ago and encompassing the present day. Sometimes called the Recent Epoch.

hornfels A THERMAL METAMORPHIC ROCK representing high-temperature metamorphism of SHALE.

horse latitudes Regions of light winds resulting from the divergence of the Trade Winds and the Westerlies.

horst A block of land, surrounded by FAULTS, which has been uplifted, or has been left upstanding as the surrounding areas were downfaulted. A horst differs from a BLOCK MOUNTAIN in that it does not need to be a hill—it may have been worn flat by erosion but the original structure can still be seen.

hot spot A region of intense activity beneath the earth's CRUST that is not associated with a PLATE margin. Such a region could give rise to VOLCANOES such as the Hawaiian island chain.

humus Partially decomposed organic matter in the SOIL, derived from the vegetation growing on it, and contributing to the soil's fertility.

hydroelectricity Electricity produced from the energy of water descending a slope. The water is trapped behind dams and channeled through turbines that drive dynamos. Mountainous areas with fast-flowing rivers are the best sites for hydroelectric power stations.

I

ice age A period of time during which temperatures were very low and a considerable proportion of the earth's surface was covered by GLACIERS. The most important ice age was that of the PLEISTOCENE EPOCH, which lasted from about 2,000,000 to 10,000 years ago, but others occurred during the Upper PENNSYLVANIAN and Lower PERMIAN PERIODS and in PRECAMBRIAN times.

icecap An area of permanent ice.

igneous rock A rock formed by the solidification of a molten mass, e.g., GRANITE, BASALT.

interglacial A period of warm climate between two ICE AGES.

intermediate igneous rock An IGNEOUS ROCK containing between 55% and 65% silica, e.g., DIORITE, ANDESITE.

intertidal zone The part of a beach that lies between high- and low-water levels.

intrusion A mass of IGNEOUS ROCK that has solidified underground. The rock of an intrusion tends to be coarse-grained because of its slow cooling.

inversion, magnetic The reversal of the earth's magnetic field, North Pole becoming South Pole and vice versa, known to have happened frequently throughout geological time.

ion An atom (or group of atoms) that has lost or gained one or more electrons, so that it has an electric charge.

ionosphere The layer of the atmosphere between 55 and 250 miles (90 and 400 kilometers) above the earth's surface. It contains a large proportion of ionized particles and has a disruptive effect on radio waves.

isostasy The theoretical balance between large portions of the earth's CRUST, regarded as buoyant and floating at different levels according to their density.

isothermal On a weather map, a line joining all places with the same temperature.

isotope Different forms of the atoms of a particular ELEMENT, arising from differences in the number of neutrons in the nucleus. The term is most often used in connection with those elements, such as uranium, which have isotopes that are unstable and emit radioactive particles.

J

jet stream A particularly fast wind that occurs at an altitude of 6.2 to 7.5 miles (10 to 12 kilometers).

Jurassic The PERIOD of geological time from 208 to 144 million years ago, characterized by the large extent of shallow seas and the heyday of reptiles.

K

kame An outwash fan formed by meltwater from the snout of a GLACIER.

L

latent heat The heat released or absorbed by a substance as it changes state, e.g. when ice melts it absorbs heat, whereas heat is released when water freezes.

laterite A red SOIL rich in iron and aluminum found in tropical climates where silica and organic materials have been leached away.

latitude The distance on the earth's surface measured in degrees north and south of the EQUATOR.

lava Molten material, derived from MAGMA, that reaches the surface in a volcanic eruption. It solidifies into an EXTRUSIVE IGNEOUS ROCK such as BASALT.

leaching The removal of certain elements of the SOIL by the passage of ground water.

limestone A SEDIMENTARY ROCK consisting largely of CALCITE. It may be CLASTIC, ORGANIC, or CHEMICAL.

lithification The process whereby an accumulation of loose fragments is converted into a SEDIMENTARY ROCK. The fragments are first compressed by the weight of subsequent sediments and then cemented by the deposition of MINERALS between the grains.

lithosphere The outer rigid layer of the earth from which the PLATES are made. The lithosphere consists of the CRUST and the topmost part of the MANTLE, and moves about on top of the ASTHENOSPHERE.

longitude The distance on the earth's surface measured in degrees east and west of a line joining the geographic North and South poles and passing through Greenwich in England.

longshore drift The movement of sand and gravel along a beach by means of sea currents flowing parallel to the shore.

M

magma Molten material beneath the earth's surface from which IGNEOUS ROCKS are formed.

magnetosphere The region in space in which the earth's magnetic field can be detected.

mantle The silica-rich layer of the earth's structure that lies between the CRUST and the CORE. It is partly liquid and partly solid and produces the CONVECTION CURRENTS that move the PLATES of the surface.

marble A THERMAL METAMORPHIC ROCK representing metamorphosed LIMESTONE and consisting almost entirely of CALCITE.

marling The mixing of sand and clay, individually useless for agriculture, to produce a workable SOIL.

massive rock A SEDIMENTARY ROCK that has no distinct beds. It indicates a long period of uninterrupted sedimentation and hence a period of constant conditions.

meander A wide loop or bend in a river. A meander is not a permanent feature because its course changes by erosion on the outside of the curve and deposition on the inside.

Mercalli scale A scale of earthquake intensity based on damage done. The modern version is:
I   Not felt.
II   Felt by people in upper stories.
III Hanging objects swing.

IV   Windows and doors rattle.
V   Sleepers awakened.
VI   People alarmed, books fall off shelves.
VII   Chimneys fall, mudbanks collapse.
VIII   Houses damaged, wet ground cracks.
IX   Serious damage to buildings and underground pipes.
X   Most buildings destroyed, water thrown out of canals.
XI   Railroad lines bent.
XII   Total destruction, objects thrown into air.

mesopause The layer of the atmosphere between 30 and 50 miles (50 and 80 kilometers) above the ground.

Mesozoic The ERA of geological time from 245 to 66 million years ago, and encompassing the TRIASSIC, JURASSIC, and CRETACEOUS PERIODS.

metamorphic rock A rock formed by the alteration of a preexisting rock by great heat or great pressure. At no time in the process does the rock become molten.

meteorite A fragment of interplanetary matter that falls to the earth's surface.

millstone grit A sequence of coarse SANDSTONES of PENNSYLVANIAN age, so called because they were once used in the manufacture of millstones.

mineral A naturally-formed inorganic substance with a fixed chemical composition. Minerals are the building blocks from which rocks are made and they may form in CRYSTALS.

Miocene The EPOCH of geological time from 24 to 5 million years ago, during which the climax of Alpine and Himalayan mountain-building occurred.

Mississippian The PERIOD of geological time 360 to 320 million years ago, significant for the widespread deposition of limestones.

Mohorovičić discontinuity The boundary between the earth's CRUST and MANTLE. It can be detected by the change in the path of seismic waves that pass across it and is named after the Yugoslavian geophysicist Andrija Mohorovičić who discovered it in 1909. *See* SEISMOLOGY.

molecule The smallest amount of a substance that exhibits all the chemical properties of that substance and that is capable of independent existence.

mollusk A member of the invertebrate phylum Mollusca, e.g., squids, clams, and snails.

monsoon Climatic conditions found especially to the north of the Indian Ocean in which the winds blow from the sea in the summer and from the continent in winter.

moraine Debris produced by the erosive power of a GLACIER. It may refer to the material carried by the glacier, or that left behind after the glacier has melted.

mudstone A very fine CLASTIC SEDIMENTARY ROCK consisting of lithified mud. Mudstone is distinguished from SHALE by being flaky, rather than splitting into thin BEDS.

mulch A layer of loose material placed around plants to help to stabilize or to feed the SOIL.

mylonite An extreme form of dislocation metamorphism in which the rock is crushed and stretched out along a fault plane.

N

nappe A large-scale FOLD, thrown up by mountain-building and so contorted as to resemble a crumpled cloth.

native mineral An ORE MINERAL consisting of the pure form of a metallic ELEMENT, not combined with other substances. Silver and copper can occur as native minerals.

navigation The art of directing a course and of checking a position at any given time.

névé Compacted snow, distinguishable from GLACIER ice by the presence of trapped air. Sometimes used synonymously with FIRN.

nomad A person who migrates with the seasons.

O

oasis A moist, fertile place in a desert, usually surrounding a well or a spring.

obsidian An IGNEOUS ROCK that is so fine-grained that it contains no CRYSTALS, forming instead a natural GLASS.

Oligocene The EPOCH of geological time from 37 to 24 million years ago.

ooze Loose sediment found on the abyssal plain of the ocean and formed from organic remains.

ophiolite A suite of rocks containing basic and ultrabasic material that are thought to be parts of the oceanic CRUST thrust above sea level.

orbit The circular or elliptical path of an astronomical body around another. A body goes into orbit when its CENTRIFUGAL FORCE balances the gravitational attraction of the other body. *See also* GRAVITY.

Ordovician The PERIOD of geological time from 505 to 438 million years ago. All life was then in the sea and fish were beginning to evolve.

ore mineral A MINERAL from which a metal can be extracted economically, e.g., hematite (iron), galena (lead).

organic sedimentary rock A SEDIMENTARY ROCK formed from the remains of living organisms, e.g., coal, LIMESTONE.

original horizontality, principle of The principle which states that sedimentary BEDS are horizontal when first formed.

orographic rain Rain produced when moist air is forced upwards by the passing of winds over mountain ranges. As the air rises, it cools below its DEW POINT and the moisture condenses, falling as rain.

outcrop A rock exposed at the surface of the earth, not covered or obscured by SOIL.

oxbow lake A curved lake or patch of marshy ground formed when a river's MEANDER is cut off and abandoned.

ozone A form of oxygen (O_3) with three atoms per MOLECULE rather than the usual two. It is concentrated in the atmosphere between 15 and 30 miles (24 and 50 kilometers) above the surface, and filters out harmful ULTRAVIOLET radiation from the sun.

P

Paleocene The EPOCH of geological time from 66 to 58 million years ago. The start of the TERTIARY PERIOD.

paleogeography The study of the landforms, depositional environments, distribution of land and sea, and other geographical phenomena of times past.

paleontology The study of FOSSILS and ancient life forms.

Paleozoic The ERA of geological time lasting from the CAMBRIAN to the PERMIAN PERIODS.

Pangaea The SUPERCONTINENT that existed when all the continental masses were united at the time between the PENNSYLVANIAN and CRETACEOUS PERIODS.

peat Partly decayed organic material with a high carbon content, often found in beds where the lack of oxygen prevents complete breakdown.

peneplain A flat area of land formed when all mountains and hills have been eroded away.

Pennsylvanian The PERIOD of geological time 320 to 286 million years ago, significant for the formation of coal. In Europe, this and the MISSISSIPPIAN are together regarded as the Carboniferous.

peridotite A coarse-grained ULTRABASIC IGNEOUS ROCK consisting almost entirely of olivine.

perigee The point in the orbit of a satellite or the moon moving around the earth at which it is closest to our planet. *See also* APOGEE.

period The standard unit of geological time, usually defined by some particular form of animal life that existed at the time. Periods are divided into EPOCHS and several periods make an ERA.

permafrost A layer of permanently frozen ground in TUNDRA regions.

permeability The degree to which water or other fluids can filter through a rock, via interconnected pore spaces between the rock's grains.

Permian The PERIOD of geological time from 286 to 245 million years ago, characterized by widespread deserts. This period marked the end of the PALEOZOIC ERA.

photosynthesis The series of chemical reactions that take place in green plants by which food is manufactured from MINERALS, water, and carbon dioxide using the energy of the sun. Oxygen is formed as a by-product.

phyllite A REGIONAL METAMORPHIC ROCK, intermediate in metamorphic grade between SLATE and SCHIST. Mica CRYSTALS are prominent.

plane table survey A mapping technique in which sightings of prominent points are taken along lines drawn directly onto paper pinned to a horizontal table.

plankton The portion of marine life that drifts passively in the water. It can be of plant or animal forms.

plate A portion of the earth's outer layer, consisting of CRUST and topmost MANTLE, which moves as a unit in response to CONVECTION CURRENTS in the mantle itself.

plateau A flat-topped highland area.

Pleistocene The EPOCH of geological time from 2 to 0.25 million years ago and encompassing the recent ICE AGE.

Pliocene The EPOCH of geological time from 5 to 0.75 million years ago, bringing to an end the TERTIARY PERIOD.

podsol A SOIL that occurs in cool moist conditions (usually supporting forests of CONIFEROUS TREES) that has its upper layers leached to a light gray color. See LEACHING.

porosity The proportion of empty space between the grains of a rock.

porphyry An IGNEOUS ROCK consisting of large CRYSTALS embedded in a matrix of fine crystals. It is formed by two separate phases of cooling.

Precambrian That extent of geological time before the CAMBRIAN PERIOD and lasting from about 4.5 billion to 500 million years ago. Precambrian FOSSILS are very rare.

precession A rotational movement of the AXIS of a spinning object.

precipitation The fall of water from the atmosphere, whether in the form of rain, sleet, snow, or hail.

Q

quartzite A THERMAL METAMORPHIC ROCK representing metamorphosed SANDSTONE and consisting almost entirely of quartz.

Quaternary The most recent PERIOD of geological time, beginning 2 million years ago with the onset of the PLEISTOCENE ICE AGE.

R

radar A method of detecting objects or measuring distances by timing the echo of a transmitted radio wave. The word is an acronym for *RA*dio *D*etection *A*nd *R*anging.

radioactive dating The dating of a rock by estimating the amount of radioactive decay that has taken place in its radioactive MINERALS, and calculating the time that such decay would take.

radioactivity The spontaneous breakdown of certain ELE-

MENTS or ISOTOPES accompanied by the emission of energetic radioactive particles.

rare gas A gas which, because of its stable atomic structure, does not readily combine chemically with other elements. Neon, argon, and krypton are rare gases.

refraction The bending of a wave (of sound, light, or other forms of energy) as it passes from a medium of one density to a medium of another density.

regional metamorphic rock A METAMORPHIC ROCK formed by the alteration of a preexisting rock by great pressure, e.g., SLATE, SCHIST.

remanent magnetism Magnetism induced by the earth's magnetic field that was sealed into a rock when it was formed. The direction of the earth's magnetic field has changed several times in the past, and remanent magnetism can be used to find the positions of the magnetic poles at different stages of geological time.

reservoir rock A rock that is sufficiently porous and permeable to contain oil or natural gas, which can be extracted from such a rock. *See* POROSITY; PERMEABILITY.

resin A sticky substance secreted by some plants. It is usually an oxidized or polymerized form of sap.

resurgence The reappearance of a stream that has previously vanished underground. Resurgences are often found in LIMESTONE areas after the stream has flowed down and through a cave system.

rheid flow The movement of a substance by means of slippage between its microscopic layers.

rhyolite A fine-grained ACID IGNEOUS ROCK; the extrusive equivalent of GRANITE.

Richter scale Scale of earthquake magnitude expressed as a function of the total energy released by the earthquake.

rift valley A valley formed by the subsidence of land between two FAULTS.

rock-forming mineral A MINERAL that occurs as the dominant constituent of a rock, as opposed to the less abundant, potentially valuable ORE MINERALS.

rotation, crop A method of maintaining the fertility of farmland by planting a different crop each year and allowing certain periods of rest.

run-off The proportion of rainwater that reaches streams, either by flowing over the ground or by seeping through the SOIL, and does not remain for long in the land on which it falls.

S

salinization The degradation of farmland by the increase of its salt content.

saltation The movement of a particle along a surface in a series of jumps, propelled by a current of water or the wind.

sandstone A medium-grained CLASTIC SEDIMENTARY ROCK consisting of lithified sand. Usually the dominant mineral is quartz.

scarp A steep slope that cuts across rock STRATA, as opposed to a DIP, which is a slope that follows the strata.

schist A high-grade REGIONAL METAMORPHIC ROCK with a coarse grain and distinct banding of MINERALS.

sea-floor spreading The aspect of PLATE tectonics in which the oceans become larger by the emplacement of new material at ocean ridges and the movement of the old material away from the ridges.

seamount A mountain rising from the floor of the sea but not reaching the surface.

sedimentary cycle The complete process in which rocks are broken down to fragments by erosion, the fragments transported and deposited, the deposits turned into SEDIMENTARY ROCK, and the rock uplifted and eroded once more.

sedimentary rock A rock formed from the LITHIFICATION of loose material, whether derived from rock debris, skeletal matter, or CRYSTALS precipitated from sea-water.

seismology The study of shock waves passing through the earth. The shock waves can be natural, produced by earthquakes, or artificial, produced by explosives. The REFRACTION, reflection, and attenuation of these waves can be used to determine what kinds of materials they passed through.

sextant A device for position finding that measures the angle between the sun (or other celestial object) and the horizon at a particular time of day.

shale A very fine CLASTIC SEDIMENTARY ROCK formed by the LITHIFICATION of mud. It is distinguished from MUDSTONE by its ability to split into thin BEDS.

sial The material that forms the continental CRUST, being rich in silica and aluminum. It is lighter than the SIMA crust that forms the ocean floors and so tends to float on it.

silicate A compound of silica (SiO_2) and one or more metals. Silicates are important as ROCK-FORMING MINERALS, e.g., olivine.

Silurian The PERIOD of geological time from 438 to 408 million years ago, characterized by the first appearance of fish and land plants.

sima The material that forms the oceanic CRUST, being rich in silica and magnesium. It is denser than the continental SIAL.

slate A REGIONAL METAMORPHIC ROCK representing low-grade metamorphism of SHALE and characterized by its perfect cleavage produced by parallel bands of mica CRYSTALS.

soil The loose material covering much of the earth's land surface and consisting of broken-down rock material and organic remains, mixed by the action of animals and plants, and altered by ground water circulation.

solar wind The movement of charged particles from the sun through the solar system.

solifluction The movement of SOIL down a slope, often caused by alternating freezing and thawing of surface soil in TUNDRA areas.

solstice One of two points in the calendar, one in midwinter and the other in midsummer, at the time of the longest day or the longest night of the year.

sonar A method of detecting objects or measuring distances (usually underwater) by timing the echo of a transmitted sound wave. The word is an acronym for *SO*und *N*avigation *A*nd *R*anging.

specific gravity The weight of a given volume of a substance compared with the weight of the same volume of water; relative density.

spheroid A three-dimensional shape approximating to a sphere. It may be oblate (that is, flattened) or prolate (that is, elongated).

spit A bar of sand, formed by LONGSHORE DRIFT or BEACH DRIFTING, which grows out into a bay or an ESTUARY.

stalactite A downward-pointing growth of CALCITE from the roof of a LIMESTONE cave.

stalagmite An upward-pointing growth of CALCITE on the floor of a LIMESTONE cave, caused by the continual dripping of calcite-rich ground water on a particular spot.

strata The layers of a SEDIMENTARY ROCK.

stratigraphy The study of SEDIMENTARY ROCKS, their mode of formation, their FOSSILS, and the information they yield about the earth in times past.

stratosphere The layer of the atmosphere between 10 and 30 miles (16 and 50 kilometers) above the earth's surface.

stress The force acting on a unit area of a body.

strike The direction of a horizontal line on the plane of a dipping BED. If the bed is partially submerged, the waterline follows the line of strike.

subduction zone The region between two tectonic PLATES in which one is being pushed beneath the other.

supercontinent A very large continent made up of more than one continental mass, carried together by continental drift.

supercooling The cooling of a gas below the point at which it would normally become a liquid, or of a liquid below the point at which it would normally become solid.

superposition, principle of The principle that states that, in any undisturbed sequence of SEDIMENTARY ROCKS, the rocks that were formed first lie at the bottom, and the younger rocks are toward the top.

syncline A fold in rock STRATA in which each stratum forms a trough shape.

T

tectonic Relating to the movements and the structures of the earth's rocks or CRUST.

Tertiary The PERIOD of geological time from 66 to 5 million years ago, comprising most of the CENOZOIC ERA.

texture The size of the individual grains or crystals in a rock.

thermal metamorphic rock A METAMORPHIC ROCK formed by the alteration of a preexisting rock by great heat.

thermocline A layer in the ocean about 300-650 feet (100-200 meters) deep in which there is a marked decrease in temperature with increasing depth.

thermosphere The region of the earth's atmosphere between about 53 and 353 miles (85 and 565 kilometers) above the earth's surface in which the temperature steadily increases with height.

tillite A CLASTIC SEDIMENTARY ROCK formed by the LITHIFICATION of till, the unsorted MORAINE of a GLACIER.

trace element An ELEMENT found in very small quantities in the earth's CRUST.

traction The movement of material along the bed of a stream or GLACIER by the force of the water or ice moving above it.

transform fault A FAULT between offset portions of an ocean ridge, in which new material produced at the different parts of the ridge move past each other.

transit In NAVIGATION, a bearing taken when two landmarks are in line.

trap A structure in which oil or natural gas accumulates. It may be formed by the structure of the rocks —as in a FAULT or an ANTICLINE—or by the localized extent of the RESERVOIR ROCK itself.

travertine A CHEMICAL SEDIMENTARY ROCK consisting of CALCITE deposited from a spring.

Triassic The PERIOD of geological time from 245 to 208 million years ago. In this Period there was a continuation of the desert conditions of the PERMIAN Period.

trilobite A member of an extinct class of arthropods in which the body is divided into a distinct head, thorax and segmented tail. Their FOSSILS are useful in PALEOZOIC BIOSTRATIGRAPHY.

troposphere The lowest layer of the earth's atmosphere (extending to an altitude of 10 miles [16 kilometers]) and the layer in which all major weather effects take place.

tsunami A large and destructive sea wave caused by a large-scale disturbance of the sea bed. It is often erroneously called a tidal wave.

tundra A terrain of high LATITUDES, characterized by treeless expanses and permanently frozen subsoil.

turbidity current A mixture of water and suspended material that moves through clearer water as though it were a totally different liquid. Turbidity currents have a great effect on the erosion of the continental slope.

U

ultrabasic igneous rock An IGNEOUS ROCK containing less than 45% silica. The composition is similar to that of the MANTLE, and the crustal rocks may be formed by the separation of the siliceous material from such a rock.

ultraviolet light Light invisible to the human eye, of a higher frequency than violet light but a lower frequency than X rays.

unconformity A break in the sequence of STRATA. It represents a period when sedimentation ceased for a time. Usually the first BEDS are uplifted and eroded before the next sequence is laid down. In this case, the beds below the unconformity lie at a different angle from those above.

uniformitarianism The geological principle that states that "the present is the key to the past," i.e., all previous geological features can be explained in terms of the natural processes that we can see today.

V

Van Allen radiation belts Two doughnut-shaped regions around the earth at heights of 2,000 and 11,500 miles (3,220 and 18,500 kilometers) respectively, in which radiation is trapped by the earth's magnetic field.

variation, magnetic The difference in bearing between the earth's magnetic and geographic North poles.

varve A thin layer of mud laid down in a lake of glacial meltwater. The number of varves in a sequence is thought to correspond to the number of years that the sequence took to form.

vector A line used in mathematical calculations that shows both magnitude and direction, e.g., a line plotted on a navigational chart showing a vessel's direction and speed. *See* NAVIGATION.

volcano The phenomenon or landform produced when molten material from the MAGMA erupts through the surface of the earth.

W

water cycle The condensation and evaporation of water on a world scale. Water evaporates from the oceans into the air, condenses and falls as rain over land, and returns via rivers to the oceans, where the cycle begins again.

watershed The line, along a mountain crest, which separates the springs that produce streams flowing down one side of the crest from those that produce streams that run down the other.

water table The upper surface of the region of rock or SOIL that is saturated with ground water.

weather The day-to-day combination of meteorological conditions, including PRECIPITATION, wind speed and direction, atmospheric pressure, humidity, and cloud cover. Not to be confused with CLIMATE, which is the average of these conditions over many years.

weathering The process in which rocks are broken down by the action of rain, wind, frost, and other WEATHER conditions.

X

X-ray crystallography A method of determining the CRYSTAL structure of a MINERAL by examining the angles of diffraction or reflection of X rays by a small sample of the mineral.

Index

Credits